THE IDEALS GUIDE TO

AMERICAN CIVIL WAR PLACES

THE IDEALS GUIDE TO

AMERICAN CIVIL WAR PLACES

By Julie Shively

IDEALS PUBLICATIONS, A DIVISION OF GUIDEPOSTS
NASHVILLE, TENNESSEE

ISBN 0-8249-4159-4

Published by Ideals Publications, a division of Guideposts
Suite 250, 535 Metroplex Drive
Nashville, Tennessee 37211

10 8 6 4   3 5 7 9

A special thanks to Lt Col. Keith Gibson, Director,
VMI Hall of Valor Civil War Museum, for his
invaluable contribution in reading and offering
suggestions to this manuscript.

Publisher, Patricia A. Pingry
Designer, Eve DeGrie
Copy Editor, Christine M. Landry
Editor, Nancy Skarmeas
Associate Editor, Thorunn McCoy
Editorial Research, Elizabeth Kea

Cover Photographs: Front Cover Fort McCook, Cumberland Gap, TN. D. Muench/H. Armstrong
Roberts. Back Cover: Cold Harbor, Richmond National Battlefield Park. Jeff Gnass.

Library of Congress Cataloging-in-Publication Data

Shively, Julie, 1964–
   The Ideals guide to American Civil War places / Julie Shively.
      p.   cm.
   Includes index.
   ISBN 0-8249-4159-4 (alk. paper)
   1. United States — History — Civil War, 1861–1865 — Battlefields Guidebooks. 2. Historic sites — United States Guidebooks. 3. United States — History — Civil War ,
1861–1865 — Campaigns. I. Title. II. Title: Guide to American Civil War places.
E641.S55 1999
973.7'3 — dc21   99-33645
                                                                              CIP

Color scans by Precision Color Graphics, New Berlin, Wisconsin

Printed and Bound by R. R. Donnelley & Sons

*This book is dedicated to my husband, Al, whose service in the U.S. Marine Corps—from
Vietnam through Desert Storm—gave him perspective, insight, and knowledge of wartime
decisions which, during our discussions of the various battles and campaigns of the Civil War,
were of infinite value to me. For this, and for his enduring love, he remains my personal hero.
—JS*

TABLE OF CONTENTS

INTRODUCTION

The United States Civil War spanned five years and was fought on battlefields that stretched from Pennsylvania to Florida, from North Carolina to New Mexico, and included most of the states and territories in between. Three million men saw combat, and more than 600,000 Americans were killed in battle. Thousands more died after the war from wounds or illnesses contracted during the conflict.

The election of Abraham Lincoln in 1860 made the inevitable war a reality. As president, Lincoln was committed to keeping the nation whole and set forth his aim in his first inaugural address in 1861. "One section of our country believes slavery is right, and ought to be extended, while the other believes it is wrong, and ought not to be extended. This is the only substantial dispute. . . . Such will be a great lesson of peace; teaching men that what they cannot take by an election, neither can they take it by a war—teaching all, the folly of being the beginners of a war."

Today, some of the Civil War battlefields are now housing developments, parking lots, and shopping malls. Many, however, remain intact and commemorate our country's tumultuous past. In museums and parks, those who fought are remembered, and in cemeteries, row upon row of markers provide silent testimonies of war.

Walk the battlefields of Shiloh, Vicksburg, Gettysburg, and others, and the ghosts of the past seem to rise from these hallowed grounds. Visit the Civil War museums of Virginia, Florida, Tennessee, and elsewhere, and marvel at the crude weapons of war and primitive medical devices that managed to keep some of the wounded alive. Kneel at the graves of those soldiers who fought, not for selfish or vain reasons, but the Southerners out of fear of a vanishing society and the unknown future, and the Northerners for the continuance of the Union. And silently thank both sides who—at last—began the process of real freedom for all Americans.

ABOUT THE AUTHOR

Julie Shively is a graduate of the United States Air Force Academy, a veteran C-141 pilot, and a former member of the Air Force's prestigious Eighty-ninth Airlift Wing. She holds a master's degree in education and teaches sixth grade math, science, and social studies. The author lives with her husband and daughter in northern Virginia.

CHRONOLOGICAL LIST OF MAJOR BATTLES AND ENGAGEMENTS

The following list of battles is by no means comprehensive but merely provides a glimpse of the enormity of the American Civil War.

 ## 1861

Apr. 12–15 ......Ft. Sumter, SC
July 21 ....First Manassas, VA (Bull Run)
Aug. 10 ....Springfield, MO (Wilson's Creek)
Sept. 12–20 ......Lexington, MO
Oct. 21 ....Ball's Bluff, Leesburg, VA (Edward's Ferry, Harrison's Landing)
Nov. 7 ....Galveston Harbor, TX
Dec. 20 ....Dranesville, VA

 ## 1862

Jan. 19–20 ......Mill Springs, KY (Logan's Cross Roads)
Feb. 8 ....Roanoke Island, NC
Feb. 12–16 ......Ft. Donelson, TN
Mar. 6–8 ....Pea Ridge, AR
Mar. 8–9 ....Hampton Roads, VA
Mar. 23 ....Winchester, VA (First Kernstown)
Mar. 26, 28 ......Glorieta Pass, NM (Apache Canon)
Apr. 6–7 ....Shiloh, TN (Pittsburg Landing)
Apr. 18–28 ......Forts Jackson and St. Philip, LA
Apr. 29–30 ......First Corinth, MS
May 31–June 1 ...Fair Oaks, VA
June 8 ....Cross Keys, VA (Union Church)
June 9 ....Port Republic, VA
June 27 ....Gaines' Mill, VA
June 27 ....First Cold Harbor, VA
June 27 ....Chickahominy, VA
July 1 ....Malvern Hill, VA
Aug. 9 ....Cedar Mountain, VA (Slaughter Mountain, Cedar Run, and Mitchell Station)
Aug. 28–30 ......Second Manassas, VA (Bull Run)
Aug. 30 ....Richmond, KY
Sept. 1 ....Chantilly, VA
Sep. 13–15 ......Harpers Ferry, WV
Sept. 17 ....Antietam, MD (Sharpsburg)
Sept. 19–20 ......Iuka, MS

Oct. 3–4 . . . . .Second Corinth, MS
Oct. 8 . . . . .Perryville, KY
Dec. 7 . . . . .Prairie Grove, Fayetteville, AR
Dec. 11–13 . . . . . . .Fredericksburg, VA
Dec. 28–29 . . . . . . .Chickasaw Bayou, Vicksburg, MS
Dec. 31–Jan. 2 . . .Stones River, TN (Murfreesboro)

1863

Jan. 1 . . . . .Galveston, TX
Feb. 3 . . . . .Fort Donelson, TN (Cumberland Ironworks)
Mar. 4–5 . . . . .Unionville, TN (Spring Hill, Thompson's Station)
May 1 . . . . .Port Gibson, MS
May 1–3 . . . . .Chancellorsville, VA
May 18–July 4 . . .Siege of Vicksburg, MS
June 9 . . . . .Brandy Station, VA
June 17–20 . . . . . . .Aldie, Middleburg, and Upperville, VA
June 23–30 . . . . . . .Rosecrans's Campaign: Murfreesboro to Tullahoma, TN
July 1–3 . . . . .Gettysburg, PA
July 10–Sep 6 . . . .Siege of Fort Wagner, Morris Island, SC
Sept. 18–20 . . . . . .Chickamauga, GA
Nov. 17–Dec. 4 . . .Siege of Knoxville, TN
Nov. 24–25 . . . . . . .Chattanooga, TN

1864

Apr. 8–9 . . . . .Mansfield and Pleasant Hills, LA/TX
May 5–6 . . . . .Wilderness, VA
May 7–Sept. 2 . . . .Atlanta Campaign
May 8–18 . . . . . . .Spotsylvania Court House, VA
May 9–13 . . . . . . .Sheridan's Cavalry Raid, VA
May 13–16 . . . . . . .Resaca, GA
May 15 . . . . .New Market, VA
May 23–26 . . . . . . .North Anna River, VA
May 25–29 . . . . . . .Dallas GA, Pickett's Mill, New Hope Church, and Allantoona Hills
June 1–12 . . . . . . .Second Cold Harbor, VA
June 10 . . . . .Brice's Crossroads, near Guntown, MS
June 15–Apr. 1 . . .Siege of Petersburg, VA
June 27 . . . . .Kennesaw Mountain, Marietta, GA (Big Shanty)
July 22 . . . . .Atlanta, GA
July 23–24 . . . . . . .Kernstown and Winchester, VA
July 28–Sep 3 . . . .Siege of Atlanta, GA
Aug. 5–23 . . . . . . .Mobile Bay, Forts Gaines and Morgan, AL
Aug. 31–Sept. 1 . . .Jonesboro, GA
Sept. 19–22 . . . . . .Winchester and Fisher's Hill, VA
Sept. 26–27 . . . . . .Ironton, MO (Pilot Knob)
Sept. 28–30 . . . . . .New Market Heights, VA (Laurel Hill)

Oct. 19 . . . . .Cedar Creek, VA
Nov. 29–30 . . . . . . .Spring Hill and Franklin, TN
Dec. 24–Jan. 13 . .Fort Fisher, NC

1865

Feb. 5–7 . . . . .Dabney's Mills, Hatcher's Run, VA
Feb. 27–Mar. 25 . .Sheridan's raid into VA
Mar. 26–Apr. 9 . . . .Siege of Mobile, AL
Apr. 1 . . . . .Five Forks, VA
Apr. 2 . . . . .Fall of Petersburg, VA
Apr. 3 . . . . .Fall of Richmond, VA, Confederate Capital
Apr. 6 . . . . .Sailor's Creek, VA
Apr. 9 . . . . .Appomattox Court House, VA, Lee surrenders to Grant
Apr. 14 . . . . .Assassination of President Abraham Lincoln
May 10 . . . . .Irwinsville, GA, Capture of Jefferson Davis
May 12–13 . . . . . .Palmito Ranch, TX
May 26 . . . . .Final surrender, Lt. Gen. Kirby Smith to Maj. Gen. Canby

EXPLANATORY NOTES

A compass denotes those sites directly related to the battle described in the previous pages.

■ The green marks on the maps represent the general location of the places. Although interstates, federal highways, and some state highways are included for orientation, space limitations prevent precise directions. In some states, the state map is not complete and shows only that area of the state that contains a Civil War place. In other states, some of the Civil War places are not included on the map because of space restrictions. Please refer to the information on the site provided in each state chapter for more specific directions.

Map abbreviations:

Am. . . . . . .American	Headqtrs. .Headquarters	Nat'l. . . . . .National
Btlfd. . . . . .Battlefield	Hist. . . . . . .Historic	Pk. . . . . . . .Park
Ch. . . . . . . .Church	Is. . . . . .Island	Plant. . . . . .Plantation
Conf. . . . . .Confederate	Mem. . . . . .Memorial	Pt. . . . . .Point
Ctr. . . . . . . .Center	Mon. . . . . .Monument	Soc. . . . . . .Society
CW . . . . . .Civil War	Mt. . . . . . . .Mount	St. . . . . .State
Dept. . . . . .Department	Mtn. . . . . . .Mountain	Vis. Ctr. . . .Visitor's Center
Ft. . . . . .Fort	Mus. . . . . . .Museum	

ALABAMA

The Alabama state legislature voted to leave the Union on January 11, 1861, making the state the fourth to secede. Alabama then played host to the first Confederate capital, at Montgomery, where representatives from the Confederate states elected Jefferson Davis their president and drafted a Confederate constitution. One hundred thousand Alabamans fought for the Confederate cause, and sixteen generals named the state as their birthplace. Still, Alabama's greatest contribution to the war effort was probably its industrial and agricultural resources. The state's iron-works armed the Confederate troops, while Alabama's farms fed soldiers throughout the South.

Alabama was among the least fought over Southern states during the war. No large-scale Federal campaigns penetrated into the state; instead troops, both Northern and Southern, passed though the state on their way to battle elsewhere. Alabama's most significant battle was fought over Mobile Bay and the city it protected.

Alabama today features Civil War sites as varied as the state's many contributions to the Confederacy, sites which remember the soldiers, the citizens, the laborers, and the leaders who were part of Civil War Alabama.

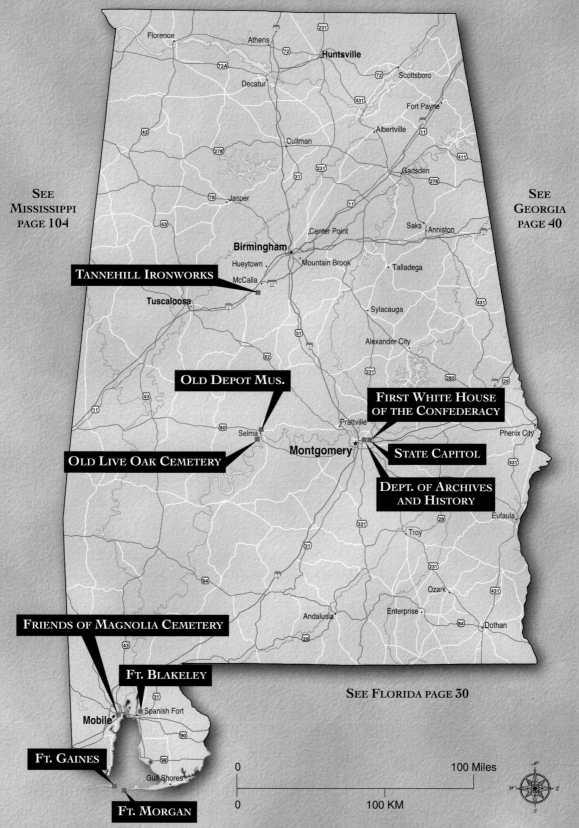

SEE TENNESSEE PAGE 168

SEE
MISSISSIPPI
PAGE 104

SEE
GEORGIA
PAGE 40

Florence
Athens
Huntsville
72A
Scottsboro
Decatur
72
431
Fort Payne
59
Albertville
11
411
Cullman
Gadsden
278
43
Jasper
78
11
Center Point
Saks
Anniston
20
Birmingham
Hueytown
Mountain Brook
Talladega
McCalla
459
Sylacauga
Tuscaloosa
431
Alexander City
82
65
231
280
84
29
Phenix City
Prattville
80
Selma
Montgomery
State Capitol
431
Dept. of Archives
and History
Eufaula
331
Troy
Ozark
431
Andalusia
Enterprise
84
Dothan
29
43
Spanish Fort
31
Mobile
90
98
Gulf Shores

TANNEHILL IRONWORKS

OLD DEPOT MUS.

**FIRST WHITE HOUSE
OF THE CONFEDERACY**

OLD LIVE OAK CEMETERY

STATE CAPITOL

**DEPT. OF ARCHIVES
AND HISTORY**

FRIENDS OF MAGNOLIA CEMETERY

FT. BLAKELEY

FT. GAINES

FT. MORGAN

SEE FLORIDA PAGE 30

0   100 Miles

0   100 KM

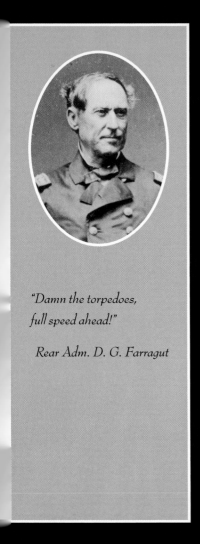

"Damn the torpedoes, full speed ahead!"

Rear Adm. D. G. Farragut

NORTHERN COMMANDERS:
Rear Adm. D. G. Farragut
Maj. Gen. G. Granger

STRENGTH: 2,400
plus naval crew

CASUALTIES: 319

THE BATTLE OF MOBILE BAY

August 5, 1864

The Union victory at Mobile Bay effectively blocked the last port available for Confederate blockade running.

In 1862, the ports of New Orleans and Pensacola fell to the Union, leaving Mobile, Alabama, as the major Confederate port in the Gulf of Mexico. Forts Morgan and Gaines protected the entrance to Mobile Bay, and the Confederates had mined the channel with torpedoes.

In the summer of 1864, the Union navy set up a blockade to prevent Confederate ships from leaving the port. When the North learned that Rear Admiral Franklin Buchanan intended to run the blockade with the ironclad *Tennessee,* the situation came to a head. Rear Admiral David Farragut ordered fourteen Union wooden ships be lashed in pairs with the larger of each pair facing Fort Morgan. Farragut planned to run the ships in a line past the Confederate forts and engage the *Tennessee.*

The Union's run began at 5:30 A.M. on August 5. The day started inauspiciously, as the USS *Tecumseh* encountered the minefield, was hit, and quickly sank. The next ship in line, the *Brooklyn,* spied buoys dead ahead, suspected them to be the minefield boundary, and reversed engines. This stalled all the ships behind and exposed them to heavy fire from Fort Morgan. Farragut, lashed to the rigging of the USS *Hartford* to keep from falling from his perch, demanded a reason for the delay. When told about the underwater torpedoes and the sailors' reluctance to move through the minefield, he called out, "Damn the torpedoes, full speed ahead!" The Federal ships passed the minefield untouched. (Fourteen of the *Hartford's* crew received Congressional Medals of Honor.)

When Farragut finally encountered Buchanan on the *Tennessee,* Farragut began what he later called "one of the fiercest naval combats on record." Throughout the day, three Union ironclads clashed with the *Tennessee* and its accompanying three gunboats, but the ship withstood the barrage. The only damage inflicted upon the *Tennessee* came from the *Manhattan's* fifteen-inch, solid shot. Overpowered and over-

Fort Gaines and Mobile Bay

"You shall not have it to say when you leave this vessel that you were not near enough to the enemy, for I will meet them, and then you can fight them alongside of their own ships; and if I fall, lay me on one side and go on with the fight."

Rear Adm. F. Buchanan

whelmed, the *Tennessee* finally surrendered. Fort Gaines followed within days, but Fort Morgan held out for more than two weeks before it also surrendered to the Union. The city of Mobile, however, remained in Southern hands until the end of the war, although its naval significance was erased by the Union victory at Mobile Bay.

SOUTHERN COMMANDERS:
Rear Adm. F. Buchanan
Capt. J. D. Johnston

STRENGTH: 2200

CASUALTIES: 312

Cannon, Fort Gaines

TANNEHILL IRONWORKS HISTORICAL STATE PARK

122632 Confederate Parkway, McCalla, AL
PHONE: 205-477-5711
HOURS: Open daily.
ADMISSION: Free.

Tannehill Ironworks was the largest producer of ordnance, skillets, pots, and ovens for the Confederate army. At its height, Tannehill produced up to twenty tons of iron a day. However, as part of Union General James Wilson's raid on Alabama war industry sites, Tannehill Ironworks was burned to the ground on March 31, 1865. Today, more than 1,500 acres are preserved for hiking, camping, and recreation. From spring through autumn, blacksmiths, millers, and craftsmen are available to demonstrate their time-honored trade. Artifacts of the nineteenth century iron industry are displayed in the Iron and Steel Museum.

THE OLD DEPOT MUSEUM

4 Martin Luther King Street, Selma, AL
PHONE: 334-874-2197
HOURS: Open daily.
ADMISSION: A fee is charged for adults; children and seniors are discounted.

The Old Depot Museum is housed in a former railway passenger station built in 1890 on the site of the Greater Naval Ordnance Works and Arsenal of the Confederacy. A cameo of Elodie Todd Dawson, Abraham Lincoln's sister-in-law and an avid Confederate, offers a poignant reminder that the Civil War split many families. Confederate bills, many printed in Selma, recall "the lost cause" in all its frailty. Nearly half of the munitions used by the Confederacy were manufactured on this site. Here the Brooke Cannon, the most powerful muzzle-loading cannon, was produced as was the ironclad *Tennessee*, of the Battle of Mobile Bay. Shells and cannonballs, remnants of the South's largest industrial complex, may be seen and touched by visitors to the museum.

Photograph on display, The Old Depot Museum

OLD LIVE OAK CEMETERY

Dallas Avenue, Selma, AL
PHONE: 334-874-2161
HOURS: Open daily.
ADMISSION: Free.

Old Live Oak Cemetery contains the remains of many Confederate soldiers as well as some notable civilians. These include Elodie Todd Dawson, staunch Confederate supporter and sister-in-law of Abraham Lincoln; N. H. R. Dawson, Confederate colonel who later was appointed U.S. Commissioner of Education; John Tyler Morgan and Edmund Winston Pettus, both Confederate generals who later became U.S. senators; Catesby ap Roger Jones, commander of the Confederate ironclad *Merrimac* and of the Greater Confederate Naval Ordnance Works at Selma; and the Reverend Arthur Small, a Presbyterian minister who died in the Battle of Selma.

FIRST WHITE HOUSE OF THE CONFEDERACY

644 Washington Avenue, Montgomery, AL
PHONE: 334-242-1861
HOURS: Open weekdays.
ADMISSION: Free.

The first Confederate government of President Jefferson Davis met here from February to May of 1861, when it then moved to Richmond, Virginia. The United Daughters of the Confederate States celebrate Robert E. Lee's birthday here every January and Jefferson Davis's birthday every June.

Jefferson Davis's bedroom

First White House of the Confederacy

ALABAMA STATE CAPITOL

600 Dexter Avenue, Montgomery, AL

PHONE: 334-242-3935

HOURS: Open daily except Sunday; closed major holidays.

ADMISSION: Free.

In February 1861, Confederate President Jefferson Davis delivered his inaugural address from the Alabama State Capitol. Built in 1851, the Greek Revival building contains twin, two-story, spiral staircases and a ninety-foot-high rotunda. The first Confederate Constitution was written in its senate.

ALABAMA DEPARTMENT OF ARCHIVES AND HISTORY

624 Washington Avenue, Montgomery, AL

PHONE: 334-833-4437

HOURS: Open Tuesday–Saturday; closed state holidays.

ADMISSION: Free.

Located across the street from the capitol, the Alabama Department of Archives and History contains exhibits on the Confederacy, the Civil War, and the presidency of Jefferson Davis. The department's collection of Civil War flags is among the largest in the state.

 # FORT GAINES HISTORIC SITE

Bienville Boulevard, Dauphin Island, Mobile, AL

PHONE: 334-861-6992

HOURS: Open daily; closed Thanksgiving and Christmas.

ADMISSION: A fee is charged for adults; children are discounted.

Latrines, Fort Gaines

Battlements and soldiers' living quarters at the fort may still be seen. A self-guided tour takes approximately one hour. Past annual events have included Confederate encampments; "Thunder of the Bay," a reenactment of the Battle of Mobile Bay; a "Damn the Torpedoes" celebration; and a women's encampment.

Cannon, Fort Gaines Historic Site

FRIENDS OF MAGNOLIA CEMETERY

1202 Virginia Street, Mobile, AL
PHONE: 334-432-8672
HOURS: Open weekdays; closed holidays.
ADMISSION: Free.

Opened in 1836, this is the second oldest municipal cemetery in Mobile. Confederate Generals Braxton Bragg, James Hagan, Adley Gladden, Danville Leadbetter, Jones M. Withers, and Thomas Kilshaw are interred here as is the youngest Confederate General, John H. Kelly. Kelly became a general at nineteen and was killed five years later at the Battle of Blakeley. Other Union and Confederate casualties from Fort Blakeley, Spanish Fort, and the Battle of Mobile Bay are buried here as well. Lieutenant J. L. Moses fired the last shot in the Battle of Blakeley and, by refusing to surrender, gave his life in the defense of Mobile. Kate Cummings, a Civil War nurse is also buried at Magnolia.

Historic Fort Blakeley State Park

33707 Alabama Highway 225, Spanish Fort, AL
Phone: 334-580-0005
Hours: Open daily; closed Christmas.
Admission: A fee is charged; children are discounted.

The state park was created in 1981 to preserve the National Register Site and its five-and-a-half miles of pristine breastworks; the park encompasses 3,800 acres. Civil War fortifications may still be seen along eight miles of nature trails. Every year a Civil War reenactment takes place in April which commemorates the fighting that began with a Federal assault on April 9, 1865, six hours after General Lee surrendered at Appomattox Court House in Virginia.

It is estimated that somewhere between 6,000 and 9,000 United States Colored Troops fought here for the Union, making this site the third largest incident of African-American troops in battle in the entire Civil War. "Greater gallantry than was shown by the officers and men could hardly be desired," wrote Gen. C. C. Andrews of the Black Division. As the African-American troops roared toward the Confederate stronghold, some Southerners, dreading to fall into their hands, ran toward the white troops and quickly surrendered to them.

Spanish Fort at Fort Blakeley State Park

FORT MORGAN HISTORIC SITE

51 Alabama Highway 180 West, Gulf Shores, AL

PHONE: 334-540-7125

HOURS: Open daily.

ADMISSION: A fee is charged; children, seniors, and groups are discounted.

Much of Fort Morgan remains in excellent condition and is still standing. A self-guided tour is available of the site. Fort Morgan features a museum, an information center, and an annual living history encampment that commemorates the Battle of Mobile Bay and the Siege of Fort Morgan.

Left: Interior wall, Fort Morgan

Photo below: Aerial view of Fort Morgan

ARKANSAS

*A*rkansas offered the Confederacy little in the way of agricultural, industrial, or transportation resources; but it did produce 60,000 volunteers to fight for the Southern rebellion. In May of 1861, the state legislature voted near unanimously to secede. The one vote for remaining loyal to the Union came from the northwestern Ozarks region, where the Confederacy was trusted as little as any other form of government. Ironically, it was in that northwestern corner of the state—not in the slaveholding counties of the south and east—that the Civil War first came to Arkansas, in battles at Pea Ridge and Prairie Grove, both of which helped the Union secure control of the state.

A frontier state at the time of the Civil War, Arkansas is still largely rural, and its battlefields have not been hemmed in or swallowed up by development. Much in Arkansas remains unchanged; especially at the Civil War battlefields, where it is not too difficult to imagine the sights and sounds of the long-ago conflict.

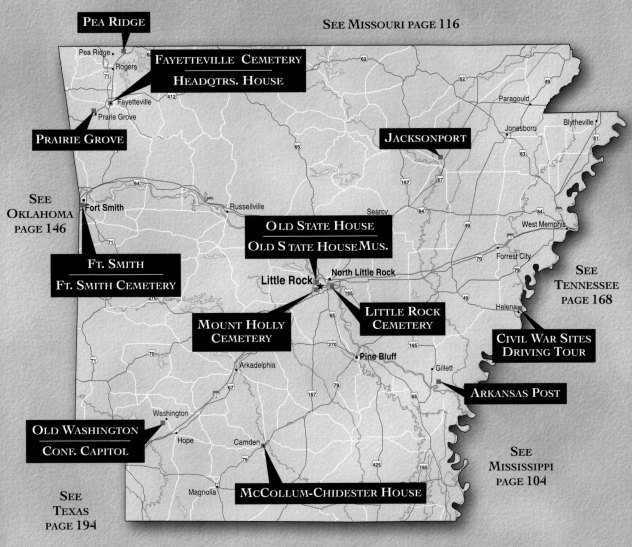

PEA RIDGE

SEE MISSOURI PAGE 116

Pea Ridge

Rogers

FAYETTEVILLE CEMETERY

HEADQTRS. HOUSE

62

62

49

Paragould

Fayetteville

412

Prarie Grove

Jonesboro

Blytheville

61

PRAIRIE GROVE

JACKSONPORT

65

167

67

63

SEE
OKLAHOMA
PAGE 146

64

Fort Smith

Russellville

40

Searcy

64

49

West Memphis

40

FT. SMITH

FT. SMITH CEMETERY

71

OLD STATE HOUSE

OLD STATE HOUSE MUS.

Forrest City

70

79

Helena

SEE
TENNESSEE
PAGE 168

270

Little Rock

North Little Rock

165

**MOUNT HOLLY
CEMETERY**

65

**LITTLE ROCK
CEMETERY**

49

**CIVIL WAR SITES
DRIVING TOUR**

71

70

270

165

Arkadelphia

Pine Bluff

Gillett

ARKANSAS POST

167

79

65

30

67

Washington

OLD WASHINGTON

CONF. CAPITOL

Hope

Camden

425

165

SEE
MISSISSIPPI
PAGE 104

79

SEE
TEXAS
PAGE 194

Magnolia

McCOLLUM-CHIDESTER HOUSE

SEE LOUISIANA PAGE 74

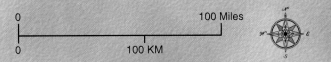

0   100 Miles

0   100 KM

NORTHERN COMMANDER: Maj. Gen. S. R. Curtis

STRENGTH: 10,250

CASUALTIES: 1,384

THE BATTLE OF PEA RIDGE (ELKHORN TAVERN)

March 6–8, 1862

Although it took place in Arkansas, this battle secured Missouri for the Union and led to Union victory in Arkansas.

General Sterling Price, former governor of Missouri and Confederate sympathizer who led a Pro-Confederate State Guard, menaced the Union army after the battle of Wilson's Creek and threatened to disrupt the Union advance down the Mississippi River. The North had to suppress Price who had joined the Confederate troops in February 1862. On the other side, the Confederates were determined to invade and retake Missouri through the new Confederate Army of the West under Major General Earl Van Dorn. In December of 1861, Brigadier General Samuel R. Curtis took command of the Union army in Missouri, and his first objective was to drive Rebel factions from the state. With this in mind, Curtis marched to Springfield and forced Confederate sympathizers, led by Price, into Arkansas. Once there, Price's men joined with Confederates under General Ben McCulloch; their combined forces came under the command of General Van Dorn.

On March 6, Curtis and his troops marched near Pea

Pea Ridge National Military Park

Cannon at Elkhorn Tavern, Pea Ridge National Military Park

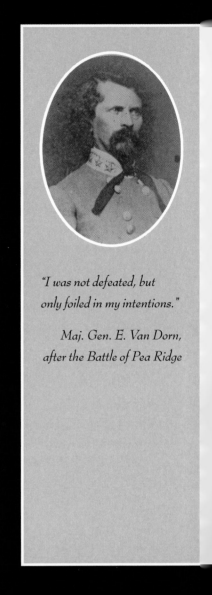

"I was not defeated, but only foiled in my intentions."

Maj. Gen. E. Van Dorn,
after the Battle of Pea Ridge

Ridge to Elkhorn Tavern, along Little Sugar Creek. That evening, Van Dorn also reached Little Sugar Creek but chose to come around the rear of the Union from the north. Curtis learned of the flanking movement and turned his twenty-one guns about. Price and McCulloch split up due to their difference in speed, so McCulloch turned toward Leetown. Curtis attacked both Confederate divisions the morning of March 7. Darkness finally halted the fighting. During the night, Curtis and Van Dorn repositioned their men to continue fighting around Elkhorn Tavern in the morning. The Confederates held their own until their artillery ammunition ran out due to ordnance trains being separated from the main body of the army. Then the Southern rout began into the heart of Arkansas. This ended any serious threat to Missouri.

SOUTHERN COMMANDERS:
Maj. Gen. E. Van Dorn
Maj. Gen. S. Price

STRENGTH: 16,500

CASUALTIES: 1,500

PEA RIDGE NATIONAL MILITARY PARK

U.S. Highway 62, Pea Ridge, AR

PHONE: 501-451-8122

HOURS: Open daily; closed Thanksgiving, Christmas, and New Year's Day.

ADMISSION: A fee is charged for adults or per car; children and seniors are discounted.

With more than 4,300 acres of the Pea Ridge Battlefield contained within its boundaries, this military park might be one of the best-preserved Civil War battle sites in the U.S. The park includes a reconstruction of Elkhorn Tavern on its original site. The tavern is open for tours from Memorial Day until Labor Day weekend. Markers outline key events of the battle on a seven-mile self-guided tour. A ten-mile hiking trail is also available. The Visitor's Center features a twelve-minute slide presentation on events before, during, and after the battle; and a museum houses exhibits pertaining to the battle. Living history programs occur throughout the year.

PRAIRIE GROVE BATTLEFIELD STATE PARK

14262 West U.S. Highway 62, Prairie Grove, AR

PHONE: 501-846-2990

HOURS: Open daily.

ADMISSION: Admission to park is free. Museum charges a fee; children are discounted.

The 400-acre Prairie Grove Battlefield State Park includes a nineteenth-century museum village, a Visitor's Center, Hindman Hall Museum, and the Morrow House. This house served as headquarters for Confederate General Hindman prior to the Battle of Prairie Grove. Among the exhibits at the Hindman Hall Museum are a diorama of the battle, Civil War artifacts, and displays on the soldier's life. A driving tour and one-mile walking trail are also available.

Photo above: Hindman Hall Museum

Photo below: Morrow House

FAYETTEVILLE NATIONAL CEMETERY

700 South Government Avenue, Fayetteville, AR
PHONE: 501-444-5051
HOURS: Open daily.
ADMISSION: Free.

Fayetteville National Cemetery was established in 1867, and the bodies of 1,975 soldiers were moved from the battlegrounds of Pea Ridge, Prairie Grove, and Fayetteville to this final resting place; 1,100 of the interred are unknown. Each year Memorial Day services commemorate the soldiers buried here.

HEADQUARTERS HOUSE

118 East Dickson Street, Fayetteville, AR
PHONE: 501-521-2970 (Washington County National Historical Society)
HOURS: Open Monday and Saturday mornings and Thursday afternoons.
ADMISSION: A fee is charged; children are discounted.

Headquarters House was built in 1853 by a Northern sympathizer and judge who was imprisoned for his political views. At various times, the

Headquarters House

house served as headquarters for both the Union and Confederate commanders. The Battle of Fayetteville was partially fought on the house grounds, and a hole made by a minié ball is still visible in one of the doors. Reenactments of the Battle of Fayetteville occur here each April.

FORT SMITH NATIONAL HISTORIC SITE

47 South 3rd Street, Fort Smith, AR
PHONE: 501-783-3961
HOURS: Open daily; closed Christmas and New Year's Day.
ADMISSION: Free.

Originally a Union fort, Fort Smith fell into Confederate hands in 1861, then was recaptured by Union forces in 1863. Until the end of the war, it remained as a base for Federal

Fort Smith National Historic Site

operations in Arkansas. The Visitor's Center offers self-guided walking tours, artifacts, exhibits, and a fifteen-minute film on the history of the fort. Marked walking trails along the Arkansas River lead to the site of the first fort.

Bastion #3, Fort Smith National Historic Site

FORT SMITH NATIONAL CEMETERY

522 Garland Avenue, Fort Smith, AR
PHONE: 501-783-5345
HOURS: Open daily.
ADMISSION: Free.

More than 1,500 unknown soldiers are buried at Fort Smith National Cemetery. Also interred at the cemetery are Confederate Generals James B. McIntosh who fought and died at Pea Ridge, Richard C. Gatlin who was the Adjutant General of North Carolina, and Alexander Early Steen who fought and died at Prairie Grove. The cemetery's office houses a few exhibits on the area's military history.

OLD WASHINGTON HISTORIC STATE PARK
CONFEDERATE STATE CAPITOL

Franklin Street, Washington, AR
PHONE: 870-983-2684
HOURS: Open daily; closed Christmas, New Year's Day, and Thanksgiving.
ADMISSION: Park is free; a fee is charged for house tours.

The Old Washington Historic State Park served as the state capital between 1864–65. The park features a nineteenth-century museum village, which includes the building that served as the Confederate capitol in Arkansas and a weapons museum. There is an annual reenactment of the Civil War experience at the park in late autumn.

1836 Courthouse, Old Washington Historic State Park

McCollum-Chidester House Museum

926 Washington Street, Camden, AR
Phone: 870-836-9243
Hours: Open Wednesday–Saturday, April–October.
Admission: A fee is charged; children are discounted.

The city of Camden was occupied by Northern forces in 1864. During the occupation, Gen. Frederick Steele, commander of the force, used this house as his headquarters.

McCollum-Chidester House Museum

Little Rock National Cemetery

Minnesota Monument

2523 Confederate Boulevard, Little Rock, AR
Phone: 501-324-6401
Hours: Open daily.
Admission: Free.

The grounds of Little Rock National Cemetery were originally used as a Union camp. After Union troops evacuated, the Confederates used the area in which to bury their dead. In 1868, the land was purchased by the U.S. government to use as a cemetery for the Union troops. A wall was constructed between the Union and Confederate dead but was removed in 1913. Approximately 5,000–6,000 soldiers are buried here. The Confederate markers are slightly more pointed than the Union gravestones. Legend has it that the Confederates used pointed stones to prevent Union soldiers from sitting on the markers. Services are held on Memorial Day and on Confederate Civil War Memorial Day in April.

Mount Holly Cemetery

12th Street and Broadway, Little Rock, AR
Phone: Not Available.
Hours: Open daily.
Admission: Free.

Mount Holly Cemetery, established in 1843, is the final resting place of executed Confederate spy David O. Dodd and five Confederate generals.

Photo right: Mount Holly Cemetery

OLD STATE HOUSE MUSEUM

300 West Markham Street, Little Rock, AR
PHONE: 501-324-9685
HOURS: Open daily; closed major holidays.
ADMISSION: Free.

The building that houses Old State House Museum was used as the state's capitol from 1836–1911. In 1861 it was the site of the Arkansas Secession Convention. In 1863 the Confederate government fled as Union troops moved into Little Rock. During the subsequent occupation, the building served as the seat of the occupational government until the end of the war. The Old State House Museum houses a collection of Confederate battle flags. A new exhibit, *Into Secessia*, presents a Federal perspective on Little Rock history. A Visitor's Center has information on self-guided tours

Old State Museum

ARKANSAS POST NATIONAL MEMORIAL

1741 Old Post Road, Gillett, AR
PHONE: 870-548-2207
HOURS: Open daily; closed major holidays.
ADMISSION: Free.

During the Civil War, the Confederates tried to maintain control of the Arkansas River by erecting an earthen fort at this site. In 1863 the Union destroyed the fort and gained control of the river.

The museum features a fourteen-minute film documenting the fort's history. The memorial also a two-and-half-mile walking trail that runs along the edge of the bayou.

The Arkansas River as seen from Arkansas Post National Memorial

JACKSONPORT STATE PARK

205 Avenue Street off Arkansas Highway 69, Jacksonport, AR
PHONE: 870-523-2143
HOURS: Open daily; museum and boat open various days.
ADMISSION: Free.

Because of its access to both the Mississippi and Arkansas Rivers, Jacksonport was of prime importance during the war and was occupied by both the Confederate and Union armies. Five generals used the town as their headquarters. On June 5, 1865, Confederate Gen. Jeff Thompson, the

Jacksonport State Park

"Swamp Fox of the Confederacy," surrendered 6,000 troops to Lt. Col. C. W. Davis at the Jacksonport Landing. The 162-acre park sits on the White and Black Rivers. On the grounds are a museum whose Civil War room exhibits extensive memorabilia and a Civil War monument. Camping is allowed for a fee.

CIVIL WAR SITES DRIVING TOUR

226 Perry Street, Helena, AR
PHONE: 870-338-9831
HOURS: Open weekdays.
ADMISSION: Free.

The Civil War Sites Driving Tour features important sites of the July 4, 1863, Battle of Helena, won by Union forces. The tour also features the Confederate Cemetery, where Confederate casualties from the Battle of Helena are interred. Brochures of the driving tour, which features four Union battery sites located on private property, are available at Helena City Hall.

FLORIDA

*D*espite having seen little battle, Florida's borders contain a diverse collection of Civil War history. Throughout the state, Florida's Civil War past is evident in its fortresses, museums, and historical sites. Although it was the southernmost state of the Confederacy, many of Florida's strategic forts and cities were controlled by Union forces. Dry Tortugas Fort, the largest all-masonry fort in the Western Hemisphere, was held by the North throughout the war.

With access to both the Atlantic Ocean and the Gulf of Mexico, Florida's peninsular location has made it a key tactical position since the Spanish first arrived in 1513. Castillo de San Marcos, the country's oldest surviving fort, was occupied by both Confederate and Union forces. Similarly, Fort Clinch in Fernandina Beach and Fort Barrancas in Pensacola were also controlled by both armies at different times during the Civil War. St. Marks Lighthouse, now a National Wildlife Refuge, was the site of a Confederate lookout tower, which Union forces attempted to burn in 1863.

The war's grip stretched as far south as Key West, where Fort Zachary Taylor boasts the nation's largest collection of Civil War armament. Each February a reenactment of the Battle of Olustee commemorates the only major battle fought in Florida. After defeat, Union forces returned to Jacksonville, and the state of Florida was secured as part of the Confederacy.

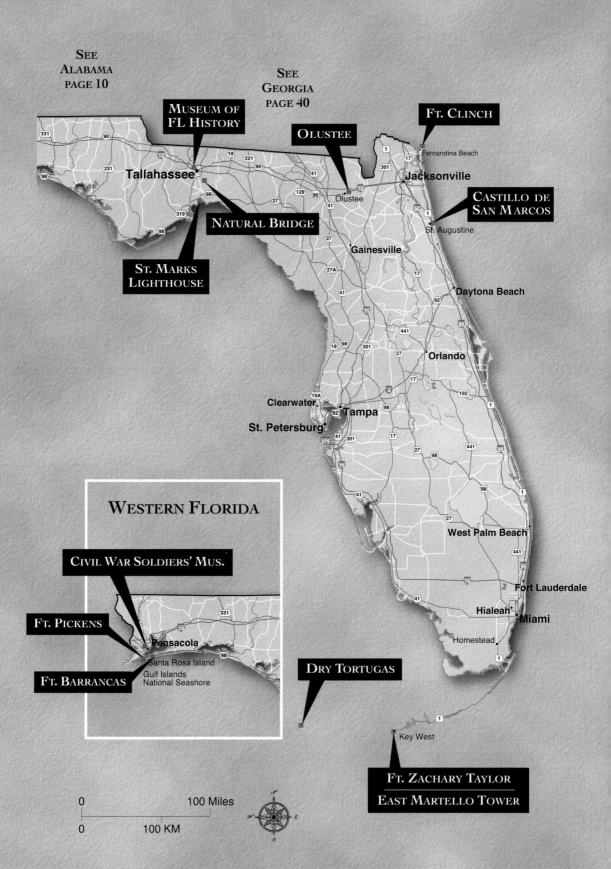

SEE
ALABAMA
PAGE 10

SEE
GEORGIA
PAGE 40

MUSEUM OF
FL HISTORY

OLUSTEE

FT. CLINCH

Fernandina Beach

Tallahassee

Jacksonville

CASTILLO DE
SAN MARCOS

NATURAL BRIDGE

St. Augustine

ST. MARKS
LIGHTHOUSE

Olustee

Gainesville

Daytona Beach

Orlando

Clearwater

Tampa

St. Petersburg

WESTERN FLORIDA

CIVIL WAR SOLDIERS' MUS.

West Palm Beach

FT. PICKENS

Pensacola

Fort Lauderdale

Hialeah

Miami

FT. BARRANCAS

Santa Rosa Island
Gulf Islands
National Seashore

Homestead

DRY TORTUGAS

Key West

0   100 Miles

0   100 KM

FT. ZACHARY TAYLOR
EAST MARTELLO TOWER

"Have met the enemy at Olustee and now falling back. Many wounded. Think I may be compelled to go to Baldwin, but shall go to Barber's immediately. . . . A devilish hard rub."

Brig. Gen. T. A. Seymour

NORTHERN
COMMANDER:
Brig. Gen. T. A. Seymour

STRENGTH: 5,500

CASUALTIES: 1,861

THE BATTLE OF OLUSTEE

February 20, 1864

The only major Civil War battle in Florida.

In December of 1863, President Abraham Lincoln issued the Proclamation of Amnesty and Reconstruction, offering pardon and amnesty to all Confederate supporters, except for government and military leaders, who would pledge their support to the Union. Included in the proclamation was a provision for Union loyal governments to be set up in states where ten percent of voters had pledged such loyalty. Lincoln had high hopes for Florida, where Union support ran high in the northern part of the state.

In February of 1864, Lincoln sent General Truman A. Seymour's Union troops to northern Florida. Included in Seymour's division were the men of the Fifty-fourth Massachusetts

Olustee Battlefield State Historic Site

Infantry, the African-American unit that had fought at Fort Wagner, South Carolina, under Colonel Robert Gould Shaw.

Seymour's force of approximately 5,000 soldiers landed at Jacksonville and moved inland. Seymour hoped to block the Southern supply line which extended into Florida. Despite the Federal blockade, the peninsula provided numerous ports for Confederate privateers and navy ships.

On February 20, Seymour's men met a Confederate force under Brigadier General Joseph Finegan east of Lake City at Olustee. The two sides, evenly matched in strength, fought through the afternoon in a bloody conflict. The Confederate forces, however, proved stronger, and the Union troops retreated to Jacksonville. The Confederates did not pursue; and once safely inside Jacksonville, the Union controlled the city for the remainder of the Civil War.

After Olustee, fighting in Florida increased. Smaller battles were fought in Gainesville, Marianna, Fort Myers, and Natural Bridge. The Confederate District of Florida surrendered to the Union on May 10, 1865.

"I pressed forward my cavalry force last night in the direction of Baldwin. I have received no report from them yet, but think that the enemy has abandoned Baldwin and retired to Jacksonville."

Brig. Gen. J. Finegan

SOUTHERN COMMANDER:
Brig. Gen. J. Finegan

STRENGTH: 5,000

CASUALTIES: 946

Cannon, Olustee Battlefield State Historic Site

THE CIVIL WAR SOLDIERS' MUSEUM

108 South Palafox Place, Pensacola, FL
PHONE: 850-469-1900
HOURS: Open Tuesday–Saturday; closed major holidays.
ADMISSION: A fee is charged.

This museum houses arms, equipment, and personal effects of soldiers from both sides of the Civil War. The museum's collection also includes exhibits on Civil War medicine and on Pensacola's Civil War history. A video entitled "Pensacola During the Civil War" is shown.

FORT BARRANCAS

40 Gulf Islands National Seashore, Florida Highway 292 to U.S. Naval Air Station, south end of Navy Boulevard U.S. Naval Air Station, Pensacola, FL

PHONE: 850-455-5167
HOURS: Open daily.
ADMISSION: Free.

Fort Barrancas has been restored and is a part of the Gulf Island National Seashore. The original fort was occupied by Confederate forces from 1861 until they withdrew in May 1862. Although artillery fire was exchanged with nearby Fort Pickens, Fort Barrancas was never attacked. Self-guided tours of the fort are available.

Fort Barrancas from across the bay

FORT PICKENS

1801 Gulf Breeze Parkway, Santa Rosa Island, Gulf Breeze, FL

PHONE: 850-934-2600 (Gulf Island National Seashore)
HOURS: Open daily.
ADMISSION: A fee is charged by the car; over 62 are free.

Built in 1829, this fort was occupied by Union troops throughout the war, despite an initial inclination to surrender the fort to the Confederacy. Fort Pickens is the site of the first Civil War battle in Florida. When Federal forces refused to evacuate the fort, Confeder-

Photo right: Casemates, Fort Pickens

Cannon, Fort Pickens

ate troops attacked unsuccessfully. In 1862 Southern leaders moved their troops to more active areas and abandoned their positions in the Pensacola area. A Visitor's Center and guided tours are available.

MUSEUM OF FLORIDA HISTORY

500 South Bronough Street, Tallahassee, FL
PHONE: 850-488-1484
HOURS: Open daily; closed Thanksgiving and Christmas.
ADMISSION: Free.

This state history museum includes Civil War military armament, soldier's personal effects, and Confederate battle flags. Nearby, the Old Capitol building houses Civil War exhibits.

Photo above: Civil War-era pistol, Museum of Florida History

Photo right: Civil War encampment, Museum of Florida History

NATURAL BRIDGE BATTLEFIELD STATE HISTORIC SITE

Natural Bridge Road, Woodville, FL
PHONE: 850-922-6007
HOURS: Open daily.
ADMISSION: Free.

On March 6, 1865, Confederate troops, including cadets and home guards, defeated Union troops as they attempted to cross St. Marks River at Natural Bridge. This historic site features a monument outlining the battle and a listing of the names of the Confederate soldiers who took part in the battle. Self-interpretive plaques are also available. Each March the site hosts a reenactment of the Battle of Natural Bridge.

Confederate monument, Natural Bridge Battlefield State Historic Site

ST. MARKS LIGHTHOUSE

St. Marks National Wildlife Refuge, on Country Road C-59, south of Tallahassee, FL
PHONE: 850-925-6121
HOURS: Open daily.
ADMISSION: A fee is charged.

In June 1862, the Union navy shelled the Confederate breastworks around St. Marks Lighthouse. The Confederates extinguished the light, abandoned the lighthouse, and attempted to blow it up to prevent Union occupation; the blast only damaged the base of the tower. Because a Federal ship had already run aground, the Union desired to use the lighthouse as a lookout and signal point; however, the lighthouse was not fully restored until after the Civil War. Although visitors are not permitted in the structure, the wildlife refuge around the site is open.

Photo right: St. Marks Lighthouse

OLUSTEE BATTLEFIELD STATE HISTORIC SITE

U.S. Highway 90, Olustee, FL

PHONE: 904-758-0400

HOURS: Open daily.

ADMISSION: Free.

The Olustee Battlefield State Historic Site represents the largest Civil War battle in Florida. Trails with interpretive markers offer a self-guided walk through the battle site. Each February the Battle of Olustee is reenacted. A small museum features several Civil War artifacts.

FORT CLINCH STATE PARK

2601 Atlantic Avenue, Fernandina Beach, FL

PHONE: 904-277-7274

HOURS: Open daily.

ADMISSION: A fee is charged; children under 6 are free.

The Union began construction of Fort Clinch in 1847 but never completed it. The partially finished building was occupied by Confederate forces from 1861 until threat of a Union naval expedition forced evacuation in March 1862. For the remainder of the war, Union troops occupied Fort Clinch. Guided tours of the fort are available. A reenactment of sentry duty and drills takes place on the first weekend of each month. Special Union garrison reenactments are scheduled for the first weekend in May, and Confederate garrison reenactments take place during the last week in October.

Fort Clinch State Park

CASTILLO DE SAN MARCOS NATIONAL MONUMENT

1 South Castillo Drive, Augustine, FL
PHONE: 904-829-6506
HOURS: Open daily; closed Christmas.
ADMISSION: A fee is charged for adults; children and seniors are discounted.

The Castillo de San Marcos (called Fort Marion during the Civil War) was originally built by the Spanish between 1672 and 1695. Confederate forces occupied the fort from 1861 until a threat from Union naval forces caused them to withdraw in 1862. Several times a day, rangers give informative talks and guided tours; information and exhibits are available inside the fort.

DRY TORTUGAS NATIONAL PARK

Dry Tortugas Island, FL
PHONE: 305-242-7700; (includes transportation information to island)
HOURS: Open daily.
ADMISSION: Free.

The largest all-masonry fort in the Western Hemisphere, Fort Jefferson was garrisoned by Union troops throughout the Civil War. It also served as a military prison. Exhibits and self-guided tours of the fort are available.

FORT ZACHARY TAYLOR STATE HISTORIC SITE

End of Southerd Street at Fort Zachary Taylor, Key West, FL
PHONE: 305-292-6713
HOURS: Open daily.
ADMISSION: A fee is charged.

Fort Zachary Taylor State Historic Site

Construction on Fort Zachary Taylor began in 1845 and was completed in 1866. To aid in the coastal blockade, Union troops quickly secured Fort Zachary Taylor at the outset of the war and occupied it for the war's entirety. Cannon inside the fort comprise one of the largest groups of Civil War heavy artillery in existence. Tours of Fort Zachary Taylor are given daily. In February the park hosts a heritage festival at the site which provides a living history showcase.

EAST MARTELLO TOWER

3501 South Roosevelt Boulevard, Key West, FL
PHONE: 305-296-3913
HOURS: Open daily; closed Christmas.
ADMISSION: A fee is charged; children are discounted.

The unfinished East and West Martello Towers were built to defend Fort Zachary Taylor from a Confederate attack which never occurred. Although no battles took place at the tower, the site provides an accurate picture of Union fortifications. Today the East Martello Tower houses a general art gallery and a Key West Museum. The museum contains some Civil War artifacts and replicas of the tower's armaments.

East Martello Tower

GEORGIA

Georgia, the most populous and prosperous state in the Deep South, was early to secede from the Union and quick to make its first contributions to the Confederacy in the form of materiel and food. Georgia's factories provided powder, arms, shoes, and uniforms; its farms produced corn and hogs. In addition, with 1,400 miles of railroad tracks, Georgia could move food, supplies, and men quickly and efficiently. Whereas there were early Civil War naval battles off the Georgia coast, it was not until the fall of 1863 at Chickamauga that large-scale land warfare came to Georgia, and not until the following spring when Union General William T. Sherman began his long march through the state—first from Chattanooga to Atlanta, and then from Atlanta to Savannah—that interior Georgia felt the full brunt of the Civil War. When Sherman left Savannah in January of 1865, Georgia's active role in the Civil War was over.

In all, more than 550 battles or skirmishes were fought on Georgia soil, and the state sent 100,000 men to fight for the Confederacy. Georgia's support of the Confederate cause was complete, and thus the destruction and devastation of the Civil War touched the state in every corner. Although much of Georgia's Civil War heritage has been lost to development and neglect, Civil War sites are abundant throughout the state, and in recent decades Georgia has made renewed efforts to preserve the evidence and artifacts of its Civil War past.

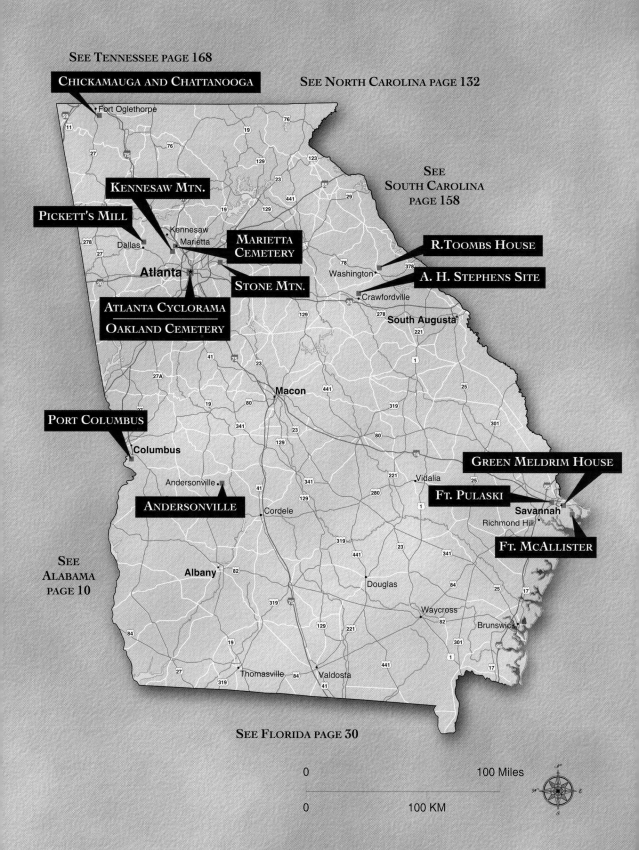

SEE TENNESSEE PAGE 168

CHICKAMAUGA AND CHATTANOOGA

SEE NORTH CAROLINA PAGE 132

Fort Oglethorpe

SEE
SOUTH CAROLINA
PAGE 158

KENNESAW MTN.

PICKETT'S MILL

R.TOOMBS HOUSE

Kennesaw

Marietta

**MARIETTA
CEMETERY**

A. H. STEPHENS SITE

Dallas

Washington

Crawfordville

Atlanta

STONE MTN.

ATLANTA CYCLORAMA

OAKLAND CEMETERY

South Augusta

Macon

PORT COLUMBUS

GREEN MELDRIM HOUSE

Vidalia

Columbus

FT. PULASKI

Andersonville

Savannah

ANDERSONVILLE

Richmond Hill

Cordele

FT. McALLISTER

SEE
ALABAMA
PAGE 10

Albany

Douglas

Waycross

Brunswick

Thomasville

Valdosta

SEE FLORIDA PAGE 30

0   100 Miles

0   100 KM

NORTHERN COMMANDER:
Maj. Gen. W. S. Rosecrans

STRENGTH: 62,000

CASUALTIES: 16,170

THE BATTLE OF CHICKAMAUGA

September 18–20, 1863

This battle near the Tennessee border was the last great Confederate victory.

The city of Chattanooga, in southeastern Tennessee near the Georgia border, was a link to the Deep South by rail and, therefore, a strategic military objective for the Union. In 1863 the city was protected by Confederate General Braxton Bragg. Through a series of blunders, both sides stumbled into the Battle of Chickamauga.

In early September 1863, Union General Ambrose Burnside took Knoxville, northeast of Chattanooga. Meanwhile, Major General William Rosecrans's army began to advance upon Chattanooga from the Tennessee River. Outnumbered and outflanked, General Bragg withdrew from Chattanooga south to LaFayette, Georgia, to regroup, obtain reinforcements, and prepare for an attack. Rosecrans learned of the Confederate retreat and concentrated his army, moving them north on the LaFayette Road toward Chattanooga. Bragg, lacking accurate information as to the Union army's

Second Minnesota Monument, Chickamauga and Chattanooga National Military Park

Chickamauga and Chattanooga National Military Park

whereabouts, belatedly seized all the crossings over Chickamauga Creek to keep Rosecrans from the LaFayette Road and to force the Union army away from Chattanooga.

On the evening of September 18, a Union brigade came upon Confederate soldiers who had captured Reed's Bridge on the northern end of the Chickamauga Creek. Believing that this was the only Confederate unit across the creek, the Union army rejoined its corps and, in the morning, turned east into the forest between LaFayette Road and Chickamauga Creek. Throughout the day, both sides fed the battle just to maintain stability. Neither side wanted a fight in the thick terrain. Fighting began at dawn and ended in a stalemate; the Union still held LaFayette Road, but in a defensive position.

The next morning, fighting resumed with no advancement on either side until, acting on false information, Rosecrans moved a division of his men to plug a reported hole in his line. The hole did not exist, but one was created by the move, and the Confederates moved through the gap and cut the Union army in half. The Union army broke and retreated. When the Confederate army did not actively pursue them, Union forces reorganized and marched into Chattanooga; they had lost the battle but had gained the city.

Bragg came under sharp criticism for his decision not to pursue and destroy Rosecrans's army. Left unharassed, the Federals fortified Chattanooga. Chickamauga was the bloodiest two-day battle of the war. Combined, the two sides lost almost 35,000 men.

SOUTHERN COMMANDER: Gen. B. Bragg

STRENGTH: 65,000

CASUALTIES: 18,454

CHICKAMAUGA AND CHATTANOOGA NATIONAL MILITARY PARK

3370 LaFayette Road, Fort Oglethorpe, GA

PHONE: 706-866-9241

HOURS: Open daily, except Christmas.

ADMISSION: Free.

* Note: See Tennessee for additional information concerning the battles of Chickamauga and Chattanooga.

Chickamauga and Chattanooga National Military Park consists of two units overlapping the Georgia and Tennessee borders. The 2,493 acres of the battlefield in this unit include Lookout Mountain, Orchard Knob, Missionary Ridge, and Wauhatchie. This park is the first of four National Military Parks authorized by Congress between 1890 and 1899. The park was officially dedicated in September of 1895.

Each year special programs, such as guided tours of several battlefield areas and Civil War encampments, are presented at Chickamauga Battlefield and Lookout Mountain to commemorate the battles of Chickamauga and Chattanooga. These events take place near the anniversary of the battles (September for Chickamauga and November for Lookout Mountain). Close to Christmas a special program of candlelight tours is held on a weekend at the Cravens House. For the occasion, the house is decorated with Victorian-era Christmas decorations. On the Saturday

First Wisconsin Cavalry Monument (foreground) and Wilder Brigade Monument (background), Chickamauga and Chattanooga National Military Park

Brotherton Cabin, Chickamauga and Chattanooga National Military Park

nearest to July 4, Chickamauga Battlefield hosts an evening "Pops in the Park" concert presented by the Chattanooga Symphony Orchestra. Several weekends during the summer, reenactment organizations present special demonstrations and Civil War encampments at Chickamauga Battlefield and Lookout Mountain. The Visitor's Center features exhibits on the Battle of Chickamauga, the Fuller Gun Collection, a Civil War timeline, and a multi-media program depicting the Battle of Chickamauga.

Photo above right: Chickamauga and Chattanooga National Military Park Headquarters

Photo below right: Chickamauga and Chattanooga National Military Park

> "We gain ground daily, fighting all the time . . . . Our lines are now in close contact and the fighting incessant, with a good deal of artillery. As fast as we gain one position the enemy has another all ready. . . . Kennesaw . . . is the key to the whole country."
>
> *Maj. Gen. W. T. Sherman*

NORTHERN COMMANDER:
Maj. Gen. W. T. Sherman

STRENGTH: 110,000

CASUALTIES: 3,000

THE BATTLE OF KENNESAW MOUNTAIN

June 27, 1864

Kennesaw Mountain was a decisive battle in General William T. Sherman's campaign to capture Atlanta for the Union.

In his campaign to reach and take Atlanta for the Union during the spring of 1864, Major General William T. Sherman, with a force of 100,000 men, began his advance toward the city on May 4 from the northwest corner of Georgia, 100 miles from Atlanta. His route was laid out along the railroad lines connecting Atlanta with Nashville, which were his connection to his supply base in Tennessee. Blocking his way was rugged terrain and 65,000 Confederate soldiers under the command of General Joseph E. Johnston.

Sherman's advance was marked by strategy more than by battle. The Confederates would set up lines of defense, the Union would outflank them, then the Confederates would move south to reset their defenses. By mid-June, Sherman was only thirty miles from Atlanta. On June 27, the general decided to make an aggressive assault on the Confederates so intent upon blocking his way. He chose Kennesaw Mountain, just outside Atlanta, as the site of this assault.

Kennesaw Mountain National Battlefield Park

Illinois Monument, Kennesaw Mountain National Battlefield Park

At 8:00 A.M., the Union struck twice at Confederate defenses on Kennesaw. The day was stiflingly hot and humid, and because the Union was unfamiliar with the thick, dense, and swampy terrain, they met with little success. The lines collided and came to a standstill, in many places falling into hand to hand combat, naming the most bloody area "Dead Angle."

By midday, the battle was over; the Confederates had held their ground against the powerful Union forces, and Union losses were triple that of the South. Still, the loss was only a minor setback for the Union. By September Sherman had taken Atlanta.

"More of their best soldiers lay dead and wounded than the number of British veterans that fell in General Jackson's celebrated battle of New Orleans."

Gen. J. E. Johnston

SOUTHERN COMMANDER:
Gen. J. E. Johnston

STRENGTH: 65,000

CASUALTIES: 1,000

Pickett's Mill State Historic Site and Battlefield

4432 Mt. Tabor Church Road, Dallas, GA
PHONE: 770-443-7850
HOURS: Open daily except Monday; closed major holidays.
ADMISSION: A fee is charged; children are discounted.

Pickett's Mill is the site of a May 27, 1864, battle between General Johnston's Confederates and General Sherman's Union troops during Sherman's March to Atlanta. This battlefield, located just north of Atlanta, is wonder-

Pickett's Mill State Historic Site and Battlefield

fully preserved. Original earthworks are intact, and brochures are available for a self-guided tour. Visitors may view a film on the battle and tour the site on several walking trails. Each year a commemoration of the battle takes place the first weekend after Memorial Day.

Kennesaw Mountain National Battlefield Park

900 Kennesaw Mountain Drive, Kennesaw, GA
PHONE: 770-427-4686
HOURS: Open daily; closed Christmas.
ADMISSION: Free.

Self-guided auto tours are the best way to tour this park, and each stop has wayside exhibits. The Visitor's Center provides information for touring the park, as well as a twenty-minute movie. A

battlefield tour interprets the site, and many trails provide hiking opportunities. Included within the park are earthworks, cannon emplacements, a monument to Georgia's soldiers, and a monument to the 400 Illinois soldiers who died here.

Kennesaw Mountain National Battlefield Park

MARIETTA NATIONAL CEMETERY

500 Washington Avenue, Marietta, GA
PHONE: 770-428-5631
HOURS: Open daily.
ADMISSION: Free.

This is the burial site of more than 13,000 Union casualties from the battles of New Hope Church, Pickett's Mill, and Kennesaw Mountain. Several special services are held during the year and include Four Chaplains' Day in February, Memorial Day in May, POW/MIA Day in September, Veterans Day in November, and Pearl Harbor Day in December.

Marietta National Cemetery

ATLANTA CYCLORAMA AND CIVIL WAR MUSEUM

800 Cherokee Avenue SE, Atlanta, GA
PHONE: 404-658-7625
HOURS: Open daily; closed major holidays.
ADMISSION: A fee is charged; children and seniors discounted.

Atlanta Cyclorama

This Civil War cyclorama, *The Battle of Atlanta*, is the largest painting in the U.S. It was completed in 1886 by German artists. Also on site are exhibits related to Atlanta's involvement in the Civil War as well as a Civil War diorama. The cyclorama and the remains of a Confederate fort are located in the center of Atlanta's Grant Park, named for Col. Lemuel Grant, a native of the city.

HISTORIC OAKLAND CEMETERY

248 Oakland Avenue SE, Atlanta, GA
PHONE: 404-658-6019
HOURS: Open daily.
ADMISSION: Free; a fee is charged for walking tours.

Established in 1850, this eighty-eight-acre cemetery contains the graves of over 3,000 known and 3,500 unknown Confederate soldiers who died defending the city of Atlanta. In addition, approximately forty Union soldiers are interred here. A Confederate obelisk is dedicated to the countless unknown civilians who were killed during the Union siege of Atlanta. Other notable Atlantans who are interred here include Margaret Mitchell, author of *Gone with the Wind*; Bishop Wesley Gaines, bishop of AME church and founder of Morris Brown College; Carrie Steele Logan, founder of Carrie Steele Pitts Home, an orphanage for black children; and Bobby Jones, the golfer. Guided walking tours are available on Saturday and Sunday.

STONE MOUNTAIN PARK AND MUSEUM

U.S. Highway 78, 16 miles east of Atlanta, GA
PHONE: 770-498-5690
HOURS: Open daily.
ADMISSION: A fee is charged.

This 3,200-acre park features a large monument to Confederate leaders. Carved into the face of the mountain are Confederate Generals Lee and Jackson and Confederate President Jefferson Davis. An antebellum mansion and a Civil War museum are also located in the park.

ROBERT TOOMBS HOUSE STATE HISTORIC SITE

216 East Robert Toombs Avenue, Washington, GA
PHONE: 706-678-2226
HOURS: Open daily except Monday; closed major holidays.
ADMISSION: A fee is charged; children are discounted.

After the Civil War, Confederate General Robert Toombs, an outspoken secessionist who was appointed by Confederate President Jefferson Davis to act as Secretary of State to the Confederacy, refused to take the Oath of Allegiance to the United States. When Federal troops came to arrest him, Toombs fled to Cuba. He returned in 1867 when his last child died. President Johnson did not arrest Toombs nor require him to swear an oath. Toombs's restored home contains family furnishings and may be viewed in self-guided tours.

Robert Toombs House State Historic Site

ALEXANDER H. STEPHENS HISTORIC SITE

456 Alexander Street NW, Crawfordville, GA

PHONE: 706-456-2221

HOURS: Open daily, except Monday.

ADMISSION: A fee is charged.

Liberty Hall, the home of Confederate Vice President Alexander H. Stephens, contains many period furnishings, as well as some which belonged to the Stephens family. Also of interest are Stephens's grave and a small Civil War museum.

Liberty Hall,
Alexander H. Stephens Historic Site

THE BATTLE OF FORT PULASKI

April 10–11, 1862

This battle displayed the deadly accuracy of modern weapons, specifically the rifled cannon.

Fort Pulaski, located on Cockspur Island off Georgia's northern coast, sits at the mouth of the Savannah River and guards the city of Savannah. The British originally realized Cockspur's strategic position and constructed Fort George, which was abandoned in 1776. After the War of 1812, Congress authorized reconstruction of Fort George which was completed in 1847 and renamed Pulaski. In 1861 volunteer militia from Savannah began repairs on the fort in the name of the Confederate States of America.

On November 7, 1861, Union forces captured Hilton Head Island, South Carolina, and prepared to take Cockspur Island through siege. Their first step was to erect batteries on neighboring Big Tybee Island. The walls of Fort Pulaski were seven-feet thick, and the fort was defended by forty-eight guns. Confederate General Robert E. Lee, who in 1830 as a lieu-

NORTHERN COMMANDER:
Maj. Gen. D. Hunter

STRENGTH: 1,000

CASUALTIES: 1

Cannon on Terreplein, Fort Pulaski National Monument

Cannon and casemates, Fort Pulaski National Monument

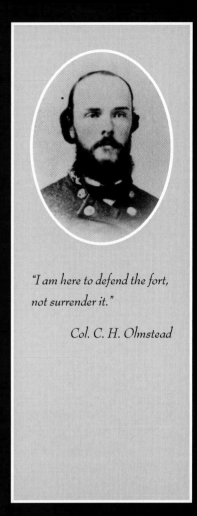

tenant designed the dike system at Fort Pulaski, declared that a Union cannon could make it difficult for Fort Pulaski but could not breach its walls. His opinion was based on his knowledge of the fort's construction and also the one-mile separation between Cockspur and Big Tybee. Lee was correct as far as traditional, smooth-bore cannon were concerned. On Big Tybee, however, the Union had a rifled cannon with spiraled grooves to give the projectiles more distance and accuracy.

Under the cover of darkness, the Union worked to construct eleven batteries—two of which contained the deadly rifled cannon—on Big Tybee Island. After months of preparation, Union guns opened fire on April 10, 1862, concentrating on the southeast side of Fort Pulaski. The cannon picked away at the wall until, by nightfall, the fortress was half its thickness on its besieged side. During the night, the Confederates repositioned their cannon, replacing those destroyed by Union fire. In the morning, however, the Union continued its relentless firing. By noon, the southeast wall of the fort was breached, and Union gunfire was exploding against the powder magazine. Confederate Colonel Charles H. Olmstead knew there was nothing else to do but surrender.

At 2:00 A.M. on April 11, fearing a devastating explosion from the magazine, Olmstead reluctantly raised the white flag. Losses were limited to one killed on each side; nearly four hundred Confederates, however, were taken prisoner, and both sides learned the deadly power of the rifled cannon.

SOUTHERN COMMANDER:
Col. C. H. Olmstead

STRENGTH: 385

CASUALTIES: 1

PORT COLUMBUS CIVIL WAR NAVAL CENTER

202 4th Street, Columbus, GA
PHONE: 706-327-9798
HOURS: Open daily, except Monday; closed major holidays.
ADMISSION: Free.

This museum features the remains of two Confederate gunboats, the CSS *Chattahoochee* and the CSS *Jackson,* as well as weapons, uniforms, paintings, and other artifacts related to both Confederate and Union forces. The museum also houses an exhibit illustrating the ingenuity of the Confederate navy (of which fifty percent were in the United States Navy prior to the war) to counter the Union naval warfare.

ANDERSONVILLE NATIONAL HISTORIC SITE

Georgia Highway 49, 11 miles from Georgia Highway 26, Andersonville, GA
PHONE: 912-924-0343
HOURS: Open daily; museum closed Christmas and New Year's Day.
ADMISSION: Free.

POW Commemorative Courtyard,
Andersonville National Historic Site

The largest and most notorious of Civil War prisons, Andersonville saw nearly 50,000 prisoners pass through its gates. Nearly 13,000 died here. The Confederate officer in charge, Capt. Henry Wirz, was the only Civil War soldier to be tried and hanged as a war criminal. Modern historians are uncertain whether the deplorable conditions were deliberate or resulted from a lack of supplies—common throughout the South—and an ignorance of sanitary conditions. Although the new museum honors all American prisoners of war from all the nation's wars, there are extensive Civil War artifacts, as well as a library with an oral history archive of former POWs. Many former American prisoners of war volunteer to serve as hosts at the National Prisoner of War Museum.

The museum's slate, granite, and steel structure is entered through a narrow walkway that passes beneath a guard tower. Portions of the original palisade and gate have been rebuilt, and white stakes show the location of the stockade and the "deadline," a line which a prisoner could not cross without being shot. The 12,920 prisoners who died in Andersonville are buried near the prison site, and the cemetery entrance is marked with a statue of three staggering prisoners.

The film, *Echoes of Captivity*, is shown at the museum, and an orientation film is shown at the Visitor's Center. Cassettes detailing a self-driving tour are also available.

FORT PULASKI NATIONAL MONUMENT

U.S. Highway 80 East, Savannah, GA

PHONE: 912-786-5787

HOURS: Open daily; closed Christmas.

ADMISSION: A fee is charged; children are free.

The Visitor's Center of the 5,623-acre Fort Pulaski National Monument features a video giving the history of the fort and the battle. The museum features exhibits of the construction era of the fort and artifacts from the Civil War. Audio stations provide interesting commentary during the self-guided walking tour of the fort. Walls marked by Union fire testify to the ferocity of the battle.

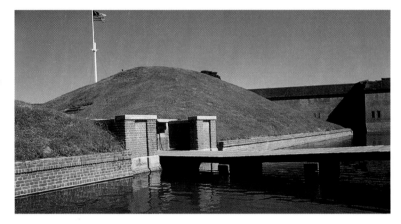

Fort Pulaski National Monument

GREEN MELDRIM HOUSE

1 West Macon Street, Savannah, GA

PHONE: 912-233-3845

HOURS: Open daily; closed Monday.

ADMISSION: A fee is charged.

Built in the early 1850s, Green Meldrim House was occupied by Union Gen. William T. Sherman, who made it his headquarters. Tours of the Gothic Revival house, which has been designated a National Historic Landmark, are available.

FORT MCALLISTER STATE HISTORIC PARK

3894 Fort McAllister Road, Richmond Hill, GA

PHONE: 912-727-2339

HOURS: Open daily; closed Monday.

ADMISSION: A fee is charged; children are discounted.

After withstanding Federal naval assault for more than two years, Fort McAllister was captured by the Union during Sherman's March to the Sea in December 1864. The park features the preserved fort itself, as well as a museum with exhibits of Civil War artillery, a gun collection, and uniforms. Also on display are artifacts from the CSS *Nashville*, a luxury liner reoutfitted by the Confederate army as a supply ship. Free brochures are available for self-guided tours.

GEORGIA — CIVIL WAR PLACES

ILLINOIS

Many of the Civil War places in Illinois center around its distinguished resident, Abraham Lincoln. The Lincoln Home National Historic Site in Springfield contains many of the family's personal belongings. The sixteenth president, his wife, and three of their sons are buried at nearby Oak Ridge Cemetery. On the steps of the nearby Old State Capitol, Lincoln delivered the immortal lines, "A house divided against itself cannot stand." Fewer than three years later, the first shots of the Civil War would tear the country in two. Even Lincoln's own family would not be immune from the division.

Illinois served as a strategic point, guarding the gateway to the Great Plains and its store of agricultural resources. Its position on the Mississippi River also proved helpful in moving supplies to southbound Union forces. Cairo, at the confluence of the Mississippi and Ohio Rivers, served as a major Union supply depot during the war. Upstream lies Galena and General Grant's home. Still further upstream, a prisoner of war camp was located at Rock Island Arsenal.

At a cemetery in Carbondale, Illinois, General John A. Logan began Decoration Day on May 30, 1868, to commemorate the Civil War dead. This holiday is now officially recognized as Memorial Day and serves as a tribute to all Americans who have sacrificed for their country.

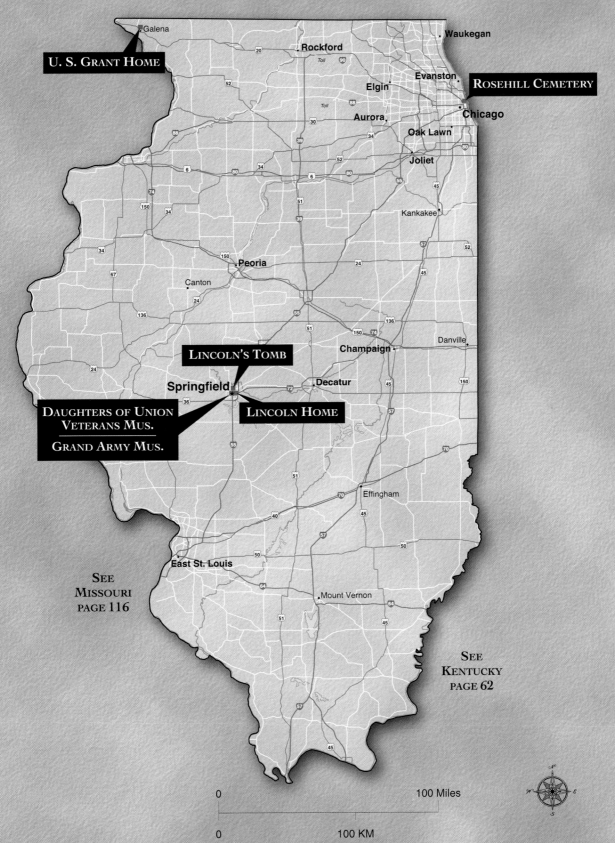

Galena

U. S. GRANT HOME

Rockford

20

Toll
90

Waukegan

52

Elgin

Evanston

ROSEHILL CEMETERY

88

Toll

88

30

Aurora

Chicago

6

39

34

Oak Lawn

80

150

80

34

52

Joliet

74

34

6

90

55

45

51

Kankakee

39

57

52

150

24

45

67

Peoria

24

Canton

136

24

55

51

136

150

74

Danville

24

LINCOLN'S TOMB

Champaign

150

Springfield

72

Decatur

45

36

**DAUGHTERS OF UNION
VETERANS MUS.**

LINCOLN HOME

57

GRAND ARMY MUS.

55

70

51

70

Effingham

40

45

**SEE
MISSOURI
PAGE 116**

57

50

East St. Louis

50

50

64

Mount Vernon

64

51

45

**SEE
KENTUCKY
PAGE 62**

57

45

0   100 Miles

0   100 KM

U. S. GRANT HOME STATE HISTORIC SITE

500 Bouthillier Street, Galena, IL
PHONE: 815-777-0248
HOURS: Open daily; closed federal and state holidays.
ADMISSION: A donation is requested.

This home was presented to General Grant by the citizens of Galena upon his return from serving in the Civil War. Although Grant lived in the home for only a short time, he used it as his legal voting residence. Ninety percent of the furnishings are original and include Grant's satchel, cane, and favorite chair. Tours are available.

U. S. Grant Home State Historic Site

ROSEHILL CEMETERY

5800 North Ravenswood Avenue, Chicago, IL
PHONE: 773-561-5940
HOURS: Open daily.
ADMISSION: Free.

The Rosehill Cemetery is the final resting spot for seventeen generals and hundreds of Civil War soldiers, including members of the Eighth Illinois Cavalry. A Civil War memorial area is located near the Ravenswood Avenue entrance. Self-guided walking tours are available, and stops on the tour include a bolder taken from the Georgia battlefield and placed on the grounds as a tribute to Gen. George Henry Thomas, the "Rock of Chickamauga." Thomas was so designated because of his glorious feat in holding the left wing against tremendous odds at the Battle of Chickamauga. Maps for the tour are available in the administration building.

DAUGHTERS OF UNION VETERANS OF THE CIVIL WAR MUSEUM

503 South Walnut Street, Springfield, IL
PHONE: 217-544-0616
HOURS: Open weekdays.
ADMISSION: Free.

The Daughters of Union Veterans of the Civil War began in 1865 and seeks to preserve the memory of all Union veterans. The museum's collection includes Civil War medals, swords, guns, photographs, and official records. Also on exhibit are uniforms, including an African-American soldier's uniform. Civil War records of every member of the organization are also located at the museum.

GRAND ARMY OF THE REPUBLIC MEMORIAL MUSEUM

629 South 7th Street, Springfield, IL
PHONE: 217-522-4373
HOURS: Open daily Tuesday–Saturday, March–December.
ADMISSION: Free.

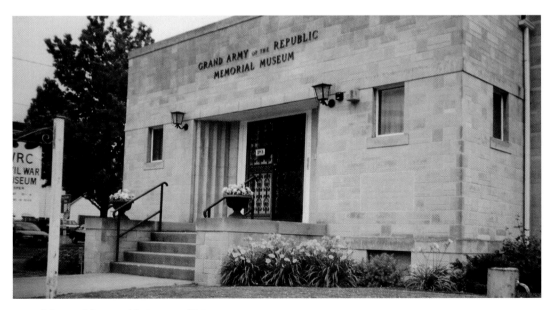

Grand Army of the Republic Memorial Museum

The Grand Army of the Republic Memorial Museum is maintained by the Women's Relief Corps, an auxiliary group to the Grand Army of the Republic. The organization was begun in 1866 and composed of Union veterans. The GAR is still active today in veterans' affairs. The museum contains collections of Civil War memorabilia, battlefield relics, weapons, official Civil War records, two Mathew Brady photographs, and one of the flags that flew at Ford's Theatre the night Lincoln was assassinated.

LINCOLN HOME NATIONAL HISTORIC SITE

413 South 8th Street, Springfield, IL
PHONE: 217- 492-4241
HOURS: Open daily; closed major holidays.
ADMISSION: Free.

At the park's center stands the two-story home of Abraham Lincoln, the only home he ever owned. The home was constructed in 1839 as a one-story cottage, and the Lincolns lived in the house from 1844 until his election to the Presidency in 1861. The home, which has been restored to its 1860s appearance, portrays Lincoln as husband, father, politician, and President-elect. It stands in the midst of a four-block historic neighborhood which the National Park Service is

Lincoln Home National Historic Site

restoring it to its Lincoln-era appearance. The film, *At Home with Mr. Lincoln*, is shown continuously at the Visitor's Center.

LINCOLN'S TOMB

Oak Ridge Cemetery, 1500 Monument Avenue,
Springfield, IL
PHONE: 217-782-2717
HOURS: Open daily.
ADMISSION: Free.

President Abraham Lincoln's tomb is located within Oak Ridge Cemetery and includes a monument and small sculptures of Lincoln at various stages of his life. The 117-foot granite tomb contains the bodies of Lincoln and his wife, Mary, and three of their four sons: Edward, William, and Thomas (Tad). During the summer, a Civil War Retreat Ceremony is held at the tomb each Tuesday evening.

Photo right: Lincoln's Tomb, Oak Ridge Cemetery

Photo below: Grand Army of the Republic Monument, Oak Ridge Cemetery

KENTUCKY

*T*he birthplace of both Abraham Lincoln and Jefferson Davis, Kentucky was truly divided by the Civil War: cities, towns, and families found themselves at odds—often violently—over loyalties to the North or the South. Kentucky began the war with a proclamation of neutrality and a warning to both Union and Confederate troops that the state was off limits. But neutrality proved impossible to maintain; by September of 1861 Confederate troops had moved to secure the city of Columbus and Federal soldiers had responded in an effort to drive them out. For the remainder of the war, Kentucky remained torn in its loyalties. Whereas the state never officially left the Union, a group of pro-Confederates organized a convention, voted to secede, and added a star to the Confederate flag.

The Civil War came to Kentucky most violently at Perryville, the site of a 1862 battle that helped the Union secure control of Kentucky although it did little to end fighting and internal contention. In all, 75,000 Kentuckians fought for the Union, and 30,000 fought for the Confederacy. Modern Kentucky remembers this tumultuous time in state history with a small but varied list of battlefields and other historical sites.

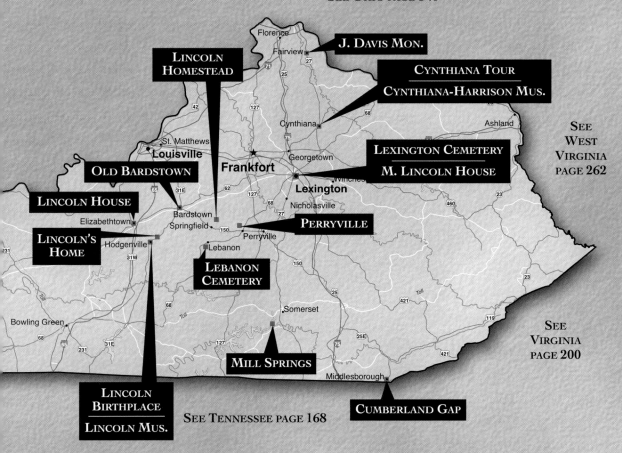

See Ohio page 140

Florence

Fairview

J. Davis Mon.

Lincoln Homestead

Cynthiana Tour

Cynthiana-Harrison Mus.

Cynthiana

Ashland

See West Virginia page 262

St. Matthews

Louisville

Georgetown

Lexington Cemetery

M. Lincoln House

Frankfort

Old Bardstown

Lincoln House

Lexington

Winchester

Elizabethtown

Bardstown

Springfield

Nicholasville

Perryville

Lincoln's Home

Hodgenville

Perryville

Lebanon Cemetery

Lebanon

Bowling Green

Somerset

Mill Springs

Middlesborough

Lincoln Birthplace

Lincoln Mus.

See Tennessee page 168

Cumberland Gap

See Virginia page 200

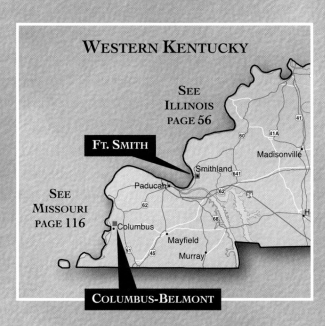

Western Kentucky

See Illinois page 56

Ft. Smith

Madisonville

Smithland

Paducah

See Missouri page 116

Columbus

Mayfield

Murray

Columbus-Belmont

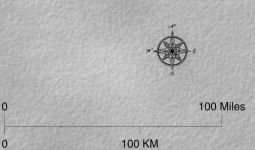

0   100 Miles

0   100 KM

NORTHERN COMMANDER: Maj. Gen. D. C. Buell

STRENGTH: 55,000

CASUALTIES: 4,211

THE BATTLE OF PERRYVILLE

October 8, 1862

One of the bloodiest battles of the Civil War for its size, Perryville ensured that Kentucky would be controlled by the Union.

At the beginning of the Civil War, Kentucky declared its neutrality and warned both Union and Confederate soldiers not to cross its borders. The peace did not last long, however, as both sides saw strategic benefit to controlling Kentucky. In 1862 Confederate Generals Braxton Bragg and Edmund Smith fought their way into Kentucky. Union Major General Don Carlos Buell followed. The two sides met before daylight at Perryville on October 8. By dawn, the fighting had ceased. The battle resumed at 2:00 P.M. and fighting escalated as the afternoon wore on.

One Union general described the action as "the bloodiest

Monument on the Perryville Battlefield

Perryville Battlefield State Historic Site

battle of modern times." At the end of battle, the Confederates had fared well. Bragg, however, realized that only a portion of the Union army had seen battle, so he began a midnight retreat to Harrodsburg. There he joined Smith but disregarded the wishes of his officers to reengage the now outnumbered Union troops. Buell permitted the Confederates to withdraw unmolested, an action that resulted in his being dismissed as Union commander.

The victory left Kentucky in Federal hands for the remainder of the war. The Battle of Perryville was the most important Civil War engagement fought in Kentucky. Some historians believe that this battle was as decisive as any other during the entire four-year conflict, for it marked a fatal loss of initiative for the South.

"We have so far received no accession to this army. . . . Enthusiasm runs high but exhausts itself in word. . . . Unless a change occurs soon we must abandon the garden spot of Kentucky."

Gen. B. Bragg

SOUTHERN COMMANDERS:
Gen. B. Bragg
Maj. Gen. E. Smith

STRENGTH: 16,000

CASUALTIES: 3,145

Cannon on the Perryville Battlefield

COLUMBUS-BELMONT STATE PARK

350 Park Road, Junction of Kentucky Highways 80 and 58, Columbus, KY
PHONE: 270-677-2327
HOURS: Open daily May–September; weekends only October–April.
ADMISSION: A fee is charged.

On this site, Confederate troops used a massive anchor and chain to block Union gunboats from traveling up the Mississippi River. Self-guided hiking trails encompass two-and-a-half miles of trenches from the Battle of Columbus. A museum, which was once used as a hospital, displays Civil War artifacts; a video presentation describes the Battle of Belmont. Each October the site hosts "Civil War Days," which features a reenactment of the Battle of Belmont.

Photo right: Anchor from the Battle of Columbus

Photo below: Columbus-Belmont State Park Museum

FORT SMITH

Kentucky Highway 60 to Level Street, Smithland Cemetery, Smithland, KY
PHONE: 270-928-2446 (Smithland City Hall)
HOURS: Open daily.
ADMISSION: Free.

Fort Smith served as the Union protection of the Cumberland River. The Battle of Fort Smith launched the offensive to Fort Donelson, Tennessee. The original earthworks of the fort are well-preserved, and markers help interpret the site. The fort is located in the Smithland Cemetery. Brochures on the fort and booklets on other historic Civil War sites in Smithland are available from the City Hall.

LINCOLN HERITAGE HOUSE

Freeman Lake Park, Elizabethtown, KY
PHONE: 270-765-2175; 800-437-0092
HOURS: Open daily except Monday June–October.
ADMISSION: A fee is charged.

The Lincoln family cabin on this site was partially built by Thomas Lincoln, Abraham's father. There is also an early 1800s cabin that is the Sarah Bush Johnston Lincoln Memorial. Sarah became ten-year-old Abraham Lincoln's beloved stepmother when she married Thomas Lincoln. On the site, there is also a one-room schoolhouse which first opened in 1892.

ABRAHAM LINCOLN BIRTHPLACE NATIONAL HISTORIC SITE

2005 Lincoln Farm Road, Hodgenville, KY
PHONE: 270-358-3137
HOURS: Open daily; closed Christmas and Thanksgiving.
ADMISSION: Free.

This site of Lincoln's birth contains 110 acres of the original Thomas Lincoln Farm. It features a symbolic birthplace cabin, a picnic area, a sinking spring where the family drew its drinking water, and hiking trails. The Visitor's Center contains exhibits and a film.

Abraham Lincoln Birthplace National Historic Site

THE LINCOLN MUSEUM

66 Lincoln Square, Hodgenville, KY
PHONE: 270-358-3163
HOURS: Open daily; closed Christmas and Thanksgiving.
ADMISSION: A fee is charged.

Listed in the National Register of Historic Places, this museum features twelve rooms which interpret different stages of Lincoln's life as well as American history. Art collections, memorabilia, a film, and changing exhibits are included in the museum.

The Lincoln Museum

LINCOLN'S BOYHOOD HOME

U.S. Highway 31, 6 miles north of Hodgenville, KY

PHONE: 270-549-3741

HOURS: Open daily April–November.

ADMISSION: A fee is charged.

The Lincolns lived here, at what is called Knob Creek, from 1811 to 1816. A replica of the Lincoln cabin rests on its original site. Guided tours are provided. A small museum, a gift shop, a picnic area, and a pavilion are open to the public.

Lincoln's Boyhood Home at Knob Creek

CIVIL WAR MUSEUM AT OLD BARDSTOWN VILLAGE

310 East Broadway, Bardstown, KY

PHONE: 502-349-0291

HOURS: Open daily except Sunday March– December; weekends only January and February.

ADMISSION: A fee is charged.

The museum houses a large collection of Civil War artifacts, including collections of authentic uniforms, battle flags, and weaponry.

Civil War Museum at Old Bardstown Village

LEBANON NATIONAL CEMETERY

Kentucky Highway 208, Lebanon, KY
PHONE: 502-893-3852
HOURS: Open daily.
ADMISSION: Free.

This still-active cemetery covers five acres and is the final resting place of many Union soldiers who fell at the Battle of Perryville in 1862.

LINCOLN HOMESTEAD STATE PARK

Kentucky Highway 438, Springfield, KY
PHONE: 606-336-7461
HOURS: Open daily May–September.
ADMISSION: A fee is charged.

This park preserves the pioneer heritage of the president's parents, Thomas Lincoln and Nancy Hanks. Featured are a reproduction of the cabin that was the boyhood home of Lincoln's father and the actual house in which the President's mother lived during her courtship by Thomas Lincoln. Split-rail fences and pioneer furniture made by Thomas Lincoln and his contemporaries complete the picture of life in the rugged Lincoln home.

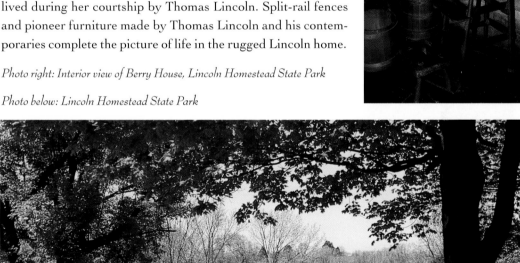

Photo right: Interior view of Berry House, Lincoln Homestead State Park

Photo below: Lincoln Homestead State Park

PERRYVILLE BATTLEFIELD STATE HISTORIC SITE -

Kentucky Highway 1920, Perryville, KY

PHONE: 606-332-8631

HOURS: Open daily April–October.

ADMISSION: A fee is charged; children and groups are discounted.

Perryville Battlefield State Historic Site contains 196 acres of the original battleground. Perryville Battlefield Walking Tour is a self-guided tour with eight stops interpreting the battle of October 8, 1862. The walking tour only encompasses a fraction of the entire battlefield, however, and it should be used in conjunction with the more comprehensive self-guided driving tour. The Civil War comes to life in the Perryville Battlefield Museum. Examine actual battle artifacts, a Civil War display, and a map with the layout of the battle. Several states have erected monuments which honor their fallen dead from the Perryville Battle; these dot the battlefield site. In 1902 a Confederate monument was erected; in 1931 a Union monument was built. The entire town of Perryville is on the National Register of Historic Homes.

Perryville Battlefield Museum

JEFFERSON DAVIS MONUMENT STATE HISTORIC SITE –

U.S. Highway 68, Fairview, KY

PHONE: 502-886-1765

HOURS: Open daily May–October.

ADMISSION: Free.

The nineteen-acre Jefferson Davis Monument State Historic Site contains a 351-foot limestone obelisk dedicated to Jefferson Davis, president of the Confederacy. Davis was born on this site on June 3, 1808. Walls of the obelisk are seven-feet thick at the base and taper to two-feet thick where the point inclines. The monument's elevator takes visitors to the observation room high atop the structure which offers a panoramic view of the countryside. On the first weekend in June, a Jefferson Davis Birthday Celebration is held at the site.

Ironically, just eight months after the birth of Davis and fewer than 100 miles away, another Kentuckian was born—Abraham Lincoln. The two were destined to become Civil War adversaries.

Jefferson Davis Monument State Historic Site

CYNTHIANA BATTLES TOUR

203 West Pike Street, Cynthiana, KY
PHONE: 606-234-5236 (Cynthiana Chamber of Commerce)
HOURS: Open daily.
ADMISSION: Free.

The Cynthiana Chamber of Commerce offers a free brochure describing the battles in the Cynthiana area. The tour is not marked, but directions and a map are in the brochure. A reenactment of the battle is held every July.

CYNTHIANA-HARRISON COUNTY MUSEUM

13 South Walnut, Cynthiana, KY
PHONE: 606-234-7179
HOURS: Open Friday and Saturday only.
ADMISSION: Free.

The Cynthiana-Harrison County Museum contains several Civil War artifacts. Information regarding a walking tour is available through the museum; the tour highlights Battle Grove Cemetery and its Confederate memorial, the second oldest such memorial in the U.S., as well as historic homes in the area.

The 1849 Lexington Cemetery

833 West Main, Lexington, KY

PHONE: 606-255-5522

HOURS: Open daily.

ADMISSION: Free.

The 1849 Lexington Cemetery is the burial site of Confederate Gen. John Hunt Morgan, statesman Henry Clay, and the Mary Todd Lincoln family.

The Mary Todd Lincoln House

578 West Main, Lexington, KY

PHONE: 606-233-9999

HOURS: Open Thursday–Saturday.

ADMISSION: A fee is charged.

In 1832 Robert Todd moved his family, including the future wife of the sixteenth president, to this late-Georgian house. Abraham Lincoln visited here on three occasions. Many Lincoln and Todd family items are on display.

Photo right: Front parlor, The Mary Todd Lincoln House

Photo below: The Mary Todd Lincoln House

MILL SPRINGS BATTLEFIELD

Kentucky Highway 235, Somerset, KY
PHONE: 606-679-1859
HOURS: Open daily.
ADMISSION: Free.

The Mill Springs Battlefield is the site of the first major Union victory of the Civil War. The first Confederate general of the the west, Felix K. Zollicoffer, was killed in this battle. An eight-mile driving tour with interpretive signs is available at the battlefield site. The battle is commemorated each Memorial Day.

CUMBERLAND GAP NATIONAL HISTORIC SITE

Kentucky Highway 25 E, Middlesboro, KY
PHONE: 606-248-2817
HOURS: Open daily; except Christmas.
ADMISSION: Free.

Although this 20,000-acre park is located at the juncture of Tennessee, Kentucky, and Virginia, the Visitor's Center is in Kentucky. No major battles were fought here, but the Cumberland Gap National Historic Site marks the gateway to the West and stands where Daniel Boone led 200,000–300,000 settlers through the gap in the Appalachian Mountains. Civil War earthwork fortifications remain. Union cannon guard Fort McCook and Fort Lyon. The cannon at Fort McCook is an example of a bronze-barreled, rifled cannon which allowed for greater accuracy.

Cannon at Fort McCook, Cumberland Gap National Historic Site

LOUISIANA

Louisiana voted to secede from the Union in January of 1861. An agricultural state with a heavy reliance on slave labor and a state where white residents were nearly outnumbered by African-Americans, Louisiana was ready and willing to take up arms to protect its citizens' right to own slaves. No state west of the Mississippi River was more important to the Confederacy than Louisiana, both for the port city of New Orleans and for the lower reaches of the Mississippi River that flowed within its borders. The Union valued Louisiana for the same reasons; thus, the state was the site of early and frequent Civil War conflict, most of it centered in the southern third of the state.

Nearly 66,000 Louisianans fought for the Confederacy; as many as 15,000 are believed to have paid the price of their lives. Commitment to the Confederate cause never wavered in Louisiana. While the Union had great success in gaining control of New Orleans and the river, the Confederate army in Louisiana did not give up fighting until many weeks after General Lee's surrender at Appomattox Court House. After the war, Louisiana held on to its uniquely southern character and has preserved its past with care.

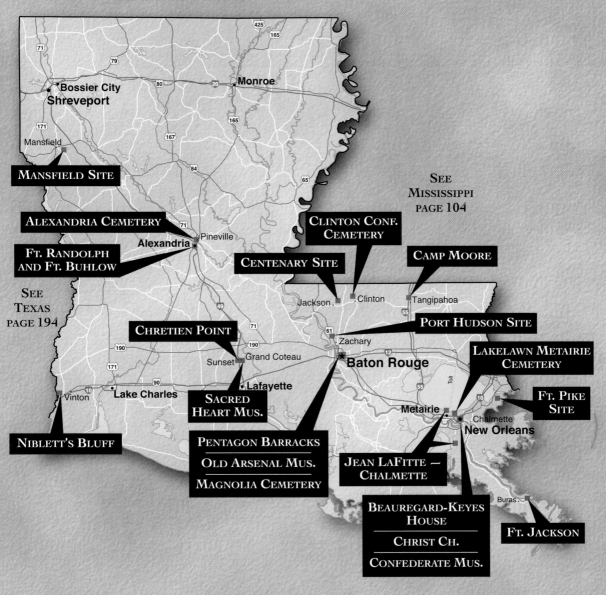

SEE ARKANSAS PAGE 20

Bossier City
Shreveport

Monroe

Mansfield

MANSFIELD SITE

ALEXANDRIA CEMETERY

Pineville
Alexandria

FT. RANDOLPH AND FT. BUHLOW

SEE MISSISSIPPI PAGE 104

CLINTON CONF. CEMETERY

CAMP MOORE

CENTENARY SITE

Jackson   Clinton   Tangipahoa

SEE TEXAS PAGE 194

CHRETIEN POINT

Sunset   Grand Coteau

Zachary

PORT HUDSON SITE

LAKELAWN METAIRIE CEMETERY

★ Baton Rouge

FT. PIKE SITE

Lafayette

Lake Charles

Vinton

SACRED HEART MUS.

Metairie   Chalmette
New Orleans

NIBLETT'S BLUFF

PENTAGON BARRACKS
———
OLD ARSENAL MUS.
———
MAGNOLIA CEMETERY

JEAN LAFITTE — CHALMETTE

BEAUREGARD-KEYES HOUSE
———
CHRIST CH.
———
CONFEDERATE MUS.

Buras

FT. JACKSON

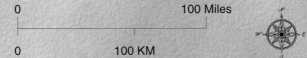

0   100 Miles

0   100 KM

N
W   E
S

NORTHERN COMMANDERS:
Maj. Gen. N. Banks
Rear Adm. D. D. Porter

STRENGTH: 19,000

CASUALTIES: 4,000

RED RIVER CAMPAIGN: BATTLES OF MANSFIELD AND PLEASANT HILL

April 8–9, 1864

The Battles of Mansfield and Pleasant Hill were the climax of the Union Red River Campaign.

The Red River runs from the northwest corner of Louisiana southeast to the Mississippi River. The Union's prime military objective in the Red River Campaign of 1863 was to capture Shreveport and break up Confederate military operations in the west. However, the political objectives—opening Louisiana and Texas to Reconstruction and capturing large quantities of cotton for Northern textile mills—actually drove the operation.

On March 11, 1864, Brigadier General Andrew J. Smith and his men captured Fort de Russy at the confluence of the Red and Mississippi Rivers. They then steamed north up the Red River to Alexandria which they occupied on March 15. Ten days later Major General Nathaniel Banks arrived by land with 20,000 infantry soldiers. Low water hampered the water

Interpretive Center, Mansfield State Historic Site

Mansfield State Historic Site

operations, and Banks left the river for Shreveport by way of Pleasant Hill and Mansfield.

In the meantime, Confederate forces under Major General Richard Taylor (the son of President Zachary Taylor) had dug in at Mansfield with 8,800 troops to wait for his chance to hit the Union force. His chance came on April 8 against General Banks's advance force of 7,000 troops. The first day ended in a Confederate victory with the Union falling back to its reinforcements of 5,000 troops at Pleasant Hill. During the night, the Confederates were also reinforced. When they met the next day, it was with comparatively equal strength of 12,000. Fighting resumed at 5:00 P.M., April 9 at Pleasant Hill. The Confederates were successful in the center of the Union line, but an unsuccessful Confederate flanking movement brought the battle to a draw. The Red River Campaign, although not a decisive Confederate victory, caused General Banks to withdraw to Nachitoches and give up on the capture of Shreveport.

SOUTHERN COMMANDERS:
Lt. Gen. E. K. Smith
Maj. Gen. R. Taylor

STRENGTH: 21,300

CASUALTIES: 3,500

MANSFIELD STATE HISTORIC SITE

Louisiana Highway 175, Mansfield, LA

PHONE: 318-872-1474

HOURS: Open daily.

ADMISSION: A fee is charged; children under 12 and seniors are free.

Within the forty-four acres of the remaining battlefield is a museum with maps, interpretive programs, and monuments. Local historians are in the process of constructing a series of marble road markers to interpret the Battle of Mansfield, also called Sabine Crossroads. A self-guided driving tour that commemorates the bloodiest battle fought in Louisiana is also available. The Battle of Mansfield/Pleasant Hill is reenacted each April.

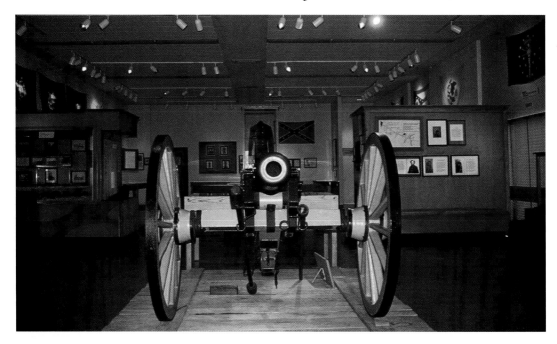

Mansfield State Historic Site

ALEXANDRIA NATIONAL CEMETERY

209 East Shamrock Street, Pineville, LA

PHONE: 318-449-1793

HOURS: Open daily.

ADMISSION: Free.

Alexandria National Cemetery was established in 1867. More than 1,500 Union soldiers are buried at this cemetery; a monument commemorates their valor. The cemetery also contains the graves of soldiers who fought in various American wars.

Entrance to Alexandria National Cemetery

Alexandria National Cemetery

FORT RANDOLPH AND FORT BUHLOW

Off U.S. Highway 71, Alexandria, LA
PHONE: 800-742-7049 (Tourist Information Center)
HOURS: Open daily.
ADMISSION: Free.

Plaque at Forts Randolph and Buhlow

Fort Randolph and Fort Buhlow stand 500 yards apart on the Pineville side of the Red River. These earthen forts were built as a defense against an expected third Red River Campaign, a campaign which never came. Artillery placements from Fort Buhlow can still be seen. Fort Randolph is currently under restoration and should be open by January 2000.

NIBLETT'S BLUFF

3409 Niblett's Bluff Road, Vinton, LA
PHONE: 318-589-7117
HOURS: Open daily.
ADMISSION: Free.

Niblett's Bluff was the site of an 1863 Confederate encampment. Slave laborers used wooden shovels to erect the fortifications. From the self-guided trails, the breastworks are still visible.

CHRETIEN POINT

665 Chretien Point Road, Sunset, LA

PHONE: 318-662-5876
HOURS: Open daily.
ADMISSION: A fee is charged; children and seniors are discounted.

This antebellum plantation home was the site of a battle during the Red River Campaign of November 1863. Although the house was not burned, Union forces destroyed all the outbuildings and confiscated the animals. Bayou Bourbeaux, located one mile to the rear of the plantation, was the site of a

Chretien Point

major battle of the Red River Campaign. Guided tours featuring costumed interpreters who describe the battle are available. The home's stairway, windows, and other architectural features were copied for the *Gone With the Wind* movie set.

ACADEMY OF THE SACRED HEART MUSEUM

1821 Academy Road, Grand Coteau, LA

PHONE: 318-662-5275
HOURS: Open weekdays.
ADMISSION: A fee is charged; children and seniors are discounted.

After 30,000 Union troops surrounded the Academy of the Sacred Heart, the Mother Superior of its sister convent in New York City wrote to the wife of Gen. Nathaniel Banks, the commander of the Union forces. Banks's own daughter attended the Convent of the Sacred Heart in New

Academy of the Sacred Heart Museum

York. Banks honored the Mother Superior's request that the Grand Coteau school be cared for by issuing a safeguard. This military order stated that any harm done to the nuns or students would be a crime punishable by death. In addition, he ensured that the school was kept supplied with food throughout the war. The original correspondence from Banks is on display in the museum. Guided tours are also available.

CENTENARY STATE HISTORIC SITE

3522 College Street, Jackson, LA
PHONE: 225-634-7925
HOURS: Open daily; closed Thanksgiving, Christmas, and New Year's Day.
ADMISSION: A fee is charged; children under 12 and seniors are free.

This former college site interprets the history of education in Louisiana. The college's buildings were used as hospitals by Confederate soldiers in 1862–1863. A Confederate cemetery on the grounds contains the remains of an estimated seventy-five unknown soldiers. A small skirmish was fought on the grounds on August 3, 1863. Each May, period interpreters conduct a memorial service.

Centenary State Historic Site

CLINTON CONFEDERATE STATE CEMETERY

Marston Street, Clinton, LA
PHONE: Not Available.
HOURS: Open daily.
ADMISSION: Free.

Although established as a Confederate cemetery, hundreds of troops from both sides rest at the Clinton Confederate State Cemetery. Many of those interred are casualties of the Port Hudson Battle. The railroad brought many of the sick and wounded to Clinton.

CAMP MOORE

70640 Camp Moore Road, Tangipahoa, LA
PHONE: 504-229-2438
HOURS: Open Tuesday–Saturday.
ADMISSION: A fee is charged; children under 6 are free.

Camp Moore was used as a Confederate training ground at the beginning of the war. Today, over 400 Confederate soldiers are buried in the camp cemetery. A museum exhibits the camp's history and displays relics from the training camp.

Camp Moore

PORT HUDSON STATE HISTORIC SITE

U.S. Highway 61, Zachary, LA
PHONE: 225-654-3775
HOURS: Open daily; closed Thanksgiving, Christmas, and New Year's Day.
ADMISSION: A fee is charged; children under 13 and seniors are free.

The Port Hudson State Historic Site encompasses 640 acres of the historic battlefield. Earthwork fortifications survive and may be viewed from one of the walking trails. Exhibits at the Interpretive

Fort Desperate, Port Hudson State Historic Site

Center give an overview of Port Hudson's significance during the war and provide information concerning the forty-eight-day siege. A national cemetery includes more than 3,000 Union soldiers, most of whom are unknown. The Battle of Port Hudson was one of the first battles in which free African-American soldiers engaged in combat on the side of the Union.

MAGNOLIA CEMETERY

North 19th Street at Florida Boulevard, Baton Rouge, LA
PHONE: 225-387-2464 (Foundation for Historical Louisiana)
HOURS: Open daily.
ADMISSION: Free.

Established in 1854, Magnolia Cemetery rests on the site of the heaviest fighting of the Battle of Baton Rouge; it is also the only area of the battlefield totally intact. During the battle, tombstones provided soldiers much needed cover. Confederate soldiers who died during the battle are buried in a mass grave. Southerner Alexander Todd, half-brother of Mary Todd Lincoln, died in the battle. Each August a commemorative ceremony is held at the cemetery.

Nearly 2,000 Union soldiers who died in the Battle of Baton Rouge are interred across the street at National Cemetery.

Photo right: Magnolia Cemetery

PENTAGON BARRACKS

959 North 3rd Street, Baton Rouge, LA
PHONE: 225-342-1866
HOURS: Open daily except Monday.
ADMISSION: Free.

Construction on the Pentagon Barracks began in 1819, and the buildings were not completed until 1829. The barracks were used as a garrison both before and after the Civil War. At various times, the Pentagon Barracks served as home to Robert E. Lee, Thomas Jackson, Ulysses S. Grant, George Custer, and Jefferson Davis. The barracks are still intact, and building "C" contains a museum and interpretive center. Tours are available.

OLD ARSENAL POWDER MAGAZINE MUSEUM

East Side State Capitol Grounds, Baton Rouge, LA
PHONE: 225-342-0401
HOURS: Open daily except Sunday; closed major holidays.
ADMISSION: A fee is charged; children are discounted.

When Louisiana seceded from the Union, the governor ordered the arsenal seized and the weapons, ammunition, and powder given to Southern armies. Union forces occupied the arsenal in May 1862 after Baton Rouge was captured. In August a Confederate army under General Breckinridge

Old Arsenal Powder Magazine Museum

unsuccessfully tried to drive the Union soldiers into the Mississippi River. A self-guided tour through the museum and grounds is available.

**NORTHERN
COMMANDERS:**
Maj. Gen. B. F. Butler
Comdr. D. D. Porter
Adm. D. G. Farragut

STRENGTH: 13,000

CASUALTIES: 229

EXPEDITION TO CAPTURE NEW ORLEANS

April 15–28, 1862

Union victory at New Orleans opened the Mississippi River to Northern ships from the Gulf of Mexico and split the Confederacy in half, east and west.

Despite its immense commercial and strategic importance as the gateway to the Mississippi Valley, a campaign to take New Orleans was not approved until November 15, 1861. Federal authorities devised a joint army-navy operation to capture New Orleans. The port was guarded at the mouth of the Mississippi River by two Confederate forts on either side of the river, Fort St. Phillip and Fort Jackson. In addition, the river had been barricaded by a chain floated on barges and hulks. The ram *Manassas*, the unpowered *Louisiana*, and the unfinished *Mississippi*, along with an assortment of other ships and firebarges, were part of the Confederate's river defenses. The forts were manned by about 500 men and eighty guns—all designed to block any Union advance on New Orleans.

Union Commodore David D. Porter countered these defenses by towing mortar boats just below the forts where they barraged the forts with thirteen-inch shells. Much damage was inflicted, but the forts held out for six days, longer than Admiral

Chalmette Battlefield

Cannon in foreground, Beauregard House in background, Chalmette Battlefield

David G. Farragut had anticipated. An impatient Farragut ordered Union ships through the gap in a Confederate boom laid across the river. Under continual mortar fire, Union ships advanced, one by one, upstream. Five days late, a makeshift Confederate naval defense met the Union navy. Farragut sank six of the eight ships, then dropped anchor in the New Orleans port, capturing it without any further conflict.

With New Orleans captured, the demoralized troops in Forts Jackson and St. Phillip mutinied and forced a surrender from their commanders. Union forces led by General Benjamin F. Butler garrisoned the forts and occupied the city. General Butler's harsh treatment of the citizens of New Orleans prompted a court of inquiry to be held and earned him the nickname "Beast" Butler.

SOUTHERN COMMANDERS:
Maj. Gen. M. Lovell
Brig. Gen. J. K. Duncan

STRENGTH: 500

CASUALTIES: 50

CHRIST CHURCH CATHEDRAL

2019 St. Charles Avenue, New Orleans, LA
PHONE: 504-895-6602
HOURS: Open weekdays.
ADMISSION: Free.

Christ Church Cathedral contains the grave of the "Fighting Bishop," Leonidas Polk. The West Point educated Polk became an Episcopal minister and eventually was named Bishop of Louisiana in 1841. In 1861 his friend and former classmate Jefferson Davis urged Polk to accept a commission in the Confederate army. Polk was killed in 1864 during the Atlanta Campaign.

Photo above: Christ Church Cathedral

Photo left: Leonidas Polk's grave, Christ Church Cathedral

LAKELAWN METAIRIE CEMETERY

5100 Pontcharcrain Boulevard, New Orleans, LA
PHONE: 504-486-6331
HOURS: Open daily.
ADMISSION: Free.

Confederate Generals P. G. T. Beauregard and Richard Taylor are buried here. Monuments to the Louisiana Division of the Army of Tennessee, the Louisiana Division of the Army of Northern Virginia, and the Washington Artillery Unit can also be viewed. Tapes are available to be used on a self-guided tour.

FORT PIKE STATE HISTORIC SITE

Louisiana Highway 90, east of New Orleans, LA

PHONE: 504-662-5703

HOURS: Open daily; closed major holidays.

ADMISSION: A fee is charged; children and seniors are discounted.

During the Civil War, Fort Pike switched hands twice without any guns from the fort being fired. The fort was first captured by Confederates before the start of the war. In 1862 the North recaptured the fort and used it as a base for raids along the gulf. There is a museum at Fort Pike State Historic Site, and tours of the fort are available.

CONFEDERATE MUSEUM

929 Camp Street, New Orleans, LA

PHONE: 504-523-4522

HOURS: Open daily except Sunday; closed major holidays.

ADMISSION: A fee is charged; children and seniors are discounted.

Confederate veterans of Louisiana founded the museum in 1891 as a repository of their memorabilia from the war. The collection includes more than 125 original Southern battle flags, rifles, guns, swords, more than 500 rare photographs, and uniforms of Confederate officers and soldiers, including the frock coats of Generals P. G. T. Beauregard and Braxton Bragg.

BEAUREGARD-KEYES HOUSE AND GARDEN

1113 Chartres Street, New Orleans, LA

PHONE: 504-523-7257

HOURS: Open daily except Sunday.

ADMISSION: A fee is charged; children and seniors are discounted.

Confederate General P. G. T. Beauregard lived at this late Federal-Greek Revival home from 1866–68. Novelist Frances Parkinson Keyes also lived here during the 1940s. The home looks much as it did

Photo right: The garden area of the Beauregard-Keyes House

Beauregard-Keyes House

during the Civil War and contains many of the general's personal belongings. Each hour costumed interpreters lead tours of the house and its beautiful and peaceful walled garden.

 # JEAN LAFITTE NATIONAL HISTORICAL PARK AND PRESERVE — CHALMETTE BATTLEFIELD AND NATIONAL CEMETERY

8606 West St. Bernard Highway, Chalmette, LA

PHONE: 504-281-0510
HOURS: Open daily; closed Christmas.
ADMISSION: Free.

The Malus-Beauregard House, built on the grounds of the Battle of New Orleans of 1815, belonged to Judge Rene Beauregard, son of Confederate General P. G. T. Beauregard. The general often visited the house to see his grandchildren. The

Photo right: Chalmette National Cemetery

Chalmette National Cemetery was established in 1864 upon the Chalmette line of Confederate earthworks, the last line of defense before New Orleans. Interred at the site are mostly Union casualties.

Beauregard House, Chalmette Battlefield

FORT JACKSON

Louisiana Highway 23, 5 miles south of Buras, LA

PHONE: 504-657-7083
HOURS: Open daily.
ADMISSION: Free.

Fort Jackson was built by the South for the defense of New Orleans and the Mississippi River from Union blockades. The fort remains intact and easily accessible. A museum contains exhibits depicting the Battle of New Orleans.

Photo right: Casemates of Fort Jackson

MARYLAND

Maryland, despite its ties to Southern culture, remained loyal to the Union throughout the Civil War and served as a bloody buffer between the North and South. Death came early to Maryland; it boasts the auspicious honor of having the first casualties of the Civil War. The Baltimore Civil War Museum commemorates four militiamen and twelve civilians who were killed by secessionist sympathizers in the Baltimore Riot of 1861.

A little over a year later, the now-quiet battlefield of Antietam was covered with bodies. More men died on September 17, 1862, than on any other day during the Civil War; the Battle of Antietam was the bloodiest day of the war. Over 350 monuments stand in tribute to those Confederate and Union soldiers who paid the ultimate price of battle. Many are buried at the Antietam Union Cemetery and at Washington Confederate Cemetery in nearby Hagerstown.

Less than two years after the Battle of Antietam, Union victory at the Battle of Monocacy helped secure the nation's capital from Confederate advance. The Monocacy National Battlefield Park contains monuments and self-guided tours that help interpret this pivotal battle.

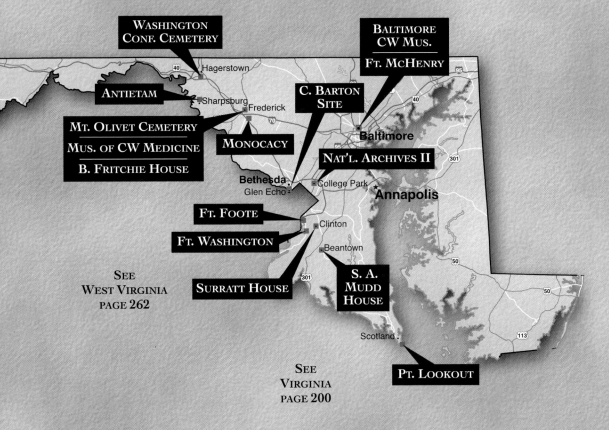

SEE PENNSYLVANIA PAGE 152

WASHINGTON
CONF. CEMETERY

BALTIMORE
CW MUS.

FT. McHENRY

Hagerstown

ANTIETAM

Sharpsburg

Frederick

C. BARTON
SITE

MT. OLIVET CEMETERY

MUS. OF CW MEDICINE

B. FRITCHIE HOUSE

MONOCACY

Baltimore

NAT'L. ARCHIVES II

Bethesda

College Park

Glen Echo

Annapolis

FT. FOOTE

Clinton

FT. WASHINGTON

Beantown

SEE
WEST VIRGINIA
PAGE 262

SURRATT HOUSE

S. A.
MUDD
HOUSE

Scotland

SEE
VIRGINIA
PAGE 200

PT. LOOKOUT

0

100 Miles

0

100 KM

NORTHERN COMMANDER:
Maj. Gen. G. B. McClellan

STRENGTH: 75,000

CASUALTIES: 12,350

THE BATTLE OF ANTIETAM (SHARPSBURG)

September 17, 1862

This battle marked the bloodiest day of the Civil War and the end of the Confederate invasion of the North.

On September 4, 1862, General Robert E. Lee crossed the Potomac River and brought his Confederate army into Northern territory. His plan was to take the fighting out of his beloved Virginia and force a showdown with Union Major General George B. McClellan at Harrisburg, Pennsylvania. En route north, however, Lee divided his army to allow General Thomas Jackson to capture the Federal garrison at Harpers Ferry, West Virginia.

McClellan learned of Lee's movements and decided to move southward to meet the Confederate troops. On September 6, McClellan began marching toward the Army of Virginia, which was concentrated at Frederick, Maryland. Cautious by nature, McClellan was slow in advancing; he was convinced that Lee's army outnumbered his own. Even when he learned the details of Lee's entire operational plan, McClellan did not act immediately. He made the additional mistake of allowing a Confederate sympathizer to be present as Lee's order was dis-

Artist's rendering of Burnside Bridge at the Battle of Antietam

cussed. When McClellan finally acted on the order, Lee had been warned.

After preliminary skirmishing, Lee positioned his army behind Antietam Creek on rising, rocky terrain, with his back to the city of Sharpsburg and waited for McClellan. On September 17, the battle began at daybreak on Lee's left flank. This section of the battle surged back and forth across a cornfield. After only four hours, the cornstalks were sheared off, and 13,000 soldiers lay dead or wounded. The center of the lines fared even worse. Confederate General Daniel H. Hill's division was forced into a sunken road. Dead men were piled on top of one another in the trench-like road, now called Bloody Lane.

After four hours of savage fighting, the Confederates were driven back. Lee's right flank fought Federals who attempted to cross a narrow bridge. Two attempts were made to cross the bridge; both times 400 Confederates from Georgia blocked the crossing. A third attempt proved successful. By 4:00 P.M., the Union had gained almost all of the high ground east and south of Sharpsburg when an unexpected Confederate attack created confusion. The South pushed the Union's left flank back to Antietam Creek, and there the fighting ended. McClellan chose not to continue fighting the next day, and Lee began withdrawing his army back across the Potomac the evening of September 18.

More men were killed at Antietam than in any other battle of the Civil War. The battle's combined total casualties remain as the single bloodiest day in U.S. history. Antietam was also a turning point in the war. Never again would the Confederates have such strength and opportunity. Shortly after Antietam, President Lincoln issued his preliminary Emancipation Proclamation, which paved the way for the official proclamation on January 1, 1863. This act changed the nature of the war by making it as much a fight against slavery as a fight against the disruption of the Union.

"I have always had a high opinion of General McClellan, and have no reason to suppose that he failed to accomplish anything that he was able to do."

Gen. R. E. Lee

SOUTHERN COMMANDER:
Gen. R. E. Lee

STRENGTH: 38,000

CASUALTIES: 13,700

WASHINGTON CONFEDERATE CEMETERY (INSIDE ROSE HILL CEMETERY)

600 South Potomac Street, Hagerstown, MD

PHONE: 301-739-3630

HOURS: Open daily.

ADMISSION: Free.

Two thousand four hundred and sixty-eight Confederate soldiers from the battles of Antietam and South Mountain have been reburied at the Washington Confederate Cemetery. Of the soldiers interred, the identities of only 346 are known. Originally buried on the field at Antietam, these Confederates were disinterred around 1871 and moved to Antietam National Cemetery.

ANTIETAM NATIONAL BATTLEFIELD PARK

Maryland Highway 65, between Interstate 70 and Maryland Highway 34, Sharpsburg, MD

PHONE: 301-432-5124

HOURS: Open daily; closed Thanksgiving, Christmas, and New Year's Day.

ADMISSION: A fee is charged; children 16 and under are free.

Antietam National Battlefield contains 3,244 acres of the original battlefield. The park features a self-guided driving tour and several walking trails. Along the tour is the rebuilt Dunker Church, around which much of the battle took place. Burnside's Bridge may also be seen along with more than 350 monuments, tablets, markers, and forty-one cannon.

The Visitor's Center showcases panoramic battle paintings by a Civil War veteran and a twenty-six-minute movie entitled *Antietam Visit*. During the summer, interpretive programs are presented by rangers or costumed interpreters.

Photo left: Monument to 128th Pennsylvania Volunteer Infantry, Antietam National Battlefield

Antietam National Cemetery is located within the confines of the National Park. Nearly 5,000 Union soldiers, of whom 1,836 remain unknown, rest on this hilltop. Most of the fallen Confederates from this battle are buried in Hagerstown and Frederick, Maryland, and in Shepherdstown, West Virginia.

Photo right: Sunken Road Monument, Antietam National Battlefield

Photo below: Cannon, Antietam National Battlefield

NORTHERN COMMANDER:
Maj. Gen. L. Wallace

STRENGTH: 5,800

CASUALTIES: 1,968

THE BATTLE OF MONOCACY

July 9, 1864

Union victory at Monocacy saved Washington, D.C., from Confederate invasion.

In 1864, acting upon orders from General Robert E. Lee, Confederate Lieutenant General Jubal Early cleared the Shenandoah Valley of Union troops and moved across the mountains to threaten Baltimore and Washington, D.C.; Confederate commanders hoped that Early's movement would draw Union troops away from General Ulysses S. Grant's siege of Petersburg.

Major General Lewis Wallace, with a small force of Union home-front guards and second-line troops, waited on the Monocacy Junction. Here, the Georgetown Pike to Washington and the National Road to Baltimore crossed the Monocacy River, as did the Baltimore & Ohio Railroad. Wallace did not know which city was the target, but he was determined to delay Early until Grant could send reinforcements.

Because Confederate forces significantly outnumbered Union, Wallace took up defensive positions behind railroad embankments, blockhouses, and the higher riverbank on the east side. For eight hours, fighting raged up and down the Union

Gambrill Mill Visitor's Center, Monocacy National Battlefield

New Jersey Monument, Monocacy National Battlefield

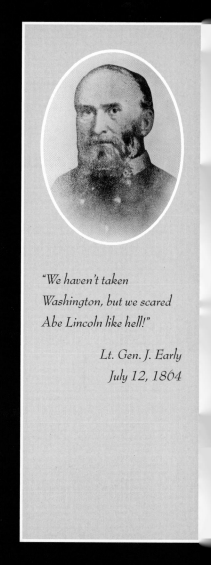

"We haven't taken Washington, but we scared Abe Lincoln like hell!"

Lt. Gen. J. Early
July 12, 1864

SOUTHERN COMMANDER:
Lt. Gen. J. Early

STRENGTH: 18,000

CASUALTIES: 800

lines. It became clear that Southern numbers were overwhelming; even with the reinforcements of two of Grant's corps. At about 4:30 P.M., Wallace ordered a withdrawal. A Confederate troop harried the retreating forces until Early called it off and moved back into the valley. Early had achieved his objective of weakening Grant's Richmond and Petersburg forces.

Although the Battle of Monocacy was a tactical victory for the Confederacy, it was a moral victory for the Union. The battle delayed Early's ability to enter Washington and made a future invasion of the Union capital unlikely.

MONOCACY NATIONAL BATTLEFIELD PARK

4801 Urbana Pike, Frederick, MD

PHONE: 301-662-3515

HOURS: Open daily from Memorial Day–Labor Day; remainder of year closed Monday and Tuesday, Thanksgiving, Christmas, and New Year's Day.

ADMISSION: Free.

The Gambrill Mill Visitor's Center features an electric map orientation program, an interactive computer program, an interpretive display, and battle artifacts. A self-guided driving tour and a walking tour are available. On the tour are monuments to the various Union regiments who combined to save Washington. Marked walking trails and roads are available.

Photo above: 14th New Jersey Monument, Monocacy National Battlefield

Photo left: Monocacy National Battlefield

MOUNT OLIVET CEMETERY

515 Market Street, Frederick MD

PHONE: 301-662-1164

HOURS: Open daily.

ADMISSION: Free.

Three-hundred-eighty soldiers from the Battle of Monocacy are buried at Mount Olivet Cemetery in a mass Confederate grave. Approximately one-third of these soldiers are unknown. Also buried at Mount Olivet is Barbara Fritchie, Union loyalist and heroine of Frederick, Maryland, whom the poet Henry Wadsworth Longfellow memorialized in his poem. From another era, but also buried here, is Francis Scott Key, author of *The Star-Spangled Banner*.

NATIONAL MUSEUM OF CIVIL WAR MEDICINE

48 East Patrick Street, Frederick, MD
Note: May 1999–September 2000 the museum will be located at 100 Adventist Drive, Frederick, MD

PHONE: 301-695-1864
HOURS: Open daily year round; closed major holidays. Walking tours of hospital sites are by appointment only.
ADMISSION: A fee is charged.

The Museum of Civil War Medicine uses its extensive collection of artifacts and illustrations to describe the care of the sick and wounded during the Civil War.

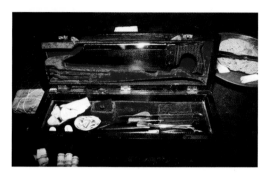

Photo above: Field hospital exhibit, Museum of Civil War Medicine

Photo left: Civil War-era medical tools, Museum of Civil War Medicine

BARBARA FRITCHIE HOUSE

154 West Patrick Street, Frederick, MD
PHONE: 301-698-0630
HOURS: Open daily except Tuesday and Wednesday, April–September; open weekends only October–November.
ADMISSION: A fee is charged.

This replica of Barbara Fritchie's home was built in 1926. According to legend, the ninety-five-year-old Fritchie boldly displayed the Union flag as Confederate soldiers entered Frederick on September 6, 1862. In tribute to her bravery, Gen. Stonewall Jackson ordered that Fritchie not be harmed. John Greenleaf Whittier immortalized her in his poem entitled "Barbara Fritchie": "'Shoot, if you must, this old gray head / But spare your country's flag,' she said."

BALTIMORE CIVIL WAR MUSEUM

601 President Street Station, Baltimore, MD
PHONE: 410-385-5188
HOURS: Open Wednesday–Sunday; closed major holidays.
ADMISSION: A fee is charged; children are discounted.

This small museum opened in 1997 and is devoted to Baltimore's role in the Civil War, specifically a riot which occurred on April 19, 1861. On their way to Camden Station, Union troops were stoned by Confederate sympathizers. The first death of the Civil War occurred in the ensuing melee. Walking tours from President Street Station to Camden Station are available on every Saturday and Sunday throughout October.

FORT McHENRY NATIONAL MONUMENT AND HISTORIC SHRINE

At the end of East Fort Avenue, Baltimore, MD
PHONE: 410-962-4290
HOURS: Open daily.
ADMISSION: A fee is charged; children under 16 are free.

Fort McHenry National Monument and Historic Site

This late 18th-century star-shaped fort is world famous as the birthplace of the American national anthem. This historic fort, whose flag inspired Francis Scott Key to write the *The Star-Spangled Banner*, was used as a prison for Confederate soldiers and sympathizers during the Civil War. A Civil War Weekend reenactment is held each spring, usually in April.

CLARA BARTON NATIONAL HISTORIC SITE

5801 Oxford Road, Glen Echo, MD
PHONE: 301-492-6245
HOURS: Open daily; closed Thanksgiving, Christmas, and New Year's Day.
ADMISSION: Free.

Clara Barton served with distinction during the Civil War and was the founder of the American Red Cross. This site was built in 1891 and used as a warehouse for disaster relief supplies until 1897. At that time, Barton remodeled the interior and used the building as her home and as the headquarters for the American Red Cross. Barton lived here until her death in 1912. Army surgeon Dr. James I. Dunn wrote to his wife about Barton, "At a time when we were entirely out of

Photo right: Clara Barton National Historic Site

dressings of every kind, she supplied us with everything, and while the shells were bursting in every direction . . . she staid [sic] dealing out shirts . . . and preparing soup. . . . I thought that night that if heaven ever sent out a homely angel, she must be one."

NATIONAL ARCHIVES II

8601 Adelphi Road, College Park, MD

PHONE: 301-713-6800
HOURS: Open daily except Sunday; closed major holidays.
ADMISSION: Free.

Free tours are available. The Still Picture Branch houses Mathew Brady's photographs of the Civil War.

SURRATT HOUSE MUSEUM

9118 Brandywine Road, Clinton, MD

PHONE: 301-868-1121
HOURS: Open Thursday–Sunday, March–December.
ADMISSION: A fee is charged.

Surratt House Museum

Built in 1852 as a middle-class plantation home, historic Surratt House also served as a tavern and hostelry, a post office, and a polling place during the crucial decade before the Civil War. During the war, it was a safe house for the Confederate underground which flourished in southern Maryland. It was also the country home of Mary Surratt, the first woman to be executed by the United States government. Surratt was found guilty of conspiring with John Wilkes Booth to assassinate Abraham Lincoln. After the assassination, Booth stopped at the Surratt House to retrieve guns and ammunition; he then went on to Dr. Samuel A. Mudd's house. Each spring the Surratt Society sponsors bus tours along Booth's escape route.

FORT WASHINGTON PARK

13551 Fort Washington Road, Fort Washington, MD

PHONE: 301-763-4600
HOURS: Open daily; closed Christmas and New Year's Day.
ADMISSION: Free.

The park has exhibits and a Visitor's Center with walking tours and seasonal living history exhibits. Fort Washington was completed October 2, 1824, and was remodeled during the 1840s to correct deficiencies in the original design. Under the command of Capt. Joseph A. Haskins, Fort Washington was held by Union forces during the Civil War.

Fort Washington Park

FORT FOOTE PARK

Fort Foote Road, Fort Washington, MD
PHONE: 301-763-4600
HOURS: Open daily.
ADMISSION: Free.

The fort's outline is marked by trees and the earthworks are still intact. Fort Foote contains the largest smooth-bore cannon and two fifteen-inch Rodman guns weighing twenty-five tons each. There is no Visitor's Center.

DR. SAMUEL A. MUDD HOUSE

At the end of Dr. Samuel Mudd Road, Beantown, MD
PHONE: 301-934-8464
HOURS: Open Saturday, Sunday, and Wednesday, April–November.
ADMISSION: A fee is charged.

The buildings and surrounding grounds have remained in the Mudd family and retain much of their original ambiance. After killing President Lincoln, John Wilkes Booth needed medical assistance for a broken leg. Doctor Mudd set Booth's leg and was later tried and convicted of conspiracy for the act. He was sentenced to life in prison, but the sentence was commuted in 1869 by President Andrew Johnson after Mudd heroically treated victims during an outbreak of yellow fever.

Dr. Samuel A. Mudd House

POINT LOOKOUT STATE PARK

Maryland Highway 5, Scotland, MD
PHONE: 301-872-5688
HOURS: Museum and Visitor's Center open daily Memorial Day–Labor Day; park open daily year round.
ADMISSION: A fee is charged; children in car seats and seniors free.

Features of the park include Hammond Hospital for the Union's Sick and Wounded and Point Lookout Prison for Confederates. By the end of the war, over 52,000 Confederates had passed through the prison, although only 20,000 were held at any one time in the twenty-acre, square prison pen. Point Lookout was the largest prisoner of war camp during the Civil War and was used mainly for enlisted men, one of whom was Confederate poet Sidney Lanier.

Today, only the earthen wall of Fort Lincoln, built by Confederate prisoners to protect the prison from an attack from Virginia, remains intact. A fishing pier stands where the prison pen once was. The park hosts a Confederate Memorial Service, Blue and Gray Days in June, and a Ghost Walk in October.

MISSISSIPPI

Situated high on the bluffs overlooking the Mississippi River, Vicksburg was a key military site. At the Vicksburg National Military Park, a sixteen-mile self-guided auto tour highlights monuments, markers, and reconstructed earthworks. Of special note is the Illinois Memorial, the largest monument on the battlefield. The remains of the Cairo, a Union ironclad, are located in one corner of the park.

Nearby, Grand Gulf Military Monument commemorates the South's attempt to secure Vicksburg. A thirty-foot observation tower offers excellent views of the park and its forts, and each year a Civil War artillery demonstration is held. Port Gibson, a charming city located thirty miles from Vicksburg, was spared devastation during the Battle of Port Gibson. General Ulysses S. Grant found the city too beautiful to burn.

Overlooking the Pearl River, Mississippi's capital, Jackson, is home to a number of historic sites, including the beautiful Oaks House Museum, the Old Capitol Museum, and the Governor's Mansion. In 1863, the city developed the nickname, "Chimneyville," after Union General William T. Sherman's troops thoroughly burned the state capital, leaving only the buildings' brick chimneys as reminders of the once grand homes.

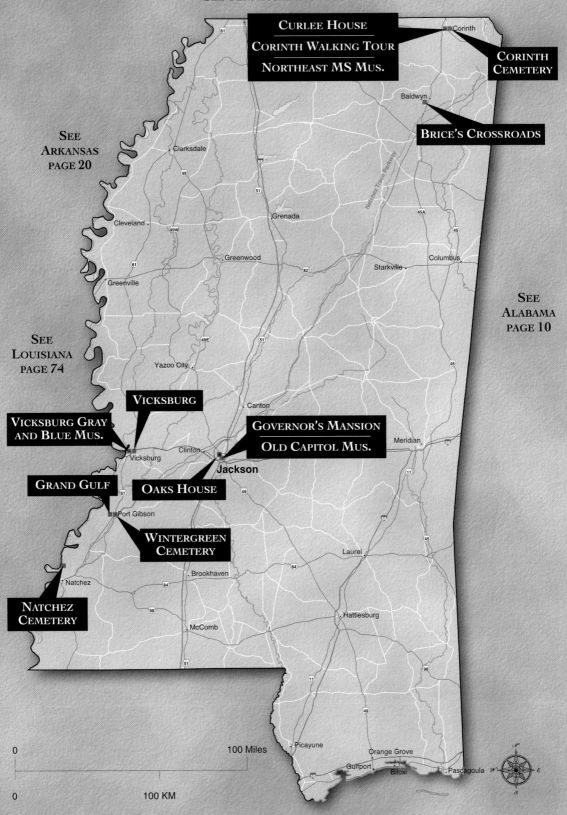

SEE TENNESSEE PAGE 168

CURLEE HOUSE

CORINTH WALKING TOUR

NORTHEAST MS MUS.

Corinth

CORINTH CEMETERY

Baldwyn

BRICE'S CROSSROADS

SEE ARKANSAS PAGE 20

Clarksdale

Natchez Trace Parkway

Cleveland

Grenada

Greenwood

Starkville

Columbus

Greenville

SEE ALABAMA PAGE 10

SEE LOUISIANA PAGE 74

Yazoo City

VICKSBURG

VICKSBURG GRAY AND BLUE MUS.

Canton

GOVERNOR'S MANSION

OLD CAPITOL MUS.

Meridian

Vicksburg

Clinton

Jackson

GRAND GULF

OAKS HOUSE

Port Gibson

WINTERGREEN CEMETERY

Laurel

Natchez

Brookhaven

NATCHEZ CEMETERY

Hattiesburg

McComb

Picayune

Orange Grove

100 Miles

Gulfport

Biloxi

Pascagoula

0

0

100 KM

"My dear general, I feel justi-fied to rely very much on you. I believe you and the brave officers and men with you will get the victory at Corinth."

Pres. A. Lincoln to
Maj. Gen. H. W. Halleck
(pictured above)

NORTHERN COMMANDER:
Maj. Gen. H. W. Halleck

STRENGTH: 23,000

CASUALTIES: 2,350

THE BATTLE AND SIEGE OF CORINTH

April 29–30, 1862

With victory at Corinth, the Union secured a vital railroad con-nection to Tennessee and Virginia and opened a route into the Deep South.

In the spring of 1862, the city of Corinth, in northeastern Mis-sissippi, became vitally important to both the Union and the Confederacy. The Union had just won significant victories in Kentucky and Tennessee and looked to the major railroad junction at Corinth as a launching point for further advances into Confederate territory. For the Confederates, Corinth was equally vital; Southern forces needed a place to consolidate and

Jacinto Courthouse in Corinth

Corinth Depot

"I feel authorized to say, by the evacuation, the plan of campaign of the enemy was utterly foiled, his delay of seven weeks and vast expenditures were of little value, and he has reached Corinth to find it a barren locality, which he must abandon as wholly worthless for his purposes."

Gen. P. G. T. Beauregard

SOUTHERN COMMANDER:
Gen. P. G. T. Beauregard

STRENGTH: 22,000

CASUALTIES: 4,800

organize their defenses as they prepared to keep Union forces out of the Mississippi River Valley. In anticipation of Union advances to this very strategic town, Confederate General P. G. T. Beauregard reinforced and deepened entrenchments around the town. The first Union attempt on Corinth came in early May, when Union Major General Henry W. Halleck led a formal siege on Corinth. Recognizing that his troops were weak from illness and had few rations, Beauregard decided not to fight. He withdrew his men to Tupelo on May 29–30, leaving Corinth for the Union.

The Union army rebuilt Corinth's railroads to use as supply lines to western Tennessee. But the Confederates were not ready to give up without one last fight. In September General Earl Van Dorn ordered an attack on Corinth, hoping to win the railroad lines which would facilitate Confederate advance into Tennessee. Although the assault was costly to the Union, after a day and a half of fighting, it also proved ineffective. The Confederates withdrew on October 4, leaving Corinth to the Union.

THE CURLEE HOUSE

723 Jackson Street, Corinth, MS
PHONE: 601-287-9501
HOURS: Open Thursday–Monday.
ADMISSION: A fee is charged.

During the Civil War, the Curlee House served as the headquarters for Confederate Generals Braxton Bragg and Earl Van Dorn, as well as Union General Henry W. Halleck. The Greek Revival house features period furnishings.

Photo right: The Curlee House

HISTORIC CORINTH WALKING TOUR AND CIVIL WAR VISITOR'S CENTER

705 Jackson Street, Corinth, MS
PHONE: 601-287-9501
HOURS: Open daily.
ADMISSION: Free.

Historic Corinth Walking Tour and Civil War Visitor's Center is housed in the former guest house of the Curlee House. The Visitor's Center provides general information about Corinth and a free brochure about the Siege and Battle of Corinth. The walking tour includes wayside exhibits with Civil War photographs and interpretive text. Also included are two batteries, described below.

BATTERY F

Bitner and Davis Streets, Corinth, MS
Battery F is one of six outer batteries built by the Union army and captured by the Confederates on October 3, 1862. This well-preserved battery protected the Memphis & Charleston Railroad.

BATTERY ROBINETT

Linden Street, Corinth, MS

Battery Robinett

Battery Robinett's peaceful five-acre park belies the fact that it contains the original Corinth battlefield, once the site of intense fighting. A reconstructed battery is available for viewing.

CORINTH NATIONAL CEMETERY

1551 Horton Street, Corinth, MS
PHONE: 901-386-8311(Memphis National Cemetery)
HOURS: Open weekdays.
ADMISSION: Free.

In 1866, Corinth National Cemetery was authorized to honor those who died in the Civil War in and around Corinth. Within the twenty acres rest 1,793 known and 3,895 unknown Union soldiers.

Photo right: Corinth National Cemetery

NORTHEAST MISSISSIPPI MUSEUM ASSOCIATION

204 East 4th Street, Corinth, MS
PHONE: 601-287-3120
HOURS: Open daily; closed major holidays.
ADMISSION: Free.

The Northeast Mississippi Museum Association houses Civil War artifacts and photographs and other information pertaining to the Battle of Corinth. It also contains models of the historic railroad crossing and Corona College whose buildings were used as a hospital by both Confederate and Union troops. The college was burned by the Union forces when they left in January 1864.

Northeast Mississippi Museum Association

BRICE'S CROSSROADS NATIONAL BATTLEFIELD SITE

Mississippi Highway 370, Visitor's Center at 607 Grisham Street, Baldwyn, MS
PHONE: 662-365-3969
HOURS: Open daily except Monday.
ADMISSION: A fee is charged; children are discounted.

The Visitor's Center of Brice's Crossroads National Battlefield Site is located in Baldwyn and shows a twenty-two-minute video that interprets the battle and displays a permanent exhibit entitled "Forrest's Finest Hour." Outside is a flag exhibit with fifteen flags of those states who fought at Brice's Crossroads. The 836-acre battlefield site has an Interpretive Center with marked walking trails detailing the Battle at Brice's Crossroads. In June 1864, 7,800 Union soldiers under General Samuel Sturgis were defeated by half as many Confederate soldiers under the command of General Nathan Bedford Forrest.

NORTHERN COMMANDER:
Maj. Gen. U. S. Grant

STRENGTH: 77,000

CASUALTIES: 10,100

THE BATTLE AND SIEGE OF VICKSBURG

March 29–July 4, 1863

Vicksburg was the last western theater stronghold to fall to the Union. This siege established Ulysses S. Grant's reputation as a brilliant field commander.

The Union considered winning Vicksburg, Mississippi, essential to winning the war. With Vicksburg in hand, the Union would control the Mississippi River and would also effectively split the Confederacy in two, cutting off western forces from those in the east. The campaign of Vicksburg encompassed the area from Vicksburg east to Jackson and south to Port Gibson.

The Union's first attempt at Vicksburg occurred in April 1862 when, after capturing New Orleans, Admiral David G. Farragut moved upstream. Then in June of the same year, Farragut's attempts failed because of a lack of troops to back up the gunship barrages. By July Farragut had returned to New Orleans, and Vicksburg was reinforced heavily by the Confed-

Vicksburg National Military Park Visitor's Center

Thayer's Approach, Vicksburg National Military Park

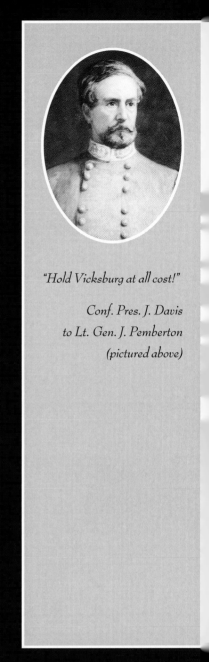

erates. Future attempts on the town would require a major Union offensive.

In the fall of 1862, Major General Ulysses S. Grant received permission to take Vicksburg. Several early assaults in November and December were effectively repulsed, however, and it was not until the spring of the following year that Grant again attacked.

In late April, Grant landed his troops at Bruinsburg, south of Vicksburg, then maneuvered east to stand between Vicksburg and Jackson. He defeated the Confederate forces led by General Joseph E. Johnston at Champion's Hill. Lieutenant General John C. Pemberton then withdrew his forces to nearby Crystal Springs.

Grant then moved onto Vicksburg itself in mid-May first attempting a direct assault. He realized, however, that siege tactics would be more effective. The siege lasted until July 4 when Pemberton, whose Confederate forces were weakened, demoralized, and starving, surrendered the city. The victory, which followed Union success at Gettysburg by one day, is seen by historians as the beginning of the end for the Confederacy.

VICKSBURG NATIONAL MILITARY PARK

3201 Clay Street, Vicksburg, MS

PHONE: 601-636-0583

HOURS: Open daily; closed Christmas.

ADMISSION: A fee is charged.

Vicksburg National Cemetery

Vicksburg National Military Park was established in 1899 to commemorate the campaign, siege, and defense of Vicksburg. Included in the park are 1,620 acres of the original battlefield, over 1,300 monuments and markers, reconstructed trenches and earthworks, one antebellum structure, and the Vicksburg National Cemetery, where more than 18,000 soldiers lie, 12,000 of whom are unknown.

The Visitor's Center runs an eighteen-minute film which gives the history of the battles and siege. There is a sixteen-mile driving tour available that passes through the siege lines and includes Big Black Battlefield, Champion Hill Battlefield, the Confederate Cemetery at Raymond, Raymond Battlefield, Grand Gulf Military Monument Park, Jackson Battlefield, Port Gibson Battlefield, and Windsor Ruins.

Model of the Cairo, *Vicksburg National Military Park*

VICKSBURG GRAY AND BLUE NAVAL MUSEUM

1102 Washington Street, Vicksburg, MS

PHONE: 601-638-6500

HOURS: Open daily except Sunday; closed major holidays.

ADMISSION: A fee is charged.

The Blue Naval Museum boasts the largest collection of Civil War gunboat models, as well as paintings, reference files, and artifacts pertaining to warships. It also features a 250-foot diorama which contains a miniature layout of Vicksburg Battlefield with 2,500 miniature soldiers. A miniature city of Vicksburg is in the planning stage.

MISSISSIPPI GOVERNOR'S MANSION

300 East Capitol Street, Jackson, MS

PHONE: 601-359-6421

HOURS: Open Tuesday–Friday; closed two weeks in December.

ADMISSION: Free.

The Mississippi Governor's Mansion was occupied in May 1863 by Mississippi Governor John Pettus. Later, when the capitol was moved, the mansion was used by Union General Sherman as

a temporary hospital. It was one of the few buildings Sherman did not destroy in Jackson. Tours of the Greek Revival home occur on the half hour, but reservations are required for groups of ten or more.

Mississippi Governor's Mansion

THE OAKS HOUSE MUSEUM

823 North Jefferson Street, Jackson, MS
PHONE: 601-353-9339
HOURS: Open Tuesday–Saturday.
ADMISSION: A fee is charged; children are discounted.

The Oaks House Museum, considered by many as the oldest home in Jackson, was briefly used as Gen. William T. Sherman's headquarters during the Vicksburg Campaign. Artifacts from the campaign may be viewed.

Dining room of The Oaks House Museum

The Oaks House Museum

OLD CAPITOL MUSEUM OF MISSISSIPPI HISTORY

100 South State Street, Jackson, MS
PHONE: 601-359-6920
HOURS: Open daily; closed major holidays.
ADMISSION: Free.

The Old Capitol Museum of Mississippi History was the site of Mississippi's Secession Convention in January 1861 and was also the seat of state government until May 1863. In October 1864, the building became the Confederate military headquarters.

Photo above: Civil War and Reconstruction Room, Old Capitol Museum

Photo left: House of Representatives Chamber, Old Capitol Museum

WINTERGREEN CEMETERY

Greenwood Street, Port Gibson, MS
PHONE: 601-437-4351 (Chamber of Commerce Tourist Information Center)
HOURS: Open daily.
ADMISSION: Free.

Established in 1807, Wintergreen Cemetery is the final resting place for most of the Confederate soldiers killed in the battle of Port Gibson. Shortly after the battle, the townspeople removed the

Confederate dead from the battlefield and interred them here in Soldiers' Row. Small footstones marked "C.S.A." were placed by the United Daughters of the Confederacy. Elsewhere in the cemetery, Confederate Generals Earl Van Dorn and Benjamin Grubb Humphreys are also interred. General Van Dorn was born near Port Gibson on September 17, 1820.

GRAND GULF MILITARY PARK
PORT GIBSON BATTLEFIELD

Grand Gulf Road, 7 miles west of U.S Highway 61, Port Gibson, MS
PHONE: 601-437-5911
HOURS: Open daily; closed state holidays.
ADMISSION: A fee is charged.

After General Grant failed to capture Vicksburg in 1862, Union troops moved south along the Mississippi River toward Grand Gulf. On April 29, 1863, Union Admiral David D. Porter's ironclads opened fire on Forts Cobun and Wade. Although Porter destroyed the guns at Wade after a five-hour bombardment, the Union was unable to silence the big guns at Fort Cobun; Porter called off the attack. After dark, the Union troops simply bypassed Grand Gulf and crossed the river at Bruinsburg. Admiral Porter later called Grand Gulf "the strongest place on the Mississippi." Forts Wade and Cobun still retain their original earthworks and ammunition magazines. The museum contains exhibits of Civil War artifacts, including Union and Confederate uniforms, cannonballs, and muskets.

NATCHEZ NATIONAL CEMETERY

41 Cemetery Road, Natchez, MS
PHONE: 601-445-4981
HOURS: Open daily.
ADMISSION: Free.

Over 3,000 Union and Confederate soldiers are interred at the Natchez National Cemetery. Soldiers who had been buried in the levees, were disinterred, and brought to this national cemetery in 1863 where they now rest in dignity. In addition, the majority of the Buffalo Soldiers—African-American soldiers from Louisiana and Mississippi who served in the West during the late nineteenth century—are interred here.

Photo right: Natchez National Cemetery

MISSOURI

Missouri's status during the Civil War is best symbolized by the fact that whereas the Confederate flag featured a star for Missouri, the state itself never officially left the Union. Torn apart over the issue of slavery before the war, Missouri found no respite from internal strife during the conflict: more incidents of guerrilla warfare occurred in Missouri than in any other state. And while 100,000 Missouri citizens fought for the Union, 40,000 of their neighbors fought for the Confederacy. Militarily, the Confederacy never got a secure foothold in Missouri, and the Union controlled the state for most of the war; nonetheless, life in Missouri was disrupted and devastated by Civil War fighting, and the internal divisiveness that marked the state before and during the war was destined to last long after.

In the southwestern corner of Missouri is a National Battlefield Site commemorating the Battle of Wilson's Creek, which took place in August of 1861. Although the Confederates won this battle, they suffered heavy losses and damage and thereafter were unable to make any significant move to control Missouri. Whereas Wilson's Creek was the largest and most important battle, Missouri was the site of more than 1,100 Civil War battles or skirmishes, and points of historic interest exist in almost every corner of the state.

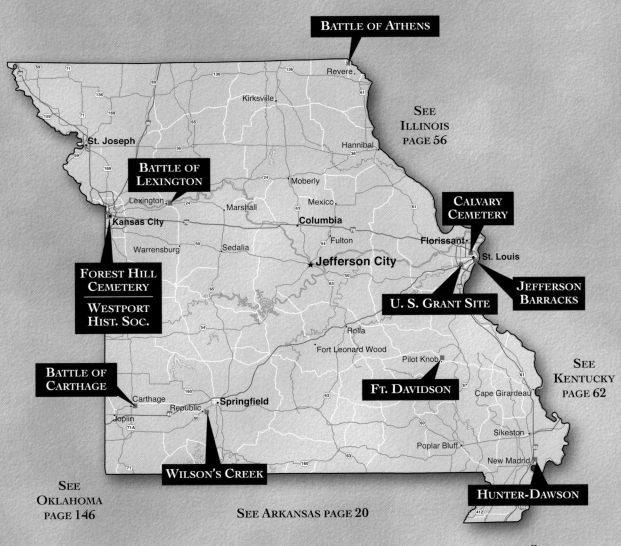

BATTLE OF ATHENS

SEE
ILLINOIS
PAGE 56

BATTLE OF
LEXINGTON

CALVARY
CEMETERY

FOREST HILL
CEMETERY

WESTPORT
HIST. SOC.

JEFFERSON
BARRACKS

U. S. GRANT SITE

BATTLE OF
CARTHAGE

SEE
KENTUCKY
PAGE 62

FT. DAVIDSON

WILSON'S CREEK

SEE
OKLAHOMA
PAGE 146

HUNTER-DAWSON

SEE ARKANSAS PAGE 20

SEE
TENNESSEE
PAGE 168

Revere

Kirksville

Hannibal

St. Joseph

Lexington

Marshall

Moberly

Mexico

Columbia

Florissant

St. Louis

Kansas City

Warrensburg

Sedalia

Fulton

Jefferson City

Rolla

Fort Leonard Wood

Pilot Knob

Cape Girardeau

Carthage

Republic

Springfield

Joplin

Sikeston

Poplar Bluff

New Madrid

0   100 Miles

0   100 KM

"Fire low—don't aim higher than their knees; wait until they get close; don't get scared; it's no part of a soldier's duty to get scared."

Brig. Gen. N. Lyon
to his men

NORTHERN COMMANDER:
Brig. Gen. N. Lyon

STRENGTH: 7,000

CASUALTIES: 1,317

THE BATTLE OF WILSON'S CREEK (OAK HILLS)

August 10, 1861

The first Civil War battle west of the Mississippi River.

Missouri included the major trails west (California, Oregon, Santa Fe, and Pony Express) as well as the three major shipping rivers of the Missouri, Mississippi, and the Ohio. Because of this strategic importance, President Lincoln gave special attention to Missouri.

In July of 1861, Union soldiers under Brigadier General Nathaniel Lyon began a march southward through Missouri to confront pro-Confederate forces organizing near Springfield. By July Lyon's Union forces were camped at Springfield, while the Confederate army, under Brigadier General Benjamin McCulloch and joined by the Missouri State Guard under Major General Sterling Price, encamped near Wilson's Creek, just south of Springfield.

Initially, McCulloch planned to attack the Union army the morning of August 10, but a light rain caused him to

The Ray House, Wilson's Creek National Battlefield

General Lyon's Marker at Bloody Hill, Wilson's Creek National Battlefield

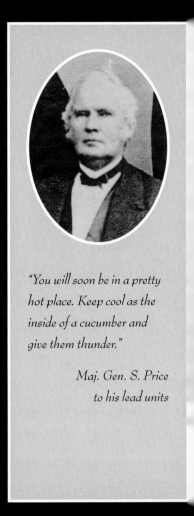

"You will soon be in a pretty hot place. Keep cool as the inside of a cucumber and give them thunder."

Maj. Gen. S. Price
to his lead units

delay. Confederate pickets, however, who had been recalled in order to prepare for battle, did not reposition themselves when the order was rescinded. Lyon realized that if he did not attack, he would be attacked by a force significantly greater in size than his own. Accordingly, he called for an attack at dawn, and on August 10, split his army into three units and attacked.

Because the pickets had not been set up, the Confederates were caught completely by surprise in the south. In the north, the Confederate cavalry stalled Lyon long enough for Price to reorganize and launch a counterattack. By midday, the Federals were nearly out of ammunition and clearly overmatched. They retreated and marched toward Springfield, without General Lyon, who had been killed during heavy hand-to-hand combat on a section of the battlefield known as "Bloody Hill."

Thirty future major and brigadier generals fought at Wilson's Creek. The Confederates won the battle, and a temporary advantage in the fight to gain control of Missouri, but they also suffered heavy losses. As a result, the South saw its plans to take Missouri stalled and eventually defeated. Additionally, two state governments were formed so that Missouri became the only state to have both seceded to the Confederacy and been reinforced by the Union.

SOUTHERN COMMANDERS:
Maj. Gen. S. Price
Brig. Gen. B. McCulloch

STRENGTH: 13,000

CASUALTIES: 1,222

WESTPORT HISTORICAL SOCIETY

4000 Baltimore Street, Kansas City, MO
PHONE: 816-561-1821
HOURS: Open Tuesday–Friday; closed major holidays.
ADMISSION: Free.

The Westport Historical Society offers free brochures detailing the Battle of Westport, the largest Civil War engagement west of the Missouri River. At Westport, Union forces repulsed Confederate forces, thus ending Price's Raid throughout Missouri. The thirty-two-mile, self-guided automobile tour follows twenty-five interpretive markers which explain the 1864 battle. Self-guided walking tours are marked through Byram's Ford and the Big Blue Battlefield.

FOREST HILL CEMETERY

6901 Troost Avenue, Kansas City, MO
PHONE: 816-523-2114
HOURS: Open daily.
ADMISSION: Free.

Forest Hill Cemetery sits on the site where the Battle of Westport took place and is the resting place for many Confederate soldiers. Also buried at Forest Hill is the leader of the "Iron Brigade," Confederate Gen. Joseph O. Shelby, who fought at the Battle of Westport. After the war, Shelby's career continued; he took his troops to Mexico to support the Emperor Maximilian and, upon his return to the U.S., became a U.S. Marshal.

BATTLE OF LEXINGTON STATE HISTORIC SITE

Missouri Highway 13, Lexington, MO
PHONE: 660-259-4654
HOURS: Open daily.
ADMISSION: No charge for the Visitor's Center and battlefield; fee charged for Anderson House; children are discounted.

Built in 1853, Anderson House was used as a hospital by both Union and Confederate forces during the Battle of Lexington. Battle damage from the September 1861 engagement is still visible in the house. The Battle of Lexington State Historic Site hosts a reenactment every three years in September.

Anderson House, Battle of Lexington State Historic Site

BATTLE OF CARTHAGE STATE HISTORIC SITE

North side of East Chestnut Street, next to Carter Park, Carthage, MO

PHONE: None available.

HOURS: Open daily.

ADMISSION: Free.

This battle was one of many Missouri skirmishes that pitted the Missouri State Guard, a pro-Southern force backed by a governor who was a Confederate sympathizer, against Union volunteer regiments. These small battles, won by Union forces, were instrumental in assuring that Missouri would remain in the Union. Over seven acres of this historic site are located where the final skirmish of the Battle of Carthage took place. An inter-

Battle of Carthage State Historic Site

pretative shelter with displays and self-guided trails explain the history of the July 5, 1861, battle. A self-guided automobile tour following various historical markers is offered.

WILSON'S CREEK NATIONAL BATTLEFIELD

6424 West Farm Road 182, Republic, MO

PHONE: 417-732-2662

HOURS: Open daily; closed Christmas and New Year's Day.

ADMISSION: A fee is charged; children under 16 are free.

Wilson's Creek National Battlefield covers 1,750 acres and features a marked, five-mile, self-guided driving tour that features eight interpretive stops detailing the progress and action of the battle. Included are Gibson's House and Mill sites; the Ray House that was used as a Confederate field hospital; Pulaski Arkansas Battery and Price's Headquarters; Sigel's Second Position, where Union forces routed 2,300 Southern cavalry; Sigel's Final Position, where the general committed the fatal

Cannon at Sharp Farm, Wilson's Creek National Battlefield

error that gave the battle victory to the Confederates; and Bloody Hill, a site where over 1,700 Union and Confederate soldiers including Gen. Nathaniel Lyon, were slain. The bed on which the body of General Lyon was laid is part of the exhibit at the Ray House. Five walking trails, ranging from a quarter-mile to three-quarters-of-a-mile each, provide further exploration. A picnic area and hiking trails also are available.

BATTLE OF ATHENS STATE HISTORIC SITE

Missouri Highway 81, County Blacktop Road CC, Revere, MO
PHONE: 660-877-3871
HOURS: Open daily.
ADMISSION: Free.

The Civil War caused bitter feelings between many of the residents of Athens. As a result of the animosity, the town of Athens was deserted during the early twentieth century. The Battle of Athens State Historic Site serves as museum both for the town's culture as well as its significance in the war. The Battle of Athens was the northernmost battle fought in Missouri during the Civil War and contributed in keeping Missouri in the Union. The battle was the clash of Confederate guardsmen pitted against Col. David Moore and his Union home guard. The Thome-Benning House, locally known as the "Cannonball House," functions as a museum and a Visitor's Center. Also on the site is the McKee House which was used by Colonel Moore as his headquarters during the Union occupation of Athens. Trails and self-guided tours are available. Every third year, a battle reenactment is held, the most recent in August 1999.

Battle of Athens State Historic Site

CALVARY CEMETERY

5239 West Florissant, St. Louis, MO

PHONE: 314-381-1313

HOURS: Open daily.

ADMISSION: Free.

Union Gen. William T. Sherman, Confederate Gov. Thomas Reynolds, and other Civil War individuals are interred in Calvary Cemetery.

JEFFERSON BARRACKS

Kingston and South Broadway, St. Louis, MO

PHONE: 314-544-5714

HOURS: Open daily except Monday; closed major holidays.

ADMISSION: Free; a fee is charged for changing exhibits.

Jefferson Barracks, built in 1826, was the site of the country's first basic training camp. Many Union and Confederate officers, including Robert E. Lee, Jefferson Davis, Braxton Bragg, and William T. Sherman passed through Jefferson, most being sent directly upon their graduation from West Point. An active army post until 1946, the barracks contain the third largest national cemetery in the U.S. The barracks were used as the only general hospital west of the Mississippi River during the Civil War. Trails, tours, a museum, and a Visitor's Center are available. Jefferson Barracks hosts periodic Civil War reenactments.

ULYSSES S. GRANT NATIONAL HISTORIC SITE

7400 Grant Road, St. Louis, MO

PHONE: 314-842-3298

HOURS: Open daily; closed major holidays.

ADMISSION: Free.

The Ulysses S. Grant National Historic Site contains five historic structures from the original 1,000-acre plantation owned by General Grant. Guided tours and information are available. Grant's birthday is celebrated in April.

1860 photograph of Ulysses S. Grant's home

Ulysses S. Grant National Historic Site

FORT DAVIDSON STATE HISTORIC SITE

Missouri Highway V, Pilot Knob, MO

PHONE: 573-546-3454

HOURS: Open daily.

ADMISSION: Free.

Fort Davidson Historic Site features the preserved remains of the earthworks of Fort Davidson. The fort was built to guard the railroad line linking Pilot Knob with St. Louis. After only about an hour, the Battle of Pilot Knob in September 1864 left 1,200 dead. Union troops were forced to abandon the fort to Southern forces. Federal troops, however, left little

Fort Davidson Historic Site Visitor's Center

for the Confederate army; before evacuating, they destroyed the guns and powder magazine.

A museum and a Visitor's Center are also located at the site. The museum features two twenty-four-pound cannon. Additionally, a slide presentation, brochures, and maps are available at the Visitor's Center. A self-guided driving tour of the valley features thirteen historic markers, one of which commemorates the spot where General Grant received word of his commission on August 8, 1861, in Irontown, Missouri. The courthouse in Irontown looks over two cannon on its grounds, and the building itself still bears battle scars.

THE HUNTER-DAWSON STATE HISTORIC SITE

112 Dawson Road, New Madrid, MO
PHONE: 573-748-5340
HOURS: Open daily; closed major holidays.
ADMISSION: A fee is charged; children are discounted.

The Hunter-Dawson State Historic Site contains an antebellum mansion that was built by the Hunter family. Originally from Virginia, the Hunter family had a son in the Confederate army. Legend has it that General John Pope used the house as his headquarters after New Madrid was occupied by Union forces. Tours of the fifteen-room house feature original furnishings.

The Hunter-Dawson State Historic Site

NEW MEXICO

During the Civil War, the Territory of New Mexico—comprised what is today the states of Arizona, New Mexico, and part of Nevada—was a thinly-populated wilderness. By 1861 the southern region of the territory was so pro-Southern, that conventions held in Mesilla and Tucson voted for secession from the Union and annexation to the Confederacy. This secessionist stance was, ironically, taken one month before the secession of Tennessee, North Carolina, Arkansas, and the Confederate capital state of Virginia.

The South sent out a military expedition to occupy and hold the territory, not for New Mexico alone, but because the territory was a steppingstone to California with its Pacific ports. With its proximity to Texas, the battle for New Mexico became a battle for the Western ambitions of Texas itself.

The Confederate venture into New Mexico ultimately ended in failure. The Union victory at the Battle of Glorieta Pass effectively halted the Confederacy's, and Texas's, movement into the West.

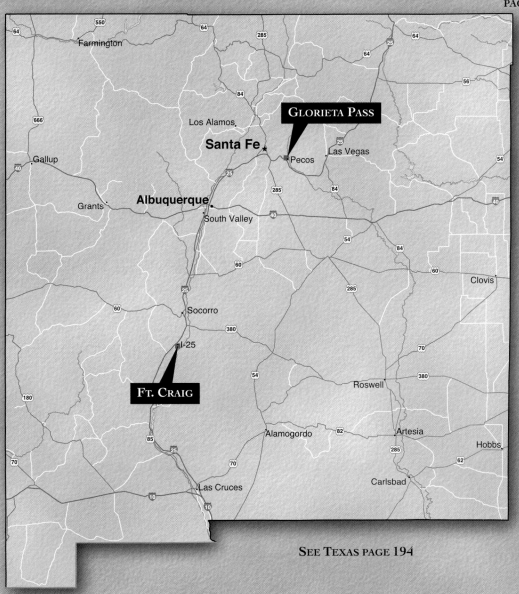

64 550 Farmington

64 285 64 25 64

56

666

84 GLORIETA PASS

Los Alamos 25

Santa Fe ★

Pecos Las Vegas 54

Gallup 40

25 285 84

Grants **Albuquerque** 40

South Valley 54

60 54 84

285 60

Clovis

25 Socorro 70

60 380

I-25 54 380

FT. CRAIG Roswell

180

82 Artesia

85 25 Alamogordo 285 Hobbs

70 70 62

Las Cruces 10 Carlsbad

10

See Texas page 194

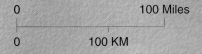

0   100 Miles

0   100 KM

"The best place to fight is at the highest possible point, right at the top of the pass. My men are used to high altitudes, Sibley's come from a low altitude. Give them ten minutes at a mile high, and one of my men will be worth ten of his."

Maj. J. M. Chivington

NORTHERN COMMANDERS:
Col. J. P. Slough
Maj. J. M. Chivington

STRENGTH: 1,300

CASUALTIES: 142

THE BATTLE OF GLORIETA PASS

March 26 and 28, 1862

Victory in New Mexico saved the Far West for the Union.

In the summer of 1861, Confederate President Jefferson Davis ordered Brigadier General Henry Hopkins Sibley to recruit a force of Texans to move into New Mexico territory and secure that territory for the Confederacy, thus opening the way into Colorado and California.

The Battle of Glorieta Pass was the climax of this Confederate thrust, which began in January of 1862. The Texans, under Sibley, had marched into New Mexico, first taking the southernmost Federal post, Fort Fillmore, and then defeating the Union at the Battle of Valverde. They then stopped for provisions about 100 miles northeast of Santa Fe on the Santa Fe Trail. Meanwhile, the Union was gathering its forces at Fort Craig. On March 22, Union Colonel John P. Slough, with 1,340 troops, set out to confront the Texans and put an end to their movement through New Mexico. The two sides met on the morning of March 26 on the Santa Fe Trail when a Confederate force of 200–300 Texans under the command of Major Charles L. Pyron encamped at Johnson's Ranch, at one end of Glorieta Pass. Union Major John M. Chivington led more

Base of Sharpshooters Ridge, Glorieta Pass Battlefield, Pecos National Historical Park

Glorieta Pass, Pecos National Historical Park

"Valverde, Glorieta, Albuquerque, Peralto... will be duly chronicled, and form one of the brightest pages in the history of the Second American Revolution."

Brig. Gen. H. H. Sibley
May 14, 1862, Proclamation

SOUTHERN COMMANDERS:
Brig. Gen. H. H. Sibley
Lt. Col. W. R. Scurry

STRENGTH: 800

CASUALTIES: 189

than 400 soldiers to the pass and, on the morning of March 26, moved out to attack. After heavy fighting all afternoon, Chivington went into camp at Kozlowski's Ranch. No fighting occurred the next day as reinforcements arrived for both sides.

Lieutenant Colonel William R. Scurry's troops swelled the Rebel ranks to about 1,100 while Union Colonel John P. Slough arrived with about 900 men. Both Slough and Scurry decided to attack and set out early on March 28 to do so. The Confederates held their ground and then attacked and counter-attacked throughout the afternoon. The fighting then ended as Slough retired first to Pigeon's Ranch and then to Kozlowski's Ranch. Scurry soon left the field also, thinking he had won the battle. Chivington's men, however, had destroyed all Scurry's supplies and animals at Johnson's Ranch. Both sides claimed victory, the Confederates because they stayed on the field, and the Union because they stopped the Confederates from continuing west.

GLORIETA PASS BATTLEFIELD

Pecos National Historical Park, New Mexico Highway 63 north of I-25, Pecos, NM

PHONE: 505-757-6414

HOURS: Open daily; closed Christmas and New Year's Day.

ADMISSION: A fee is charged.

The Glorieta Pass Battlefield is located in the Pecos National Historical Park. The pass was a strategic location during the Civil War because it was situated at the southern tip of the Sangre de Cristo Mountains, southeast of Santa Fe and on the Santa Fe Trail. In March 1862, a battle ensued for control of the pass which the Union troops won, thereby stopping Confederate incursions into the Southwest. Glorieta Pass was the turning point of the war in the New Mexico Territory. Today, much of Glorieta Pass Battlefield is pri-

Photo above: Looking down the east side of Sharpshooters Ridge, Glorieta Pass Battlefield, Pecos National Historical Park

Photo left: Atop Sharpshooters Ridge, Glorieta Pass Battlefield, Pecos National Historical Park

vately owned, but tours by park rangers are available. The Visitor's Center at Pecos National Historical Park contains exhibits and information relating to the battle.

Looking towards Sharpshooters Ridge, Glorieta Pass Battlefield, Pecos National Historical Park

FORT CRAIG

Socorro Resource Area, Bureau of Land Management, near exit 115 of Interstate 25
PHONE: 505-835-0412
HOURS: Open daily.
ADMISSION: Free.

After their defeat at Valverde on February 21, 1862, Union troops gathered at Socorro to await reinforcements before attacking the Confederate Texan Army at Glorieta. Each year Fort Craig hosts a Civil War reenactment. Although the fort itself is in ruins, the foundations of the structures are still highly visible and provide an accurate description of the largest western army fort in the Civil War-era. Trails and self-guided tours are of Fort Craig are available.

Ruins of Officer's Quarters, Fort Craig

NORTH CAROLINA

*M*any of North Carolina's Civil War battles occurred along its Atlantic coastline. Barrier islands and sandbars provided natural protection for small blockade-running ships. These ships were important in providing troops and civilians with supplies and weapons. The most significant maritime battle took place just outside Wilmington. Fort Fisher guarded the city from Union attack and provided a port for Confederate blockade runners. Many of these supply ships were destroyed by members of the Union blockade. Items, including supplies and arms, from sunken blockade runners are exhibited in Fort Fisher's Museum. Nearby, earthworks at the Brunswick Town/Fort Anderson State Historic Site further illustrate North Carolina's Cape Fear defense system.

Inland, North Carolina's largest battle took place at Bentonville. Union General William T. Sherman's army defeated Confederate General Joseph E. Johnston's army at the Battle of Bentonville. This last major battle of the Civil War is commemorated at living history exhibits held during the summer. Every five years, a reenactment of the battle takes place at Bentonville Battleground State Historic Site in Newton Grove.

SEE
TENNESSEE
PAGE 168

SEE VIRGINIA PAGE 200

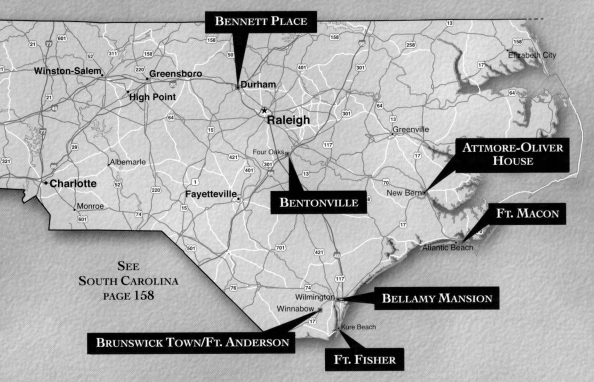

BENNETT PLACE

21 601 77

311 52

21 220 **Winston-Salem** **Greensboro**

85

High Point

40 64

21

158

50

Durham

158 95 258

401

301

13

Raleigh

158

Elizabeth City

17

64

Greenville

17

13

64

158

**ATTMORE-OLIVER
HOUSE**

29

Albemarle

321

85

Charlotte

52

Monroe 74

601

15

421

301 401 95

1

Four Oaks

117

BENTONVILLE

13

70

New Bern

8

17

FT. MACON

Atlantic Beach

Fayetteville

220

15

501

701 421

76

74

117

Wilmington
Winnabow

17

Kure Beach

BELLAMY MANSION

SEE
SOUTH CAROLINA
PAGE 158

BRUNSWICK TOWN/FT. ANDERSON

FT. FISHER

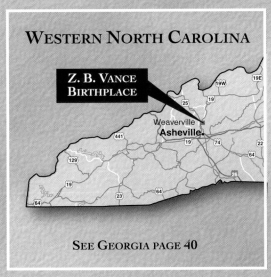

WESTERN NORTH CAROLINA

**Z. B. VANCE
BIRTHPLACE**

19W 19E

25 19

Weaverville
Asheville

441 19 74

129

22

64

19 26

23 64

64

SEE GEORGIA PAGE 40

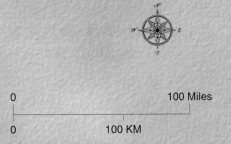

0   100 Miles

0   100 KM

NORTHERN COMMANDERS:
Maj. Gen. B. Butler
Rear Adm. D. D. Porter

STRENGTH: 6,500

CASUALTIES: 16

THE BATTLE OF FORT FISHER

December 7–27, 1864; January 6–15, 1865

At Fort Fisher, a combined effort of Union army and navy closed the last major supply port for General Lee's Army of Northern Virginia.

Wilmington, North Carolina, was among the most important blockade-running ports in the Confederate South. With railroad connections to major cities, Wilmington was essential in supplying the Confederate army. Dangerous offshore shoals and riptides kept Union blockade ships from getting too close to shore. To defend Wilmington, the Confederates built a series of forts, one of which was Fort Fisher.

Rear Admiral David D. Porter was given orders to take Wilmington but was worried about the Confederate ship, the *Albemarle*, which had proven its ability to withstand attack. A young lieutenant, William Cushing, and fourteen others volunteered to ram the *Albemarle* with a Union torpedo boat. Only Cushing and one other crew member escaped with their lives. The *Albemarle* was sunk with a single torpedo.

With the *Albemarle* cleared, Porter agreed to General Butler's suggestion to detonate a ship of explosives next to Fort Fisher and then immediately begin shelling it. This plan would cripple the fort and make it easier for a landing party of Union army forces. The explosion, however, had little effect on the

Sheppard's Battery, Fort Fisher State Historic Site

Sheppard's Battery after the Battle of Fort Fisher, taken in January 1865 by Timothy O'Sullivan, one of Mathew Brady's traveling photographers

fort, and it was ten hours before the navy began the shelling. When the Confederates did not fire back, Union commanders erroneously concluded that their guns had been silenced. On Christmas morning, Major General Benjamin Butler landed his men at Fort Fisher; he returned them posthaste when he realized that the fort was, indeed, fully functional.

Both Union commanders blamed each other for the botched attack. General Grant relieved Butler, assigning Major General Alfred Terry in his place. Coordination between the Union army and navy improved after the change of command.

On January 15, a joint attack from both the river and land began, but the sailors and marines were ill-prepared for attacking a fort. Out of 1,200 sailors and 400 marines, 350 became casualties. Still, the attention given to the river attack allowed a group of Union troops to slip through a breach caused by naval gun fire. Seven hours of hand-to-hand combat ensued before the South surrendered Fort Fisher, its last sea stronghold. The city of Wilmington, the Confederate's last open port, surrendered five weeks later on February 22, 1865.

SOUTHERN COMMANDERS:
Maj. Gen. R. Hoke
Col. W. Lamb

STRENGTH: 800

CASUALTIES: 300

THE ZEBULON B. VANCE BIRTHPLACE

Zebulon B. Vance Birthplace

911 Reems Creek Road, Weaverville, NC
PHONE: 828-645-6706
HOURS: Open daily April–October;
closed Monday November–March.
ADMISSION: Free.

This Zebulon B. Vance Birthplace commemorates the life of Zebulon B. Vance, a prominent public figure in North Carolina politics before, during, and after the Civil War. A member of the U.S. House of Representatives until North Carolina seceded, he served as colonel of the Twenty-sixth North Carolina Regiment. After the war, Vance was elected to three terms in the U.S. Senate. His birthplace is interpreted through costumed guides and includes many items authentic to the Civil War era. A springhouse, corn crib, smokehouse, loom house, slave house, and tool house are located on its grounds. Special events occur throughout the year.

BENNETT PLACE STATE HISTORIC SITE

4409 Bennett Memorial Road, Durham, NC
PHONE: 919-383-4345
HOURS: Open daily April–October; closed Monday November–March.
ADMISSION: Free.

The reconstructed Bennett Place State Historic Site marks the site where Confederate General Joseph G. Johnston surrendered to Union General William T. Sherman in April 1865. The house contains exhibits on the surrender meetings and a peace monument. A Visitor's Center contains three rooms which focus on the Bennett family, the Civil War, and the surrender at Bennett Place. A model of the Bennett farm

Peace Monument, Bennett Place State Historic Site

showing the arrival of Union and Confederate cavalry troops on April 17, 1865, and a fifteen-minute audio-visual program on the site's history are also offered.

BENTONVILLE BATTLEFIELD STATE HISTORIC SITE

5466 Harper House Road, Four Oaks, NC
PHONE: 910-594-0789
HOURS: Open daily April–October; closed Monday November–March.
ADMISSION: Free.

In March 1865, the Battle of Bentonville marked General William T. Sherman's last devastating march north through the Carolinas. Despite their numerical disadvantage, General Joseph E. Johnston's Confederate forces successfully ambushed one wing of Sherman's army on March 19, 1865; however, they were soon repulsed. For the Confederates, it was a heroic but futile effort to delay the inevitable; within a month, both Richmond and Raleigh had fallen, and Lee had surrendered.

Reenactor at Harper House, Bentonville Battlefield State Historic Site

Goldsboro Rifles' mass grave monument, Bentonville Battlefield State Historic Site

The Harper House is located at Bentonville Battlefield State Historic Site. The downstairs room contains a functioning Civil War field hospital, while the upstairs rooms contain period domestic furnishings. A Confederate mass grave, the Harper family cemetery, and a trail leading to a section of Union earthworks are also accessible to the public. Battle relics and an audiovisual program about the battle are available at the Visitor's Center. Roads in the area are marked with highway historical markers highlighting events of the battle.

THE ATTMORE-OLIVER HOUSE

511 Broad Street, New Bern, NC
PHONE: 252-638-8558
HOURS: Open daily April–mid-December.
ADMISSION: A fee is charged.

Although the Attmore-Oliver House was built in 1790, it contains some Civil War memorabilia. One room exhibit includes guns, sabers, photographs, documents, chests, medical supplies, diaries, and other items of interest from the Civil War period.

The Attmore-Oliver House

FORT MACON STATE PARK

North Carolina Highway 58, East Fort Macon Road, Atlantic Beach, NC

PHONE: 252-726-3775

HOURS: Open daily.

ADMISSION: Free.

On April 26, 1862, the Union captured Fort Macon, the Confederate fort which guarded Beaufort Harbor. The well-preserved fort features a museum. Three reenactments occur annually in April, July, and September.

Fort Macon State Park

BELLAMY MANSION MUSEUM

Corner of Market and 5th Streets, Wilmington, NC

PHONE: 910-251-3700

HOURS: Tours available Wednesday–Sunday.

ADMISSION: A fee is charged.

About six months after the Bellamy family built this antebellum mansion, the Civil War broke out. Shortly thereafter, Gen. Joseph Hawley made the house his headquarters. Tours of the Bellamy Mansion Museum can be arranged by calling the home in advance.

Bellamy Mansion Museum

BRUNSWICK TOWN/FORT ANDERSON STATE HISTORIC SITE

8884 St. Philips Road SE, Winabow, NC

PHONE: 910-371-6613

HOURS: Open daily April–October; closed Monday November–March.

ADMISSION: Free.

The 120-acre Brunswick Town/Fort Anderson State Historic Site contains the remnants of Fort Anderson's earthworks. Also featured is a Colonial Anglican church that was used as a hospital by the Confederates. The Visitor's Center features audio-visual presentations and a small museum of artifacts and relics.

River Battery, Brunswick Town/Fort Anderson State Historic Site

FORT FISHER STATE HISTORIC SITE

1610 Fort Fisher Boulevard, Kure Beach, NC

PHONE: 910-458-5538

HOURS: Open daily April–November; closed Monday December–March.

ADMISSION: Free.

Fort Fisher State Historic Site features a reconstructed palisade, mounted guns, interpretive trails, a Visitor's Center, and a Blockade Runner Museum with artifacts from sunken ships.

Fort Fisher State Historic Site

OHIO

Despite the fact that only one major battle, Buffington Island, took place in the state, Ohio contributed a great deal to the war effort. Among its famous native sons, Ohio boasts President Rutherford B. Hayes, General William Tecumseh Sherman, General Ulysses S. Grant, and General George Armstrong Custer. Museums honoring these Union commanders are found in Fremont, Lancaster, Point Pleasant, and New Rumley.

Ohio also numbers the "Fighting McCooks" as famous residents. The McCook House in Carrollton commemorates the fourteen McCook members who served the Union during the Civil War. General Robert McCook and General Joseph Hooker, the commander of the Army of the Cumberland, are buried in the Spring Grove Cemetery and Arboretum. Almost 1,000 other Civil War soldiers are interred on the cemetery's beautiful grounds. Statues and artwork dot the site's 733 acres.

Prisoner of war camps proliferated after Union commander Ulysses S. Grant ended prisoner exchanges and paroles on April 17, 1864, and many of the camps were located in Ohio. Over 2,000 soldiers rest at Camp Chase Cemetery in Columbus. The camp was used as a Union training center and then as a prisoner-of-war camp. To the north, the Johnson Island Cemetery in Lakeside-Marblehead was also the site of a prisoner-of-war camp and contains 206 Confederate graves.

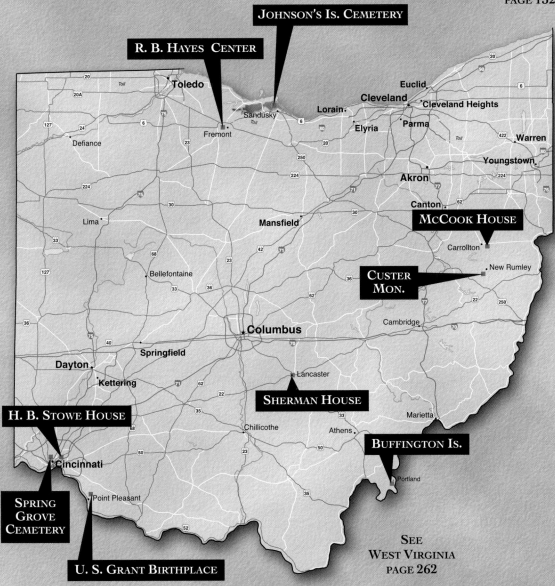

SEE
PENNSYLVANIA
PAGE 152

JOHNSON'S IS. CEMETERY

R. B. HAYES CENTER

Toledo

20

20A

75

127

24

Defiance

Sandusky

Fremont

6

Toll

Euclid

Cleveland

Cleveland Heights

Lorain

Elyria

Parma

Toll

422

Warren

Youngstown

80

Akron

77

224

Canton

62

76

McCOOK HOUSE

Carrollton

New Rumley

CUSTER
MON.

22

250

250

224

71

30

Mansfield

42

71

23

68

Lima

33

127

Bellefontaine

33

36

62

36

Cambridge

70

Columbus

75

40

Springfield

Dayton

Kettering

71

62

22

35

68

Chillicothe

Lancaster

SHERMAN HOUSE

Athens

33

Marietta

BUFFINGTON IS.

H. B. STOWE HOUSE

Cincinnati

50

50

23

Portland

35

Point Pleasant

52

SPRING
GROVE
CEMETERY

U. S. GRANT BIRTHPLACE

SEE
WEST VIRGINIA
PAGE 262

SEE
KENTUCKY
PAGE 62

0   100 Miles

0   100 KM

JOHNSON'S ISLAND CEMETERY

Off Marblehead Peninsula in Sandusky Bay, OH
PHONE: N/A
HOURS: Open daily.
ADMISSION: Free.

During the war, a Union prison for Confederate officers was located on Johnson's Island. In 1865 approximately 3,000 officers were imprisoned there. More than 200 prisoners are buried in Johnson's Island Cemetery.

RUTHERFORD B. HAYES PRESIDENTIAL CENTER

Spiegel Grove, Fremont, OH
PHONE: 419-332-2081
HOURS: Open daily; closed major holidays.
ADMISSION: A fee is charged; children and seniors are discounted.

Hayes, our nineteenth president, served in the Union army and attained the rank of brevet major general. Located on the president's former twenty-five-acre estate is the Rutherford B. Hayes Presidential Center which contains a museum, the first presidential library, the president's home, and the president's tomb. The site maintains an extensive museum that contains cannon and Civil War weaponry, personal uniforms and medals, and many other Civil War artifacts.

Photo above: The Hayes Home, Rutherford B. Hayes Presidential Center

Photo left: Hayes Museum and Library, Rutherford B. Hayes Presidential Center

McCook House

Public Square, Carrollton, OH
PHONE: 216-627-3345
HOURS: Open Friday–Sunday Memorial Day weekend–mid-October; otherwise, by appointment.
ADMISSION: A fee is charged for adults; children are discounted.

McCook House

The "Fighting McCooks" were so named from their record of contributing fourteen family members to the Union army during the Civil War. In all, seven generals, one colonel, two majors, three lieutenants, and one private bore the name of McCook. Of those, four lost their lives. The McCook House has been restored and is maintained as a memorial to their name.

Custer Monument State Memorial

Ohio Highway 646, New Rumley, OH
PHONE: 614-297-2630 (Ohio Historical Soc.)
HOURS: Open daily.
ADMISSION: Free.

George Armstrong Custer, born in 1839, graduated from West Point and became one of the youngest generals of the Union. He was flamboyant and daring in his actions in the cavalry; he was involved in the battles of Manassas, Shenandoah, Waynesboro, and Appomattox. A statue of Custer stands near the site of his birth. An exhibit pavilion is also located at the site.

Photo right: Custer Monument State Memorial

The Sherman House

137 East Main Street, Lancaster, OH
PHONE: 740-687-5891
HOURS: Open daily except Monday April–mid-December.
ADMISSION: A fee is charged; students are discounted.

The Sherman House is the birthplace of William Tecumseh Sherman, the Union's fiercest general. A museum with personal and professional memorabilia as well as other Civil War artifacts is now housed at the site. Sherman's birthday is celebrated each February.

Photo right: The Sherman House

SPRING GROVE CEMETERY AND ARBORETUM

4521 Spring Grove Avenue, Cincinnati, OH
PHONE: 513-681-6680
HOURS: Open daily.
ADMISSION: Free.

Nearly 1,000 Civil War soldiers are buried at Spring Grove Cemetery and Arboretum. Notable Union casualties interred here include Gen. Robert McCook of the "Fighting McCooks" and Gen. Joseph Hooker. A self-guided walking tour of the arboretum and cemetery is available.

Spring Grove Cemetery and Arboretum

Spring Grove Cemetery and Arboretum

HARRIET BEECHER STOWE HOUSE

2950 Gilbert Avenue, Cincinnati, OH
PHONE: 513-632-5120
HOURS: Open Tuesday–Thursday.
ADMISSION: Free.

Harriet Beecher Stowe inflamed public sentiment regarding slavery with her book *Uncle Tom's Cabin*. The Harriet Beecher Stowe House was actually built for her father when he moved his family from Connecticut. Each May a Memorial Day sunrise service takes place at the house.

ULYSSES S. GRANT BIRTHPLACE STATE MEMORIAL

1591 Ohio Highway 232, Point Pleasant, OH

PHONE: 513-553-4911

HOURS: Open daily April–October; closed Monday and Tuesday.

ADMISSION: A fee is charged for adults; children and seniors are discounted.

Grant, our eighteenth president, served in the Civil War with distinction, rising to General of the Union army and receiving Confederate General Lee's surrender at Appomattox Court House. This small-frame house faces the Ohio River and contains items belonging to Grant's parents and period furnishings. The front room, only sixteen-and-a-half feet by nineteen feet, was the entire home when the Grants lived there. After the Grants left, two large rooms, which today serve as a museum of Civil War artifacts, were added.

Ulysses S. Grant Birthplace State Memorial

BUFFINGTON ISLAND

Ohio Highway 124, Portland, OH

PHONE: 614-297-2630 (Ohio Historical Soc.)

HOURS: Open daily.

ADMISSION: Free.

A memorial commemorates Ohio's only major engagement. At Buffington Island, Confederate Gen. John Hunt Morgan and his cavalry were defeated by Union troops led by Gen. Edward Henry Hobson and Gen. James M. Shack-elford in 1863.

Photo right: Buffington Island

OKLAHOMA

During the Civil War, Oklahoma Territory sat at a difficult crossroads; to its north were the Union states of Kansas and Missouri, and to its south and east were the Confederate states of Texas and Arkansas. The South sought to enlist many of Oklahoma's Native Americans into its army. Five tribes—the Cherokee, Chickasaw, Choctaw, Creek, and Seminole—fought for the Confederate cause. The Battle of Honey Springs, in which the Confederates were routed, marked a disillusionment for the Native Americans.

The Battle of Honey Springs is commemorated at reenactments held every three years. A newly renovated battlefield park interprets the site where Native American and African-American troops outnumbered white soldiers. The Union casualties of this battle were taken to Fort Gibson where many of the original buildings are still visible, and living history programs help interpret the site. Fort Gibson National Cemetery, the only national cemetery in Oklahoma, contains the graves of over 2,000 Union soldiers.

SEE
MISSOURI
PAGE 116

FT. GIBSON CEMETERY

FT. GIBSON

HONEY
SPRINGS

SEE
ARKANSAS
PAGE 20

FT. TOWSON

SEE
TEXAS
PAGE 194

Miami

Bartlesville

Ponca City

Woodward

Enid

Stillwater

Sand Springs

Tulsa

Sapulpa

Guthrie

Edmond

The Village

Fort Gibson

Muskogee

Okmulgee

Oklahoma City

Midwest City

Rentiesville

Moore

Norman

Shawnee

Chickasha

McAlester

Ada

Altus

Fort Sill

Lawton

Duncan

Ardmore

Durant

Fort Towson

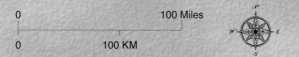

0   100 Miles

0   100 KM

"They were in the hottest of the fight and opposed to Texas troops twice their number, whom they completely routed."

Maj. Gen. J. G. Blunt on the conduct of his African-American troops

NORTHERN COMMANDER:
Maj. Gen. J. G. Blunt

STRENGTH: 3,000

CASUALTIES: 77

THE BATTLE OF HONEY SPRINGS

July 17, 1863

The largest Civil War battle fought in Indian Territory.

The Battle of Honey Springs was the largest battle in Indian Territory, the first battle in which African-Americans fought as a unit, and the largest battle in which Native Americans fought on both sides.

Union troops, consisting of a unit of African-Americans of the First Regular Kansas Volunteers (Colored) and the Second Indian Home Guard, soundly defeated a Confederate force twice their size. The battle was the climax of the struggle over Indian Territory and was unique in the Civil War because Indian and African-American troops outnumbered white troops. The victory at Honey Springs gave the Union control over Oklahoma's vast Indian Territory.

Union and Confederate troops had frequently skirmished in the vicinity of Honey Springs Depot. The Union commander in the area, Major General James G. Blunt, correctly surmised that Confederate forces, mostly Native American troops under the command of Brigadier General Douglas H. Cooper, would attack his force at Fort Gibson. He decided to defeat the Confederates at Honey Springs Depot before they were joined by Brigadier General William Cabell's brigade which was advancing from Fort Smith, Arkansas.

Blunt began crossing the swollen Arkansas River on July 15, 1863. By midnight July 16, he had a force of 3,000 white, Native American,

African-American Infantry corporal holding a Colt model 1849 pocket revolver.

UNITED STATES SOLDIERS AT CAMP "WILLIAM PENN" PHILADELPHIA, PA.

"Rally Round the Flag, boys! Rally once again,
Shouting the battle cry of FREEDOM!"

*A recruiting poster of U.S. soldiers at Camp William Penn, Pennsylvania,
calling for the enlistment of African-American soldiers in the Union army,
Artist Unknown*

and African-American troops marching toward Honey
Springs. Early in the morning of July 17, Blunt skirmished
with Rebel troops, and by mid-afternoon, full-scale fighting
ensued.

The Confederates had wet powder, causing misfires, and
the problem intensified when rain began. After repulsing one
attack, Cooper pulled his forces back to obtain new ammunition. He then learned that Blunt was about to turn his left
flank. The Confederate retreat began. Although Cooper fought
a rearguard action, many of those troops counterattacked,
failed, and fled. Any possibility of the Confederates taking Fort
Gibson was gone. Following this battle, Union forces controlled Indian Territory north of the Arkansas River.

**SOUTHERN
COMMANDER:**
Brig. Gen. D. H. C

STRENGTH: 5,70

CASUALTIES: 1£

HONEY SPRINGS BATTLEFIELD PARK

U.S. Highway 69 to Rentiesville Exit, park located north of Rentiesville, OK

PHONE: 918-473-5572

HOURS: Open daily.

ADMISSION: A fee is charged.

Renovation of the 2,997-acre Honey Springs Battlefield Park will be completed in the spring of 2000. The Oklahoma Historical Society currently administers 963 acres of the park. Self-guided trails and driving tours will interpret the site with markers and monuments which commemorate the battle. Living history exhibits, a nature trail, an archaeological site, and audio-visual programs will also be available through the Visitor's Center. The Battle of Honey Springs is reenacted every third year in mid-July. A memorial service is held every year on or near the battle's anniversary.

FORT GIBSON NATIONAL CEMETERY

423 Cemetery Road, Fort Gibson, OK

PHONE: 918-478-2334

HOURS: Open daily.

ADMISSION: Free.

Fort Gibson National Cemetery was established in 1868 and is the only national cemetery in Oklahoma. The cemetery contains 2,068 casualties of the Civil War. Most are unknown because the bodies were brought from all of the forts in the area without identification; only fifty Union soldiers are known. The cemetery is unique in that its grave markers are six-inch square markers, resembling rows of jagged teeth. Self-guided walking tours are available.

Fort Gibson National Cemetery

FORT GIBSON HISTORIC SITE

907 North Garrison, Fort Gibson, OK

PHONE: 918-478-4088

HOURS: Open daily.

ADMISSION: A fee is charged.

Fort Gibson Historic site contains seven original buildings, entrenchments, a reconstructed log stockade, a museum, and a gift shop. Information on interpretive trails and self-guided tours are available at the Visitor's Center. Each year living history and educational programs occur at the site.

Fort Gibson Historic Site

FORT TOWSON HISTORIC SITE

U.S. Highway 70, Fort Towson, OK

PHONE: 580-873-2634

HOURS: Open daily.

ADMISSION: Free.

Fort Towson was established in 1824 and closed in 1854. Confederate Maj. General Sam Bell Maxey later reopened the fort in 1864. The last surrender of the Civil War took place less than a mile from the fort on June 23, 1865. A self-guided tour includes ruins of the barracks, the officers' quarters, a bakery, and a powder magazine. A Visitor's Center is available. Every five years, a reenactment of the surrender of Fort Towson is held on the third weekend of June.

PENNSYLVANIA

The first state to answer President Lincoln's call for volunteers in April of 1861, Pennsylvania provided soldiers—nearly 325,000—but also coal, iron, petroleum, and 2,500 miles of railroad lines to the Union cause. More than sixty Union generals came from Pennsylvania, and 300,000 Union soldiers trained at a camp near Harrisburg. Located on the southern edge of Northern territory, Pennsylvania saw more action than any other Northern state. The single most significant battle of the Civil War took place in the Pennsylvania town of Gettysburg in July of 1863. Gettysburg was a devastating defeat for the Confederacy and prompted a change in Southern strategy from offense to defense. Northerners, inspired both by the battle and by Lincoln's immortal Gettysburg Address, took from Gettysburg's bloody fields new dedication to winning and ending the war.

Today, Gettysburg remains the most studied military event in American history; Pennsylvania's Civil War heritage is preserved in and around the extensive, beautiful, national park site at the Gettysburg battlefield, a site which still echoes with the words of Lincoln and pays ongoing tribute to the great sacrifices made by soldiers and citizens from both North and South.

Carbondale
Dunmore

Kingston
Nanticoke

Williamsport

Berwick
Hazleton

Sunbury
Shamokin
Pottsville

State College

Easton
Bethlehem
Allentown
Emmaus

Reading

Harrisburg
Hershey
Carlisle
Middletown
Norristown

Toll

Lancaster

Chambersburg
York

Philadelphia

Gettysburg
Hanover

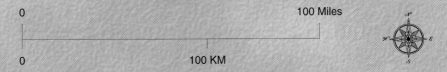

GETTYSBURG

SEE MARYLAND PAGE 90

0   100 Miles

0   100 KM

NORTHERN COMMANDER:
Maj. Gen. G. G. Meade

STRENGTH: 83,300

CASUALTIES: 23,000

THE BATTLE OF GETTYSBURG

July 1–3, 1863

A bloody, monumental battle that turned the tide of the war once and for all toward the Union.

When Robert E. Lee became the Commander of the Confederate Army of Virginia, his first priority was to defend his home state rather than his new country. Eventually, however, Lee realized that he could not ultimately win the war unless he changed his defensive stance to an offensive one; he had to take the war into the Northern states. After the Battle of Chancellorsville in June of 1863, Lee began the trek northward through Virginia, keeping the Blue Ridge Mountains between his forces and the Union army.

At this time, Major General Joseph Hooker asked Lincoln if he could be relieved after the Union defeat at Chancellorsville. Lincoln replaced him with Major General George Gordon Meade, whose orders from the overall commander, General Henry Wagner Halleck, were to "cover the capital, Baltimore, and as far as circumstances will admit."

Before leaving his command, Hooker ordered his cavalry to Emmitsburg on the Maryland-Pennsylvania border, south of Gettysburg. Meade further ordered two corps to Gettysburg. On June 30, Lee maneuvered to reach Cashtown, just

Slyder Farm, Gettysburg National Military Park

northeast of Gettysburg. All of these Northern maneuvers were unknown to Lee, who was operating without the eyes of his cavalry and believed that Meade's army was much farther south.

On July 1, Southern General Henry Heth took his division into Gettysburg to retrieve a reported store of shoes for his men. Just west of town he met with a Northern brigade. For two hours these forces fought and throughout the day, more and more Union and Confederate divisions joined the fight until Union troops retreated from Gettysburg to rally on Cemetery and Culp's Hills. Neither side had planned to fight at Gettysburg, but this unintended meeting had sparked one of the decisive battles of the war.

Fighting began the next morning with both armies at full strength. Confederate troops occupied the town and arced south on both sides, trapping the Union army inside. Meade's army formed a fishhook with Cemetery Ridge at its extreme right. Union General Sickles's corps advanced between ridges, getting caught at Devil's Den. The Confederates attacked and only quick reinforcements secured Cemetery Ridge for the Union.

July 3 dawned with both Lee and Meade determined to make a decisive stand. Lee began with a major assault on Cemetery Ridge. When this was repelled, Lee committed Major General George E. Pickett's division to the center of the line and ordered him to cross an open field and attack the center of the Union column. In what became known as Pickett's Charge, 5,000 Confederate soldiers died in an hour. Meade, content to stay on the defensive, never ordered a counterattack. On July 4, Lee began his long retreat back to Virginia. Meade let him go.

Gettysburg was a psychological turning point in the war; Union victory boosted morale and recommitted Northerners to winning the war. The battle, however, also proved negative for the Union as General Meade did not pursue Lee's Army of Northern Virginia, allowing that army to survive to fight again, thus prolonging the war.

"All this has been my fault, it is I that has lost this fight, and you must help me out the best you can."

Gen. R. E. Lee (pictured above) to Gen. C. Wilcox

SOUTHERN COMMANDER:
Gen. R. E. Lee

STRENGTH: 75,000

CASUALTIES: 28,100

GETTYSBURG NATIONAL MILITARY PARK

97 Taneytown Road, Gettysburg, PA

PHONE: 717-334-1124

HOURS: Open daily; closed major holidays.

ADMISSION: Free; a fee is charged for the orientation program.

A variety of battlefield tours, self-guided auto tours, and interpretive trails are available through the Visitor's Center. Stops along the tour include Seminary Ridge, John Burns Statue, the Eternal Peace Light Memorial, Oak Ridge, Oak Ridge Observation Tower, the North Carolina Monument, the Virginia Monument, the Eisenhower Observation Tower, Warfield Ridge, Little Round Top, Wheatfield, Trostle Farm, Peach Orchard, Forty-fourth New York Infantry Memorial, and the Angle, the site of the last major conflict at Gettysburg. In addition, the Visitor's Center offers a thirty-minute program with a large-scale, electric relief map to explain how the battle was fought, as well as a twenty-minute program that accompanies a panoramic painting of the famous "Pickett's Charge." Each year a reenactment is held on the battle's anniversary.

Tennessee Monument, Gettysburg National Military Park

Little Round Top, Gettysburg National Military Park

South Carolina Monument, Gettysburg National Military Park

Perhaps even more memorable than the battle at Gettysburg is President Lincoln's speech. His immortal words place the battle of Gettysburg and the Civil War in perspective.

> Fourscore and seven years ago our fathers brought forth on this continent, a new nation, conceived in liberty, and dedicated to the proposition that all men are created equal.
>
> Now we are engaged in a great civil war, testing whether that nation, or any nation so conceived and so dedicated, can long endure. We are met on a great battlefield of that war. We have come to dedicate a portion of that field, as a final resting-place for those who here gave their lives that that nation might live. It is altogether fitting and proper that we should do this.
>
> But, in a larger sense, we can not dedicate—we can not consecrate—we can not hallow—this ground. The brave men, living and dead, who struggled here, have consecrated it far above our poor power to add or detract. The world will little note nor long remember what we say here, but it can never forget what they did here. It is for us, the living, rather, to be dedicated here to the unfinished work which they who fought here have thus far so nobly advanced. It is rather for us to be here dedicated to the great task remaining before us—that from these honored dead we take increased devotion to that cause for which they gave the last full measure of devotion; that we here highly resolve that these dead shall not have died in vain; that this nation, under God, shall have a new birth of freedom; and that government of the people, by the people, for the people, shall not perish from the earth.

SOUTH CAROLINA

*D*ecades *before a state convention voted unanimously to leave the Union in December of 1860, South Carolina had been steadily moving toward secession. The Southern spirit of rebellion was born in South Carolina, a state where black slaves outnumbered free whites by 100,000 and where economic and cultural life was dominated by the plantation system. South Carolinians were determined to protect their way of life from Federal intrusion.*

Although South Carolina led the secessionist movement, actual combat in the state was rather limited. The Civil War brought mostly coastal fighting to South Carolina, at least until 1865, when Union troops under General William T. Sherman marched through the state bringing the terror of war to the interior. Out of the 70,000 South Carolinians who fought for the Confederacy, 13,000 gave their lives. Unlike most other Confederate states, South Carolina provided no white volunteers for the Union army.

South Carolina was transformed drastically by the war it helped begin. Civil War sites in the state today remember South Carolina's pivotal role in the rebellion, its antebellum lifestyle, and the effects of the war on its citizens.

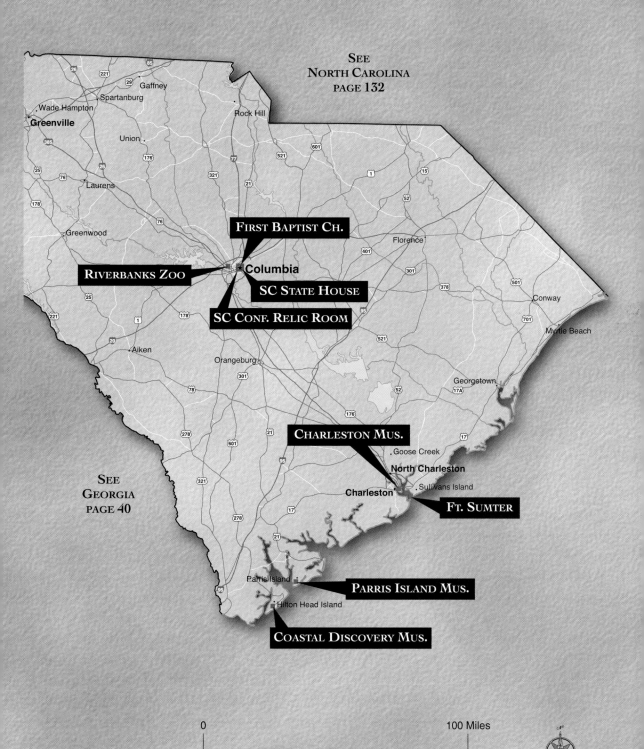

SEE
NORTH CAROLINA
PAGE 132

Gaffney

Spartanburg

Wade Hampton

Greenville

Rock Hill

Union

Laurens

Greenwood

FIRST BAPTIST CH.

Florence

RIVERBANKS ZOO

★ **Columbia**

SC STATE HOUSE

SC CONF. RELIC ROOM

Conway

Myrtle Beach

Aiken

Orangeburg

Georgetown

SEE
GEORGIA
PAGE 40

CHARLESTON MUS.

. Goose Creek

North Charleston

Charleston

. Sullivans Island

FT. SUMTER

Parris Island

PARRIS ISLAND MUS.

Hilton Head Island

COASTAL DISCOVERY MUS.

0   100 Miles

0   100 KM

N
W   E
S

NORTHERN COMMANDER:
Maj. R. Anderson

STRENGTH: 85

CASUALTIES: 11

THE BATTLE OF FORT SUMTER

April 12–14, 1861

The opening rounds of the Civil War were fired at this small fort in Charleston Harbor.

After South Carolina voted to secede in 1860, the spirit of rebellion engulfed the state, and thousands of volunteers and militia members gathered in Charleston ready to fight. The only Union presence in the area was a force of eighty-five men at Fort Moultrie, adjacent to the mainland in Charleston Harbor. With the growing number of Confederates gathering in Charleston, these Union men were quickly transferred to nearby Fort Sumter, further out in Charleston Harbor, where better defenses were in place.

Major Robert Anderson, a Kentuckian married to a Georgian, took his Union troops from Fort Moultrie to Fort Sumter, believing the move would reduce tensions through increased distance. Southerners, however, saw the move as an act of aggression, violating sitting President James Buchanan's pledge to keep the status quo in Charleston Harbor.

Fort Sumter

The situation was ripe for conflict. The Union garrison was dangerously low on supplies, and the South had erected artillery batteries around the harbor to thwart any attempt to resupply and reinforce Fort Sumter. Both sides realized the powerful implication of possessing the fort. As long as the flag of the United States flew over Fort Sumter, the South's sovereignty would be in question. In his inaugural address, President Lincoln stated that he would use "all the powers at my disposal" to "reclaim the public property and places which have fallen: to hold, occupy, and possess these, and all other property and places belonging to the government."

The day after his inauguration, Lincoln learned that Fort Sumter had only six weeks of rations left. Time was running out for a peaceful solution. Lincoln chose to resupply his men but not reinforce them. He notified the Confederates of his intention, leaving the decision to attack a ship bringing "food for hungry men" squarely in the lap of the South.

The Confederate cabinet response was the decision to open fire on Fort Sumter prior to its resupply. The only dissenting vote came from Confederate Secretary of State Robert Toombs, who reportedly told Confederate President Jefferson Davis that the action "will lose us every friend at the North. You will wantonly strike a hornets' nest. . . . Legions now quiet will swarm out and sting us to death. It is unnecessary. It puts us in the wrong. It is fatal." He was correct. The Confederates opened fire upon Fort Sumter on April 12, 1861.

On April 14, after thirty-three hours and 5,000 rounds, the American flag was lowered and the fort surrendered. Then the Confederate flag was raised over Fort Sumter. On April 15, 1861, Lincoln called for 75,000 volunteers to help quell the Southern insurrection. The Civil War had begun.

"All proper facilities will be afforded for the removal of yourself and command, together with company arms and property, and all private property to any post in the United States which you may select. The flag which you have upheld so long and with so much fortitude . . . may be saluted by you on taking it down."

Brig. Gen. P. G. T. Beauregard to Maj. R. Anderson

SOUTHERN COMMANDER:
Brig. Gen. P. G. T. Beauregar

STRENGTH: 5,000

CASUALTIES: 4

SOUTH CAROLINA CONFEDERATE RELIC ROOM AND MUSEUM

920 Sumter Street, Columbia, SC

PHONE: 803-898-8095

HOURS: Open weekdays and the first and third Saturdays of the month.

ADMISSION: Free.

With over 4,000 square feet of exhibit space, this museum focuses on state military history from the American Revolution through Desert Storm. The largest and most concentrated emphasis, however, is on the Confederate era of South Carolina.

South Carolina Confederate Relic Room and Museum

THE SOUTH CAROLINA STATE HOUSE

Intersection of Main and Gervais Streets, Columbia, SC

PHONE: 803-734-2430

HOURS: Open daily.

ADMISSION: Free.

The blue granite State House shows scars from Federal fire during the Civil War. Bronze stars mark hits from General Sherman's cannon in 1865. The grounds feature a Confederate Monument and a monument to South Carolina's Confederate Gen. Wade Hampton.

The South Carolina State House

RIVERBANKS ZOO AND GARDENS

500 Wildlife Parkway, Columbia, SC

PHONE: 803-779-8717

HOURS: Open daily; closed Thanksgiving and Christmas.

ADMISSION: A fee is charged; children are discounted.

On the west bank of the Saluda River lies Riverbanks Zoo and Gardens. The site was once the camp of Gen. William T. Sherman's troops. Because the Confederates had destroyed the only bridge over the Broad River leading into Columbia, legend has it that Sherman and his men pulled up the planks of Saluda Factory, a textile mill, and made rafts to cross the Broad River and enter Columbia. More than likely, however, they just waded across the river. Today the ruins of the factory and the original mill's small canal are joined by a new Saluda Factory Interpretive Center. The site features interpretive graphics outlining the area's Civil War history.

Ruins of bridge, Riverbanks Zoo and Gardens

FIRST BAPTIST CHURCH

1306 Hampton Street, Columbia, SC

PHONE: 803-256-4251

HOURS: Open daily; closed major holidays.

ADMISSION: Free.

The table on which the South Carolina Ordinance of Secession was drafted is exhibited at the First Baptist Church of Columbia. The secessionist convention met at the church only one day, December 17, 1860. Fear of a smallpox epidemic forced adjournment of the convention although only one case was confirmed. Later, the ordinance was signed in Charleston. Tours of the historic church are available.

First Baptist Church

NORTHERN COMMANDERS:
Brig. Gen. T. W. Sherman
Cpt. S. F. DuPont

STRENGTH: 15,000

CASUALTIES: 31

THE BATTLE OF PORT ROYAL SOUND

November 7, 1861

After this battle, the Confederacy abandoned South Carolina's outlying coastal forts to concentrate on inland defenses.

Guarded on either side by Fort Walker and Fort Beauregard, Port Royal Sound, South Carolina, proved a well-guarded coastal position. Union Captain Samuel F. DuPont, the head of the Blockade Board, was given the task of capturing the sound. Contrary to conventional wisdom, he believed that a steamship, which did not have to rely on wind or tide, could successfully engage coastal fortifications without overwhelming firepower.

In preparation for attacking Port Royal, DuPont amassed 15,000 soldiers under Brigadier General Thomas W. Sherman and thirty steam warships. When the Union ships ran the gauntlet of the two Confederate forts on November 7,

Bombardment and capture of Forts Walker and Beauregard, Port Royal

The bombardment of Port Royal

1861, the ships rained shells into the forts. Although the steamships received fire, there sustained no serious damage. Once through, the ships turned around and steamed back and forth in front of Fort Walker then Fort Beauregard. By nightfall, both forts had been abandoned. The Federal occupation of these forts established a key naval base which would aid in Scott's coastal blockade plan.

"Whenever [the enemy's] fleet can be brought, no opposition to his landing can be made. We have nothing to oppose its heavy guns, which sweep over the low banks of this country [South Carolina] with irresistible force."

Gen. R. E. Lee

SOUTHERN COMMANDERS:
Gen. R. E. Lee
Gen. B. Bragg
Com. J. Tattnall

STRENGTH: 7,000

CASUALTIES: 66

Photograph of prison, Port Royal

CHARLESTON MUSEUM

360 Meeting Street, Charleston, SC

PHONE: 843-722-2996

HOURS: Open daily; closed major holidays.

ADMISSION: A fee is charged; children are discounted.

Founded in 1773, the Charleston Museum is the first and oldest museum in the United States. It features exhibits which explain South Carolina's Lowcountry heritage, as well as interpret Charleston's varied past. The museum also houses an impressive collection of Civil War-era weapons and artifacts. Each year the museum holds a Civil War event, usually in April.

FORT SUMTER NATIONAL MONUMENT
(INCLUDES FORT MOULTRIE)

1214 Middle Street, Sullivan's Island, SC

PHONE: 843-883-3123; (for transportation to island 843-722-2628)

HOURS: Open daily; closed Christmas.

ADMISSION: A fee is charged; children and seniors are discounted. An additional fee is charged for public transportation to the island.

This national historic site includes both Fort Moultrie and Fort Sumter. A highway connects Fort Moultrie to the mainland, but Fort Sumter is accessible only by boat. Public transportation leaves from the City Marina and Patriots' Point in Charleston.

Both forts offer brochures that include self-guided walking tours. Built in 1809, Fort Moultrie stands much as it did during the war. Passageways and ramparts offer points of interest, and the fort provides beautiful views of Fort Sumter and the city.

Fort Sumter, on which construction began in 1829, is classified as a ruins due to damage from the Civil War's heavy artillery fire. Tours provide insight into the fort's history, and a museum exhibits relics from the battle which began the Civil War.

Each fort features a gift shop, a Visitor's Center, and a video detailing the fort's history.

Fort Moultrie

THE PARRIS ISLAND MUSEUM

Building 111, Panama Street, Parris Island, SC
PHONE: 843-338-2951
HOURS: Open daily; closed Thanksgiving and Christmas.
ADMISSION: Free.

The Parris Island Museum contains a small theater and a research center which houses an extensive collection of photographs, uniforms, and firearms relating to the Civil War actions in Beaufort, South Carolina, and the surrounding area. Permanent displays include maps, photographs, firearms, reference books, and uniforms pertaining to the

Parris Island Museum

Battle of Port Royal Sound, the Battle of Honey Hill, and the Siege of Charleston. Of note is an original uniform from a Fifty-fifth Massachusetts soldier and an ornately carved Sharp's carbine.

COASTAL DISCOVERY THE MUSEUM ON HILTON HEAD ISLAND

100 William Hilton Parkway, Hilton Head Island, SC
PHONE: 843-689-6767
HOURS: Open daily; closed major holidays.
ADMISSION: Free.

Coastal Discovery contains Civil War artifacts and offers tours of area forts including the remains of Fort Mitchell, Fort Walker, Port Royal, and Fort Howell.

Fort Howell was built for the purpose of protecting Mitchellville, the nation's first Freedman's community.

Above right: Engraving of Port Royal Sound during the Union occupation of Hilton Head Island

Below right: Fort Walker

TENNESSEE

The second most populous Confederate state, Tennessee also ranked second in the number of military actions during the war. Nonetheless, Tennessee was neither eager nor unanimous in its decision to secede from the American Union, and the Confederacy never enjoyed Tennessee's full support, especially in the mountainous regions of the east. Still, the Confederacy needed Tennessee. The state's farmers supplied the Southern armies with wheat, corn, horses, mules, and meat. Tennessee was also crossed or bordered by three major rivers—the Mississippi, the Cumberland, and the Tennessee—all of them possible passageways into the Deep South. In addition, cities like Nashville and Memphis were important centers for trade and transportation for all of the Southern states. All of this made Tennessee equally attractive to the Union armies, who came in full force and fought battles all over middle and southern Tennessee.

The people of Tennessee survived four solid, bloody years of battle before Confederate surrender put an end to the Civil War and restored peace within the state's borders; today, in large battlefields, small museums, and wayside monuments, the state pays tribute to those who fought and those who lost their lives.

SEE MISSOURI PAGE 116

FT. PILLOW ST. HIST. PK.

SEE ARKANSAS PAGE 20

Henning

Memphis

MUD IS. RIVER PK. AND MS RIVER MUS.

SEE MISSISSIPPI PAGE 104

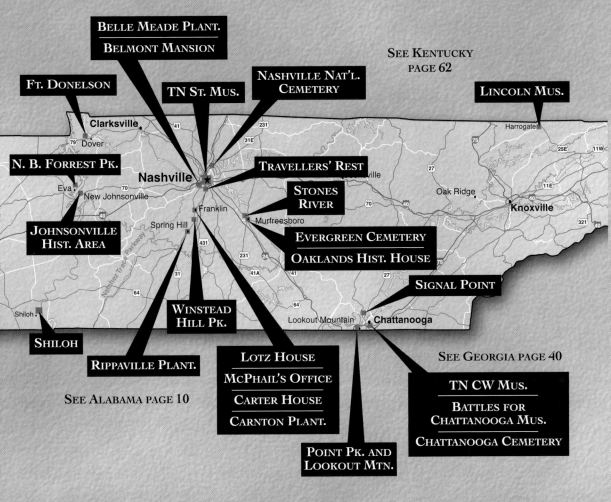

BELLE MEADE PLANT.
BELMONT MANSION

NASHVILLE NAT'L.
CEMETERY

SEE KENTUCKY
PAGE 62

FT. DONELSON

TN ST. MUS.

LINCOLN MUS.

Clarksville

Harrogate

N. B. FORREST PK.

TRAVELLERS' REST

Nashville

STONES
RIVER

JOHNSONVILLE
HIST. AREA

EVERGREEN CEMETERY

OAKLANDS HIST. HOUSE

Knoxville

Oak Ridge

SIGNAL POINT

WINSTEAD
HILL PK.

SHILOH

RIPPAVILLE PLANT.

SEE ALABAMA PAGE 10

LOTZ HOUSE

McPHAIL'S OFFICE

CARTER HOUSE

CARNTON PLANT.

Chattanooga

Lookout Mountain

SEE GEORGIA PAGE 40

TN CW MUS.

BATTLES FOR
CHATTANOOGA MUS.

CHATTANOOGA CEMETERY

POINT PK. AND
LOOKOUT MTN.

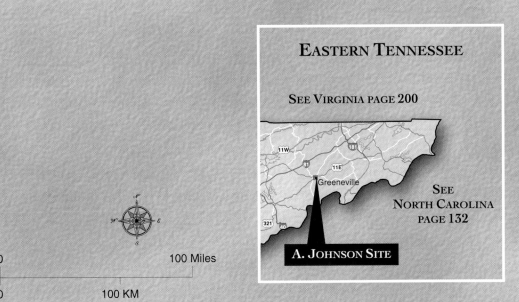

EASTERN TENNESSEE

SEE VIRGINIA PAGE 200

Greeneville

SEE
NORTH CAROLINA
PAGE 132

A. JOHNSON SITE

0   100 Miles

0   100 KM

"I saw an open field...over which the Confederates had made repeated charges the day before, so covered with dead that it would have been possible to walk across...in any direction, stepping on dead bodies without a foot touching the ground."

Maj. Gen. U. S. Grant
in his memoirs

NORTHERN COMMANDER:
Maj. Gen. U. S. Grant

STRENGTH: 62,000

CASUALTIES: 13,000

THE BATTLE OF SHILOH

April 6–7, 1862

The Union victory at Shiloh led to the fall of Nashville. Soon, all of western Tennessee fell under Union control.

Major General Ulysses S. Grant's victory at Fort Donelson opened up the Tennessee and Cumberland Rivers to the Union. Grant, using the Tennessee River, advanced 43,000 troops toward the rail connections near Corinth, Mississippi. Forty thousand Confederate forces massed for an attack to defend this vital rail line. By March Grant and his men encamped around Shiloh Church at Pittsburg Landing, Tennessee, twenty-three miles northeast of Corinth. In early April, General P. G. T. Beauregard moved to attack Grant.

After a long hard march of three days, Beauregard set up camp within a mile of Grant, who believed the Confederates were still at Corinth, and therefore had not set out his pickets and patrols. The initial attack was a complete surprise, but after the Union's first shock, they established control and set up defensive lines. These lines, however, contained gaps, which the Confederate troops quickly used to their advantage.

Union troops took up a line from the Tennessee River bluffs to Owl Creek; this line passed directly through a place called Hornets' Nest. After eleven separate assaults on Hor-

Powell's Artillery Battery marker, Shiloh National Military Park

William Manse George Cabin, Shiloh National Military Park

nets' Nest, which lasted from 10:00 A.M. until 5:30 P.M., Confederate troops finally overwhelmed Union forces. Many soldiers escaped to the rear, but 2,100 troops surrendered.

Grant's final line stretched from Dill Branch to Tilghman Branch. Union forces amassed fifty-three cannon and 20,000 troops to protect Pittsburg Landing and the Hamburg-Savannah Road. To reach this line, Confederate forces had to descend a sixty-foot bluff, cross the ravine, and climb the bank on the far side of the Tennessee River—all of this after thirteen hours of fighting. Although two brigades did reach the other side, they could not hold on and withdrew.

During the night, the Union received thousands in reinforcements. The Confederates had no additional men to give.

On the second day, the Union troops advanced and forced the Confederates back. By the afternoon, General Beauregard withdrew to Corinth. Despite the loss of one of its divisions and severe damages to the remaining four, the Battle of Shiloh was a decisive Union victory. Corinth and Memphis were within Union range.

SOUTHERN COMMANDER:
Gen. P. G. T. Beauregard

STRENGTH: 44,000

CASUALTIES: 11,700

FORT PILLOW STATE HISTORIC PARK

3122 Park Road, Henning, TN
PHONE: 901-738-5581
HOURS: Open daily; closed major holidays.
ADMISSION: Free.

In April 1864, Nathan Bedford Forrest's Confederate troops attacked Fort Pillow. Southern forces easily overran the fort, and the Union surrendered. Many Northerners were killed after the surrender. When the atrocities were investigated, the battle was declared a mas-

Fort Pillow State Historic Park

sacre by the Committee on the Conduct of the War. A Visitor's Center at Fort Pillow State Historic Park includes a small museum and information on the site. Each April the site is host to a Living History Weekend, and each November lectures on the Civil War are open to the public.

MUD ISLAND RIVER PARK AND MISSISSIPPI RIVER MUSEUM

Mud Island, Memphis, TN
PHONE: 901-576-7241
HOURS: Open daily April–October.
ADMISSION: A fee is charged; children and seniors are discounted.

The fifty-two-acre Mud Island River Park and Mississippi River Museum can only be reached by pedestrian walkbridge and monorail. The museum, located on an island in the Mississippi River, houses ship models and several Civil War exhibits, including one on the Battle of Memphis.

Mud Island River Park and Mississippi River Museum

SHILOH NATIONAL MILITARY PARK

Tennessee Highway 22, Shiloh, TN

PHONE: 901-689-5696

HOURS: Open daily; closed Christmas.

ADMISSION: A fee is charged.

The 4,000-acre Shiloh National Military Park has a museum of Civil War military equipment, a twenty-five-minute orientation film, and a bookstore. Over 150 monuments, 600 troop position markers, and 200 cannon dot the battlefield and interpret the battle. Not far from the Visitor's Center is Shiloh National Cemetery where almost 2,000 Union soldiers are buried. A nine-and-a-half-mile self-guided tour is available.

Confederate Burial Trench, Shiloh National Military Park

Bloody Pond, Shiloh National Military Park

NORTHERN COMMANDER:
Brig. Gen. U. S. Grant

STRENGTH: 27,000

CASUALTIES: 2,832

THE BATTLE OF FORT DONELSON

February 12–16, 1862

The Confederacy's first major defeat, this battle was also the first victory for Union Brigadier General Ulysses S. Grant. Winning Fort Donelson gave the Union control of the Cumberland and Tennessee Rivers, main arteries into the Deep South.

Like the Mississippi River, control of the Cumberland River was needed by both armies to achieve their tactical goals. For the South, control of the river was imperative to maintaining control of Tennessee and Kentucky. For the North, the river provided access to Mississippi and Alabama. On February 2, 1862, Brigadier General Ulysses S. Grant left Cairo, Illinois, with 17,000 Federal soldiers and a flotilla of gunboats under the command of Flag Officer Andrew H. Foote. His objective was to win control of the Cumberland River.

Confederate Monument, Fort Donelson National Battlefield

Lower River Battery, Fort Donelson National Battlefield

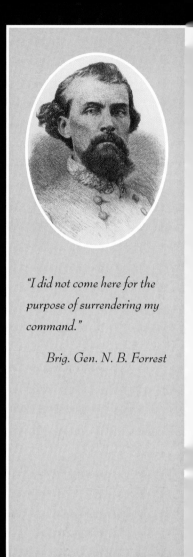

In a joint land and water operation, Grant moved on Fort Henry, eleven miles north of Fort Donelson. After a two-hour battle, Grant took Fort Henry on February 11, 1862, sending Confederate forces fleeing to Fort Donelson.

On February 13, Grant encircled Fort Donelson. Probing Confederate lines indicated that a direct assault would be fatal; instead, Grant lay siege to the Fort while Foote attacked from the river. Foote's four ironclads, however, were no match for the Confederate water batteries. All four Union gun ships were badly damaged, and Foote was wounded. On February 15, as Grant contemplated his next move, Confederate General Gideon Johnson Pillow, aided by Brigadier General Nathan Bedford Forrest's cavalry, left the fort and attacked Grant's men with such force that the Confederates soon controlled the road leading to Nashville. In a tactical error, troops did not continue their attack or push on to Nashville. Grant acted quickly and soon regained all lost ground.

On February 16, Generals Floyd and Pillow fled the fort south by water, leaving Brigadier General Simon B. Buckner in command of the demoralized fort. When Buckner requested terms for surrender, Grant's now famous reply was "no terms except unconditional and immediate surrender can be accepted." Grant and Buckner were old friends from West Point and after the surrender, discussed the battle. With Fort Donelson in hand, the Federal army was poised for a move into the Deep South.

SOUTHERN COMMANDERS:
Brig. Gen. J. B. Floyd
Brig. Gen. N. B. Forrest

STRENGTH: 21,000

CASUALTIES: 2,000
(15,000 captured)

FORT DONELSON NATIONAL BATTLEFIELD ⎯⎯⎯

U.S. Highway 79, Dover, TN

PHONE: 931-232-5706

HOURS: Open daily; closed Christmas.

ADMISSION: Free.

Fort Donelson National Battlefield covers 536 acres, about twenty percent of the core battlefield, the fort itself, and earthen rifle pits and river cannon batteries. The park also includes Fort Donelson National Cemetery, established in 1867; a Visitor's Center; and the Dover Hotel, site of Buckner's headquarters and his surrender. Two rooms of the Dover Hotel have been restored and are open to the public. Walking tours of the battlefield are marked. Additionally, a seven-mile driving tour of the battle is available. Audio tapes to accompany the self-guided auto tour are available for purchase at the Visitor's Center. Inside the Visitor's Center is a museum of Civil War relics and a slide show.

National Cemetery, Fort Donelson

NATHAN BEDFORD FORREST STATE PARK

1825 Pilot Knob Road, Eva, TN
PHONE: 901-584-6356
HOURS: Open daily.
ADMISSION: Free.

The Nathan Bedford Forrest State Park commemorates Forrest's Johnsonville raid which destroyed supplies intended to aid General Sherman's March to the Sea.

Forrest enlisted in the C.S.A. a month before his fortieth birthday. He had only about six months of school but had risen from poverty to become a wealthy businessman and Memphis alderman. His raids against the Union were so effective that Sherman declared, "Forrest is the very devil, and I think he has some of our troops under cower. . . . [He] must be hunted down and killed if it costs 10,000 lives and bankrupts the Federal Treasury. There never will be peace in Tennessee until Forrest is dead."

Photo right: Nathan Bedford Forrest State Park

JOHNSONVILLE STATE HISTORIC AREA

90 Readout Ridge, New Johnsonville, TN
PHONE: 931-535-2789
HOURS: Open daily; Visitor's Center open only during the summer months.
ADMISSION: Free.

This 800-acre Johnsonville State Historic Area rests on the Tennessee River and commemorates the November 4, 1864, Battle of Johnsonville. General Forrest attacked the Union navy and inflicted immense damage when he sank many Union boats. Twelve of these vessels still remain in the river, although one has been reclaimed. In addition, an original cannon, redoubts, and rifle pits remain as they were during the battle. During the summer, interpretive tours and a Visitor's Center are available. A self-guided tour is marked.

"You should attack before he fortifies. . . . You will now suffer incalculable injury upon your railroads if Hood is not speedily disposed of. Put forth, therefore, every possible exertion to attain this end. Should you get him to retreating, give him no peace."

Gen. U. S. Grant to
Maj. Gen. G. H. Thomas
(pictured above)

NORTHERN COMMANDERS:
Maj. Gen. J. M. Schofield
Maj. Gen. G. H. Thomas

STRENGTH: 26,000

CASUALTIES: 2,352

THE BATTLES OF FRANKLIN AND NASHVILLE

November 30, 1864, December 15–16, 1864

These decisive battles marked the end of the Confederate Army of Tennessee.

By September of 1864, General William T. Sherman had successfully taken Atlanta. The Confederate army under General John Bell Hood, however, still posed a threat to Sherman's extensive supply line.

After Union troops captured Nashville in December of

Carter House

*"And the wails and cries of
widows and orphans made at
Franklin, Tennessee, November 30th 1864, will heat up
the fires of the bottomless pit
to burn the soul of General J.
B. Hood for murdering their
husbands and fathers at that
place that day."*

*Capt. S. T. Foster
about Gen. J. B. Hood
(pictured above)*

1862, the Confederates withdrew to outlying towns and
regrouped. They did not attempt to retake the city until 1864,
when Hood chose to attack Nashville rather than pursue Sherman. Confederate cavalry, led by General Nathan Bedford
Forrest, preceded the 40,000-strong Confederate army.

On November 29, 1864, 32,000 Confederate troops cut
off 36,000 Union troops from Nashville by encircling them at
Spring Hill. Union troops under Major General John M.
Schofield slipped out of the net during the night and fled to
Franklin. Hood threw his army against the defensive works at
Franklin. At first the South appeared to have the upper hand,
driving the Union troops from Franklin and capturing all their
guns. A countercharge in the afternoon, however, drove the
Confederates back. The fighting lasted until midnight, costing
Hood almost one-sixth of his force and any hope of retaking
Tennessee. Although Hood besieged Nashville until December
16, there was no chance of victory, and the Army of Tennessee
retreated.

None of the battleground remains, but markers commemorate the Battles of Nashville and Franklin. Each year in
November, a memorial march in Franklin leaves Winstead Hill
for the Carter House at 4:00 P.M., the time the Army of Tennessee went into battle.

**SOUTHERN
COMMANDER:**
Gen. J. B. Hood

STRENGTH: 40,000

CASUALTIES: 6,261

NASHVILLE NATIONAL CEMETERY

1420 Gallatin Road S, Madison, TN

PHONE: 615-736-2839

HOURS: Open weekdays; closed major holidays.

ADMISSION: Free.

Nashville National Cemetery

Nashville National Cemetery was established in January 1867; 16,530 Union soldiers are interred here. Over 4,000 of those remain unknown. Veterans from other wars are also buried here, and each Memorial Day a service commemorates wartime casualties.

BELMONT MANSION

1900 Belmont Boulevard, Nashville, TN

PHONE: 615-460-5459

HOURS: Open daily; closed major holidays.

ADMISSION: A fee is charged.

Belmont Mansion

Built in 1850, the restored fifteen-room Belmont Mansion was the home of Adelicia Acklen. Acklen preserved the house and its contents through the Civil War, three marriages, and ten children. Union scouts used the 105-foot-tall, brick water tower, which still exists, as a lookout point and to relay signals. The mansion itself served as the headquarters for Union General Thomas J. Wood during the battle. Guided tours of the house, which is located on the campus of Belmont University, last approximately one hour.

TRAVELLERS REST

636 Ferrell Parkway, Nashville, TN

PHONE: 615-832-8197

HOURS: Open daily except Monday; closed major holidays.

ADMISSION: A fee is charged.

Once a working plantation of over 10,000 acres of corn, cotton, and fruit trees, Travellers Rest gives a taste of the pre-Civil War South. Built by Judge John Overton in 1799, the site houses an active history museum which interprets life in Middle Tennessee from 1789–1833. General Hood made this house his headquarters during the war.

BELLE MEADE PLANTATION

Belle Meade Plantation

5025 Harding Road, Nashville, TN
PHONE: 615-356-0501
HOURS: Open weekdays; closed major holidays.
ADMISSION: A fee is charged.

Belle Meade Plantation was once a thoroughbred horse farm, but during the Civil War the mansion housed General Jackson's troops. Costumed interpreters recall the days before the war with the sweeping front lawn and colonnaded facade of Belle Meade as the backdrop. This historic site includes eight buildings and an antique carriage collection.

TENNESSEE STATE MUSEUM

505 Dedrick Street, Nashville, TN
PHONE: 615-741-2692
HOURS: Open daily except Monday; closed major holidays.
ADMISSION: Free.

The battlefield of the Battle of Nashville has been consumed by suburban growth south of downtown. Only small remnants of the struggle remain. Information on the battle and the Civil War in Tennessee can be found at the Tennessee State Museum.

Confederate Cannon, Tennessee State Museum

CARTER HOUSE

1140 Columbia Avenue, Franklin, TN

PHONE: 615-791-1861

HOURS: Open daily; closed major holidays.

ADMISSION: A fee is charged.

Carter House, built in 1830 by F. B. Carter, was at the center of the Battle of Franklin. The original buildings still show battle damage. The Visitor's Center includes a video presentation, battlerama, military museum, and museum shop. Guided tours of the site are available. Carter House is part of a candlelight tour of homes during the first week of December. The Annual Battle of Franklin Illumination Tour traces the battle's progress through personal accounts given by reenactors each November.

Interior, Carter House

CARNTON PLANTATION

1345 Carnton Lane, Franklin, TN

PHONE: 615-794-0903

HOURS: Open daily; closed major holidays.

ADMISSION: A fee is charged.

In 1826 after his term as mayor of Nashville, Randal McGavock built Carnton Plantation. On the evening of November 30, 1864, after the Battle of Franklin, the McGavocks opened the home as a hospital for Confederate soldiers. In 1866 the McGavocks designated two acres adjacent to their family plot as a Confederate cemetery; nearly 1,500 Southern soldiers killed at Franklin are interred here, making this the nation's largest private Confederate cemetery.

Carnton Plantation

WINSTEAD HILL PARK

U.S. Highway 31, Franklin, TN

PHONE: Not Available.
HOURS: Open daily.
ADMISSION: Free.

From the high point of Winstead Hill Park, Gen. John Bell Hood commanded his Confederate soldiers in the Battle of Franklin. A relief map and several large granite markers at this privately-owned park provide historical interpretation of the events prior to and during the battle. A Memorial March and brief program with speakers and reenactors is conducted annually in November.

LOTZ HOUSE

1111 Columbia Avenue, Franklin, TN

PHONE: 615-791-6533
HOURS: Open daily; closed major holidays.
ADMISSION: Free.

The Lotz House contains a museum with local and regional Civil War relics. Displays include the sword used at Franklin by General Hiram Granbury.

DR. MCPHAIL'S OFFICE

209 East Main Street, Franklin, TN

PHONE: 615-591-8514
HOURS: Open daily; closed major holidays.
ADMISSION: Free.

Built in 1815, Dr. McPhail's Office served as General Schofield's Union headquarters during the battle of Franklin. It is now a Visitor's Information Center.

RIPPAVILLE PLANTATION

5700 Main Street, Spring Hill, TN

PHONE: 931-486-9037
HOURS: Open daily; closed Christmas and New Year's Day.
ADMISSION: A fee is charged.

Little has changed in the 12,000 square-foot Rippaville Plantation and its 1,500 surrounding acres since it housed the Council of War for General John Hood. Here, with troops camped on the grounds, Hood gave his generals their orders and informed them of the plan for the Battle of Franklin. Now the headquarters of the Tennessee Antebellum Trail, this 1852 plantation also serves as the regional Visitor's Center. It includes a historic house museum and a museum of the Civil War Armies of Tennessee.

NORTHERN COMMANDER:
Maj. Gen. W. S. Rosecrans

STRENGTH: 44,000

CASUALTIES: 13,000

THE BATTLE OF STONES RIVER (MURFREESBORO)

December 31, 1862–January 2, 1863

Stones River was a Southern defeat in both territory and manpower.

After the Federal victory at Perryville, Kentucky, General Braxton Bragg withdrew his troops to Murfreesboro, southeast of Nashville. In Nashville, the Union under Major General William S. Rosecrans fortified the city and prepared to attack Bragg. Confederate President Jefferson Davis ordered Bragg to hold Murfreesboro if possible. The city was on the Nashville & Chattanooga Rail Line and the Nashville Pike. Abandoning Murfreesboro could open up East Tennessee to the Union.

Bragg decided to hold his position northwest at Stones River. He disregarded the open terrain with no natural holds for his flanks, the thick patches of low trees that could hide the enemy and hamper any offensive movements, and the possibility of flooding in this low country. It was an area in which he could concentrate his force and protect the roads leading to his supply depot in Murfreesboro. At dawn on December 31, 1862, Bragg decided to attack Rosecrans's right flank in a clockwise wheeling movement. This advance caught the Union

Fortress Rosecrans, Stones River National Battlefield

Cannon, Stones River Battlefield

completely off guard, as they had planned to attack Bragg in his right flank and had concentrated forces accordingly. After falling back to the Nashville Pike, the Union did not retreat but regrouped in a sharp angle. The Confederates were unable to break this strong position.

After five days of rain, the Stones River was becoming exceedingly difficult to ford. Bragg's cold, wet, exhausted men were no match for the fresh reinforcements which joined Rosecrans; Bragg withdrew from Murfreesboro.

Both sides lost heavily, but the North gained solid control of Nashville and also won the confidence of the citizens of the state. Throughout the Union, news of the victory at Stones River lifted spirits after two tough Union defeats at Fredericksburg, Virginia, and Vicksburg, Mississippi.

Hazen Monument, Stones River National Battlefield

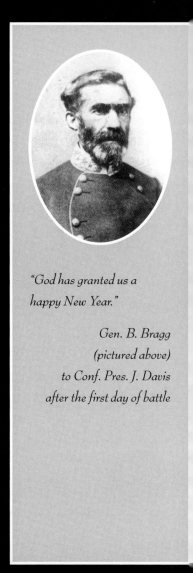

"God has granted us a happy New Year."

Gen. B. Bragg
(pictured above)
to Conf. Pres. J. Davis
after the first day of battle

SOUTHERN COMMANDER:
Gen. B. Bragg

STRENGTH: 34,000

CASUALTIES: 13,000

STONES RIVER NATIONAL BATTLEFIELD

3501 Old Nashville Highway, Murfreesboro, TN

PHONE: 615-893-9501
HOURS: Open daily.
ADMISSION: Free.

The Stones River National Battlefield includes the sites of both Rosecrans's and Bragg's headquarters, as well as Redoubt Brannan, a supply base built by the Union. Many walking trails cover the battlefield. A self-guided audio tour with nine stops is available. Audio tapes can be purchased or rented at the Visitor's Center.

Photo right: U.S. Regulars Monument, Stones River National Battlefield

Photo below: Stones River National Cemetery, Stones River National Battlefield

EVERGREEN CEMETERY

519 Greenland Drive, Murfreesboro, TN

PHONE: 615-893-5641

HOURS: Open daily.

ADMISSION: Free.

Evergreen Cemetery is home to the "circle of the unknown dead" where 2,000 unknown Confederate soldiers are buried. Also interred here is Confederate General Joseph B. Palmer.

Evergreen Cemetery

Evergreen Cemetery

OAKLANDS HISTORIC HOUSE MUSEUM

900 North Maney Avenue, Murfreesboro, TN

PHONE: 615-893-0022

HOURS: Open daily except Monday; closed major holidays.

ADMISSION: A fee is charged.

The grounds of Oaklands Historic House Museum once served as the campgrounds for both Confederate and Union forces. The home itself was used as the headquarters for Union Col. William Duffield and his regiment. Duffield surrendered Murfreesboro to Confederate Cavalryman Nathan Bedford Forrest at Oaklands. The antebellum mansion has been completely restored.

Oaklands Historic House Museum

"You ought to be court-mar-tialed, every man of you. I ordered you to take the rifle pits, and you scaled the mountain!"

Gen. G. Granger to his men after taking Missionary Ridge

NORTHERN COMMANDERS:
Maj. Gen. U. S. Grant
Gen. G. H. Thomas
Gen. J. Hooker
Gen. G. Granger
Gen. W. T. Sherman

STRENGTH: 70,000

CASUALTIES: 5,815

THE BATTLE OF CHATTANOOGA

November 24–25, 1863

Union victory at Chattanooga helped open the lower South to Union forces.

Chattanooga, situated on the south side of the Moccasin Bend of the Tennessee River just north of the Tennessee-Georgia border, was a river port to cities west of the Cumberland Plateau. It was also the site of railroad lines running to Virginia and Mississippi. In short, it was a major strategic position for both sides.

After its defeat at Chickamauga, Georgia, the Union Army of the Cumberland withdrew to Chattanooga. Its position was tenuous, however, as a result of the disorganization and disarray that followed Chickamauga. Union commander, General William S. Rosecrans was demoralized and unsure of himself, and he had lost the confidence of Union leaders. Rosecrans was replaced by General George Henry Thomas, who was ordered to hold Chattanooga at all costs. The Confederates, led by General Braxton Bragg, began a siege of Chattanooga by occupying Lookout Mountain to the southwest and Missionary Ridge to the south and east of the city. Bragg also stationed 1,000 men on the river to guard the route into the city. Although these two positions succeeded in overlooking

View of Moccasin Bend from Point Park, Lookout Mountain

Cannon atop Missionary Ridge

the railroads to the east and west and the river on the west, it proved ineffectual in controlling supplies to the city in total.

While the Union strengthened its position, Confederate forces weakened. Bragg was so stringently criticized by commanders under him, that Jefferson Davis himself visited him to offer support. The president encouraged Bragg; however, Davis also stripped the general of 15,000 men.

Major General Ulysses S. Grant took the offensive on November 23 by ordering Hooker to attack the line on Lookout Mountain where only a handful of Confederate soldiers were stationed; with that successful attack, the first part of the battle was over. On November 25, General William T. Sherman repeatedly assaulted Missionary Ridge, but the line held. Then, troops under General George Henry Thomas attacked the center of the Confederate line on the ridge. The Confederates panicked and fled; the siege was over.

Victory at Chattanooga set the stage for the Union to move on to Atlanta. It also interrupted the Confederate's east-west communication and supply lines. After his defeat at Chattanooga, Bragg resigned.

SOUTHERN COMMANDERS:
Gen. B. Bragg

STRENGTH: 50,000

CASUALTIES: 6,667

SIGNAL POINT

Atop Signal Mountain, Chattanooga, TN

PHONE: Not Available.

HOURS: Open daily.

ADMISSION: Free.

Overlooking both Chattanooga and the Tennessee River, the strategic point of Signal Mountain was controlled by the Union army from September to November of 1863. The Tennessee River was the Union supply line to Chattanooga since rugged terrain to the west of the mountain prevented easy transport to the city. Although the mountain was important in the Union victory at Chattanooga, no fighting took place in the area. It was mainly used to watch Rebel troop movements and to convey messages to Union commanders in the field.

POINT PARK AND LOOKOUT MOUNTAIN

110 Point Park Road, Chattanooga, TN

PHONE: 423-821-7786

HOURS: Open daily; closed Christmas.

ADMISSION: Park is free; a fee is charged for the museum and house.

* Note: See Georgia for additional information concerning the battles of Chickamauga and Chattanooga.

Craven House, Point Park

Point Park, located on top of Lookout Mountain, contains three gun batteries which mark a small segment of the siege lines that once encircled Chattanooga. In the center of the park is the New York Peace Memorial. At the top of the monument, Union and Confederate soldiers shake hands under one flag, signifying peace and brotherly love. A Visitor's Center, the Ochs Museum and Overlook, and Cravens House, which was used as headquarters by Confederate officers, are also located in the park. Marked trails offer walking tours, but most are strenuous.

Each year special programs, such as guided tours of several battlefield areas and Civil War encampments, are presented at Chickamauga Battlefield and Lookout Mountain to commemorate the battles of Chickamauga and Chattanooga. These events take

Point Park Entrance

place near the anniversary of the battles (September for Chickamauga, and November for Lookout Mountain). Near Christmas, Cravens House is decorated in Victorian-era decorations, and candle-light tours are offered. On the Saturday nearest to July 4, Chickamauga Battle-field hosts an evening "Pops in the Park" concert presented by the Chattanooga Symphony Orchestra. During the sum-mer, reenactment organizations present special demonstrations and Civil War encampments at Chickamauga Battlefield and Lookout Mountain. The Visitor's Center features exhibits on the Battle of Chickamauga, the Fuller Gun Collection, a Civil War timeline, and a multi-media program depicting the Battle of Chickamauga.

CHATTANOOGA NATIONAL CEMETERY

Holtzclaw Avenue, Chattanooga, TN
PHONE: 423-855-6590
HOURS: Open daily.
ADMISSION: Free.

On November 26, 1863, the day after the battle on Missionary Ridge, work began on creating a final resting place for Union soldiers who died in northwest Georgia and southeastern Tennessee. Interred at the site are James Andrews and seven of his men. In April 1862, James Andrews and twenty Union raiders stole a locomotive, named the General, at Big Shanty (now Kennesaw), Georgia. In an episode that became known as "The Great Locomotive Chase," they were pur-sued throughout northwest Georgia and captured near Ringgold. Later, Andrews and seven of the raiders were hanged in Atlanta. The "Raiders" were the first soldiers to receive the Congres-sional Medals of Honor. Andrews was a civilian and therefore not eligible. A monument to Andrews' Raiders stands near the graves of James Andrews and seven of his men, all of which are marked with a small replica of the locomotive.

Raiders' Monument,
Chattanooga National Cemetery

TENNESSEE CIVIL WAR MUSEUM

3014 St. Elmo Avenue, Chattanooga, TN

PHONE: 423-821-4954

HOURS: Open daily; closed major holidays.

ADMISSION: A fee is charged.

The Tennessee Civil War Museum is a privately-owned museum that combines state-of-the-art technology with relics to remember the accomplishments and the sacrifices of the common soldier. A full-time historian gives talks on uniforms, weapons, and personal history of the Northern and Southern soldier. Interactive touch-screen computers give historical information, and a movie presents an overview of the Civil War. Also featured is a million-dollar collection of Civil War relics.

THE BATTLES FOR CHATTANOOGA MUSEUM

1110 East Brow Road, Lookout Mountain, TN

PHONE: 423-821-2812

HOURS: Open daily; closed Christmas.

ADMISSION: A fee is charged; children under 12 are discounted.

The Battles for Chattanooga Museum is a small, privately-owned museum that features a large electric map and a light and sound show that explains the Battles of Chattanooga.

The Battles for Chattanooga Museum, foreground, and Point Park Gate, background

ABRAHAM LINCOLN MUSEUM

On the campus of Lincoln Memorial University, Harrogate, TN
PHONE: 423-869-6237
HOURS: Open daily; closed Christmas and New Year's Day.
ADMISSION: Free.

When Tennessee seceded from the Union, the Cumberland Gap area of Harrogate remained loyal. In appreciation of this loyalty, President Lincoln instructed General Oliver Otis Howard to do something for the people of the area. In 1897 Howard began Lincoln Memorial University. The museum, on the grounds of the university, contains a large collection of Union and Confederate uniforms, basic soldier's gear, and one of the largest collections of Lincoln memorabilia.

Abraham Lincoln Museum

ANDREW JOHNSON NATIONAL HISTORIC SITE

College and Depot Streets, Greeneville, TN
PHONE: 423-638-3551
HOURS: Open daily; closed Thanksgiving, Christmas, and New Year's Day.
ADMISSION: A fee is charged; children and seniors are free.

The Andrew Johnson National Historic Site features Homestead, the home of President Johnson from 1851 until his death. After Lincoln's assassination, Johnson became president and presided over Reconstruction. Also included at the site are a Visitor's Center, the Andrew Johnson National Cemetery where President Johnson is buried, and the Johnson family home.

TEXAS

On February 1, 1861, the twenty-fifth anniversary of Texas's Declaration of Independence from Mexico, Texas seceded from the United States of America and became a member of the Confederate States of America. The legendary governor, Sam Houston, had fought against the secession and for his courage, was driven from office.

Texas brought to the Confederacy considerable assets, sending to the Southern cause over 50,000 troops. In addition, the state had four times as many cattle and horses as all other Southern states combined, which promised a steady supply of meat and mounts. Few battles were fought in the state, and very little damage was done by the war; Texas rejoined the Union in 1869.

SEE
NEW MEXICO
PAGE 126

El Paso

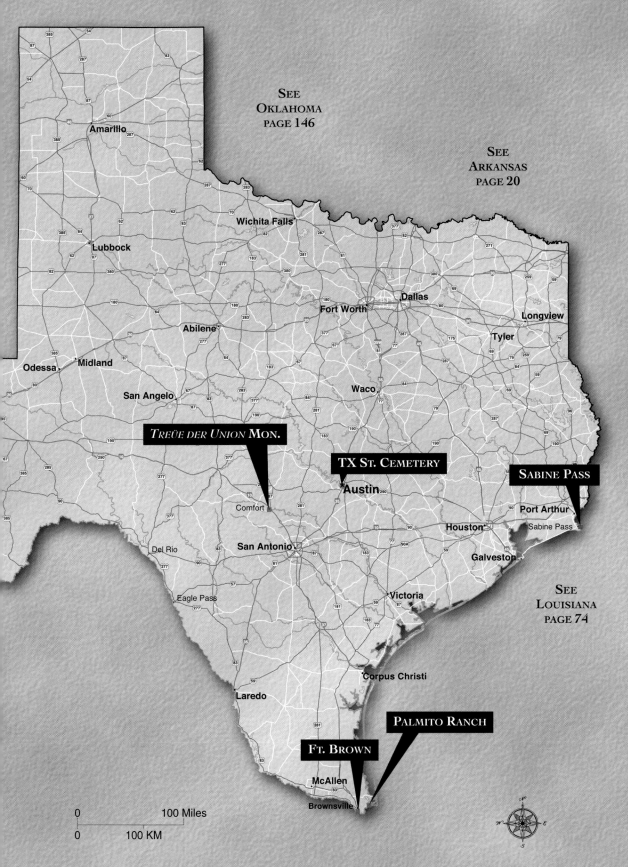

See
Oklahoma
page 146

See
Arkansas
page 20

Amarillo

Lubbock

Wichita Falls

Dallas

Fort Worth

Longview

Abilene

Tyler

Odessa

Midland

San Angelo

Waco

Treüe der Union Mon.

TX St. Cemetery

Sabine Pass

Comfort

Austin

Port Arthur

Sabine Pass

Del Rio

San Antonio

Houston

Galveston

See
Louisiana
page 74

Eagle Pass

Victoria

Corpus Christi

Laredo

Palmito Ranch

Ft. Brown

McAllen

Brownsville

0   100 Miles

0   100 KM

"An invasion of Texas was a matter of political or state policy."

Maj. Gen. N. P. Banks, head of Red River Campaign, November 1864

NORTHERN COMMANDER:
Col. T. H. Barrett

STRENGTH: 500

CASUALTIES: 118

THE BATTLE OF PALMITO RANCH

May 12–13, 1865

The last land-based engagement of the Civil War.

The Battle of Palmito Ranch took place near Brownsville, Texas, along the Rio Grande, more than a month after General Robert E. Lee's surrender to General Ulysses S. Grant at Appomattox Court House, Virginia. Lee's surrender of the Army of Virginia had brought the Civil War to its symbolic end but not its actual end. The Confederate army in Texas still continued the rebellion.

On May 11, 1865, Union Colonel Theodore H. Barrett, commander of forces at the island of Brazos Santiago, Texas, dispatched an expedition composed of 250 men of the Sixty-second U.S. Colored Infantry Regiment and fifty men of the Second Texas Cavalry Regiment under the command of Lieutenant Colonel David Branson to the mainland to attack reported Rebel outposts and camps. Branson led his men toward Palmito Ranch but encountered much skirmishing along the way. Branson sent word of his predicament to Barrett, who reinforced Branson at daybreak on May 13 with 200

Palmito Ranch Battlefield

Monument, Palmito Ranch Battlefield

men of the Thirty-fourth Indiana Volunteer Infantry.

After the fighting stopped, Barrett led his force to a bluff at Tulosa on the river where the men could camp for the night. At 4:00 P.M., a large Confederate cavalry force, commanded by Colonel John S. "Rip" Ford, approached, and Union troops formed a battle line. The Rebels hammered the Union line with artillery. To preclude an enemy flanking movement, Barrett ordered a retreat. During the two-day battle, Ford's Confederate troops held off the Union and forced them to retreat to Boca Chica and ultimately to return to the island of Brazos Santiago.

The fighting at Palmito Ranch was the last land engagement of the Civil War. By holding off the Union army, the Confederacy's Trans-Mississippi Department was able to maintain control of the lower Rio Grande and Mississippi valleys a little longer.

Despite their victory, however, the Confederates were fighting a war that had already been lost. Fewer than two weeks later, the forces that fought to victory at Palmito Ranch were part of a Confederate surrender at New Orleans that put a final and complete end to the Civil War.

SOUTHERN COMMANDER:
Col. J. S. Ford

STRENGTH: Unk[

CASUALTIES: Un[

Texas State Cemetery

909 Navasota Street, Austin, TX
PHONE: 512-463-0605
HOURS: Open daily; office open weekdays.
ADMISSION: Free.

Texas State Cemetery was established in 1851; a Confederate section was added in 1871. More than 2,000 Confederate veterans and their wives are buried in rows of white marble tablets. In 1867 General Albert Sidney Johnston's body was moved to the Texas State Cemetery. Johnston led the

Fountain on Republic Hill and General Johnston's grave, Texas State Cemetery

Confederate charge at the Battle of Shiloh and was fatally wounded there. The cemetery's Visitor's Center offers internet access to biographies, photographs, and Confederate records of the buried.

Treüe der Union (True to the Union) Monument

Just past the intersection of High Street and U.S. Highway 27, Comfort, TX
PHONE: 830-995-3131 (Chamber of Commerce)
HOURS: Open daily.
ADMISSION: Free.

This is the oldest Civil War monument in Texas and commemorates a sad moment in Civil War history. In August 1862, a group of unarmed German immigrant families, loyal to the Union, left their homes in Texas to move north. In the dark, a Confederate patrol mistook them for a Union party and killed or captured at least thirty-six men in what is now called the *Nueces* Massacre. An unknown stonecutter erected this limestone obelisk in 1866. The names of thirty-six of the known victims are inscribed on the monument.

Palmito Ranch Battlefield

Texas Highway 4, Brownsville, TX
PHONE: 800-626-2639 (Convention and Visitor's Bureau)
HOURS: Open daily.
ADMISSION: Free.

Although much of the Palmito Ranch Battlefield is privately owned and is not open to public access, historical markers along the Boca Chica Highway, or Highway 4, describe the battle and outline much of the battlefield. A Visitor's Center is not available, but information can be obtained through the Texas Convention and Visitor's Bureau.

Photo right: Palmito Ranch Battlefield

FORT BROWN

80 Fort Brown on the campus of University of Texas, Brownsville, TX

PHONE: 956-544-8200
HOURS: Buildings open during school hours; campus always open.
ADMISSION: Free.

Fort Brown

Fort Brown was established in 1846 and utilized during the Mexican War. In 1861 Texas troops controlled the fort and used it to protect the Brownsville port which received cotton and war materiel. To extend a coastal blockade, Union forces took over the fort in November 1863, but eight months later a strong Confederate army retook the fort and controlled it until the end of the war. Today, the post headquarters, medical laboratory, guardhouse, hospital, and morgue still stand. The nearby Historic Brownsville Museum contains exhibits pertaining to Brownsville's Civil War past.

SABINE PASS BATTLEGROUND STATE HISTORICAL PARK

Texas Highway 87, Sabine Pass, TX
PHONE: 409-971-2451
HOURS: Open daily.
ADMISSION: Free.

Sabine Pass was a major Confederate port for receiving supplies and materiel. Because of the Union blockade of gulf ports and those further east, the Confederates required that the Texas ports remain open. Fort Sabine and nearby Fort Griffin were constructed for this purpose. Twice, in September of 1862 and again in September of 1863, the Union attempted to gain control of the forts, with only brief success in 1862. Neither fort is still standing, but there is a monument to the Confederate Lieutenant Richard Dowling and his men who fought in the 1863 engagement. Camping and walking trails are available. Each September the park hosts a tribute to Lieutenant Dowling.

VIRGINIA

*V*irginia did not join the parade of Southern secession until April of 1861, but it quickly became the most important state in the Confederacy. Virginia saw more battles than any other state—2,150 in all—and it was the birthplace of ninety-one Confederate generals, including Robert E. Lee and Stonewall Jackson. Richmond, Virginia, the Confederate capital, lay only 100 miles from Washington, D.C., and Virginia was of strategic importance to both sides for its farms, ironworks, and rail lines.

Most of the fighting in Virginia pitted two great Civil War generals and their armies—Robert E. Lee and his Army of Northern Virginia and Ulysses S. Grant and his Army of the Potomac—against one another in a contest that has become symbolic in American minds for the war as a whole. Rightly so, for when Lee surrendered to Grant at Appomattox Court House, although other armies in other states continued to fight, the Civil War was considered finally and officially over.

Virginia's rich Civil War heritage is unmatched by any other state, North or South. The Confederacy's most important state is now the nations' most important guardian of Civil War history.

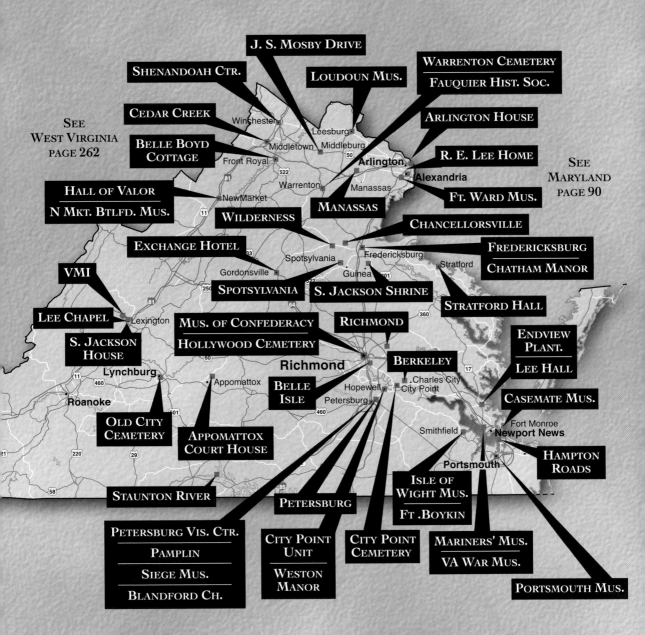

J. S. MOSBY DRIVE

SHENANDOAH CTR.

LOUDOUN MUS.

WARRENTON CEMETERY

FAUQUIER HIST. SOC.

CEDAR CREEK

ARLINGTON HOUSE

BELLE BOYD
COTTAGE

R. E. LEE HOME

SEE
WEST VIRGINIA
PAGE 262

SEE
MARYLAND
PAGE 90

HALL OF VALOR

N MKT. BTLFD. MUS.

FT. WARD MUS.

WILDERNESS

MANASSAS

CHANCELLORSVILLE

EXCHANGE HOTEL

FREDERICKSBURG

CHATHAM MANOR

VMI

SPOTSYLVANIA

S. JACKSON SHRINE

STRATFORD HALL

LEE CHAPEL

S. JACKSON
HOUSE

MUS. OF CONFEDERACY

HOLLYWOOD CEMETERY

RICHMOND

ENDVIEW
PLANT.

LEE HALL

CASEMATE MUS.

BERKELEY

OLD CITY
CEMETERY

BELLE
ISLE

HAMPTON
ROADS

APPOMATTOX
COURT HOUSE

STAUNTON RIVER

ISLE OF
WIGHT MUS.

FT .BOYKIN

PETERSBURG

PETERSBURG VIS. CTR.

PAMPLIN

SIEGE MUS.

BLANDFORD CH.

CITY POINT
UNIT

WESTON
MANOR

CITY POINT
CEMETERY

MARINERS' MUS.

VA WAR MUS.

PORTSMOUTH MUS.

Winchester

Leesburg

Middletown   Middleburg

Front Royal

Arlington

Alexandria

Warrenton

Manassas

NewMarket

Spotsylvania

Fredericksburg

Stratford

Gordonsville

Guinea

Lexington

Appomattox

Richmond

Charles City
City Point

Lynchburg

Hopewell

Roanoke

Petersburg

Smithfield

Newport News
Fort Monroe

Portsmouth

SEE NORTH CAROLINA PAGE 132

• *Because of space constraints, all of
the sites listed on the following pages
are not shown on this map*

0   100 Miles

0   100 KM

NORTHERN COMMANDER:
Brig. Gen. I. McDowell

STRENGTH: 29,000

CASUALTIES: 2,896

THE FIRST BATTLE OF MANASSAS (BULL RUN)

July 21, 1861

The Confederate victory at the first battle at Manassas made it clear that the war would be long and hard-fought.

The town of Manassas was an important railroad center between Washington and Richmond because it lay directly between the Confederate and Union capitals. It was obvious to many that conflict would occur between the two capitals, and civilians were eager to watch the fight. In the summer of 1861, 32,000 Confederate soldiers under General P. G. T. Beauregard

Stonewall Jackson Monument, Manassas National Battlefield Park

set up defensive positions alongside a stream called Bull Run.

In mid-July Union Brigadier General Irvin McDowell led 39,000 men out of Washington toward Brigadier General P. G. T. Beauregard in a three-pronged attack. When McDowell's first probe into the Confederate flank at Manassas proved unsuccessful, he paused and spent the next two days devising a new plan of attack. He ordered General Patterson to keep General Joseph E. Johnston occupied in Winchester. Johnston, however, evacuated Winchester, leaving a cavalry screen to fool Patterson. Unaware of the deception, on July 21, McDowell directed a small group to feign an attack from the north while the main assault would come from the northwest. But the decoy attack was too weak. The Confederates realized the trick and left only a few men to fight against the Union. The remainder of the brigade left to meet McDowell.

The troop strength of the Northern army eventually drove Southern forces under General Barnard Bee back to Henry House Hill where a Confederate brigade under General Thomas Jackson waited to assist them. Bee rallied his troops with the words, "There stands Jackson, like a stone wall! Rally behind the Virginians!" The troops rallied and pushed the North into confusion. Thousands of Union troops began to move toward the rear where Northern civilians were watching the battle. A general melee ensued as both soldiers and civilians clogged the road in retreat. The first land battle of the war was over; victory belonged to the Confederacy.

Manassas proved to the citizens, however, that there would be no quick end to the war, and people began to plan accordingly. For example, a Manassas citizen named Wilmer McLean had his house damaged by the shots. After the battle, he moved to what he thought would be a safer location in Appomattox Court House, Virginia.

"*The conduct of General Jackson also requires mention, as eminently that of an able, fearless soldier and sagacious commander—one fit to lead his efficient brigade. His prompt, timely arrival before the plateau of the Henry House . . . contributed much to the success of the day*"

Brig. Gen. P. G. T. Beauregard
August 26, 1861

SOUTHERN COMMANDER:
Brig. Gen. P. G. T. Beauregar

STRENGTH: 32,000

CASUALTIES: 1,982

NORTHERN COMMANDER: Gen. J. Pope

STRENGTH: 63,000

CASUALTIES: 9,931

THE SECOND BATTLE OF MANASSAS (BULL RUN)

August 28–30, 1862

The second battle of Manassas was also a victory for the Confederacy and opened the door for General Lee's invasion of the North.

A year after the First Battle of Manassas, the Northern armies had yet to win a major victory, and the South was hopeful that independence would soon be theirs. The Confederacy rested its hopes on General Robert E. Lee's Army of Northern Virginia. Lee, however, knew that if he were to succeed in northern Virginia, he had to defeat General John Pope's Union Army of Virginia before it joined the Army of the Potomac. These two forces would create a Federal fighting force twice the size of Lee's Confederate army. The fighting between Lee and Pope would climax in August 1862 at the Second Battle of Manassas.

On August 25, 1861, Jackson's foot cavalry flanked General Pope's right, cutting off his supply line from Washington. When Jackson's men fired from an unfinished railroad, Union troops from Wisconsin and Indiana (later called the Iron Brigade) quickly formed battle lines and marched to within 100 yards of the Confederates. Only darkness ended the fighting, which resulted in a thirty-three percent casualty rate. The next

Manassas Visitor Center, Manassas National Battlefield Park

Manassas National Battlefield Park

day, Pope continued the stalemate until Major General Kearny, the one-armed veteran of the Mexican War, drove against Jackson's left flank. Pope did not send reinforcements, and a Union retreat resulted. That evening, Generals Lee and Longstreet slipped in with reinforcements. On the third day, at what became known as the Deep Cut, Jackson slaughtered the Union army in thirty minutes of intense fighting. Pope fell back to fight until nightfall when he withdrew toward Washington where he was relieved of command and sent to the West to fight in the Indian wars.

Second Manassas was the climax of skirmishes between Generals Pope, Lee, and Jackson. In the end, General Pope and his men traced McDowell's steps back toward Washington.

This Union defeat was more devastating than the first; not only were the casualties higher but so were the stakes. After victory at Second Manassas, General Lee's confident Army of Northern Virginia was prepared to take the Civil War into Northern territory.

SOUTHERN COMMANDER:
Gen. R. E. Lee

STRENGTH: 55,000

CASUALTIES: 8,353

MANASSAS NATIONAL BATTLEFIELD PARK

6511 Sudley Road, Manassas, VA

PHONE: 703-361-1339

HOURS: Open daily; closed Thanksgiving and Christmas.

ADMISSION: A fee is charged.

Located twenty-six miles southwest of Washington, D.C., Manassas National Battlefield Park contains about 5,500 acres where the battles of the First and Second Manassas took place. There are two visitor centers: Henry Hill Visitor Center and Museum offers a battle map program as well as a thirteen-minute introductory slide program that provides information on both battles. Stuart's Hill Visitor Center is open only during the summer months.

A twenty-five minute self-guided walking tour covers the major areas of the battles, and ranger-led tours are available during the summer months. A twelve-mile, twelve-stop driving tour includes the Groveton Confederate Cemetery where unknown Confederate soldiers are buried in mass graves. Only a few in the cemetery are identified. Period cannon on the grounds mark some of the original

Old Stone House, Manassas National Battlefield Park

Manassas National Battlefield Park

artillery positions. Historic Stone House is open during the summer months. During the battles, this house was turned into a field hospital.

THE MANASSAS MUSEUM

9101 Prince William Street, Manassas, VA
PHONE: 703-368-1873
HOURS: Open daily except Monday; closed major holidays.
ADMISSION: A fee is charged; children are discounted.

The Manassas Museum contains exhibits and photographs depicting the history of Manassas and includes a large collection of Civil War artifacts and two video programs: *A Place of Passages* and *A Community At War*.

The Manassas Museum system also includes the train depot and earthworks. Inside the depot, which also serves as a Visitor's Center, a small exhibit area illustrates the railroad's history and influence on Manassas and the two battles which occurred here. The city is in the process of restoring the original earthworks of both the Confederate and Union forces. The Confederate earthworks are located along the railroad on the eastern side of Manassas, and the Union earthworks are also located along the

The Manassas Museum

railroad on the west side of town. Once restored, each area will contain approximately eleven to seventeen acres.

Also of note in Manassas, is the Jennie Dean Memorial which stands on the site of the Manassas Industrial School for Colored Youth. This school was established in the 1890s by Jennie Dean, a former slave, for the purpose of providing African-Americans with a proper education.

EXCHANGE HOTEL AND CIVIL WAR MUSEUM

400 South Main Street, Gordonsville, VA
PHONE: 540-832-2944
HOURS: Open mid-March–mid-December on varying days; closed July 4 and Thanksgiving.
ADMISSION: A fee is charged.

This former railroad hotel was converted into a Civil War hospital and served troops from the battles of Cedar Mountain, Chancellorsville, Trevilian Station, Mine Run, Brandy Station, Manassas, the Wilderness, and Fredericksburg. Although it was primarily a Confederate facility, it treated both sides. By the end of the war, over 70,000 men had passed through the Exchange Hotel/Hospital. Over 700 were buried on the grounds. After the war, the bodies of the Confederate dead were moved to a mass grave in Gordonsville's Maplewood Cemetery. Federal soldiers were reinterred in the national cemetery in Culpepper. Guided tours of the restored building are available. Civil War medical reenactments take place in the spring and fall.

FORT WARD MUSEUM AND HISTORIC SITE

4301 West Braddock Road, Alexandria, VA

PHONE: 703-838-4848

HOURS: Fort open daily; closed major holidays. Museum closed Monday.

ADMISSION: Free.

Fort Ward is the best preserved of the system of forts and batteries built to protect Washington, D.C., during the Civil War. The Fort Ward Museum features an orientation video on the defense of Washington, a living history series and lecture series, bus tours, and changing exhibits. The museum focuses on the history of Fort Ward, Alexandria's role as a vital crossroads and supply center, and the lifestyles of soldiers and civilians during the war. The permanent collection includes: military equipment related to the infantry; artillery; edged and shoulder weapons; flags; musical instruments; medical equipment; uniforms and clothing accessories; cooking and mess equipment; artwork, primarily period prints of both Union and Confederate significance;

Northwest Bastion, Fort Ward Museum and Historic Site

documents; photographs; and artifacts excavated at Fort Ward. The museum also contains a comprehensive research library that is open to the public during regular museum hours; however, researchers should call ahead for reservations.

Museum and Reconstructed Officer's Hut, Fort Ward Museum and Historic Site

BOYHOOD HOME OF ROBERT E. LEE

607 Oronoco Street, Alexandria, VA
PHONE: 703-548-8454
HOURS: Open daily; closed major holidays.
ADMISSION: A fee is charged.

Robert E. Lee lived in this home, which the Lee family rented, from the age of five to eighteen, when he entered the United States Military Academy at West Point. The home is furnished with period pieces, and guided tours are available.

THE LOUDOUN MUSEUM

14–16 Loudoun Street SW, Leesburg, VA
PHONE: 703-777-7427
HOURS: Open daily; closed major holidays.
ADMISSION: A fee is charged; children are discounted.

The Loudoun Museum is dedicated to the county's diverse history and contains exhibits on the area's Civil War heritage. Artifacts from the Battle of Ball's Bluff and Dranesville are housed here as are exhibits that focus on the local citizens who were torn between the forces of North and South. The museum offers a fifteen-minute movie.

BELLE BOYD COTTAGE

101 Chester Street, Front Royal, VA
PHONE: 540-636-1446 (Warren Heritage Society)
HOURS: Open Monday, Tuesday, Thursday, and Friday.
ADMISSION: A fee is charged; children are discounted.

Belle Boyd, a Confederate spy, used friendships with Union soldiers and officers occupying Front Royal to gain information about troop movements. In one instance, Boyd eavesdropped on Union Generals Shields and Banks concerning the upcoming Battle of Front Royal. The infor-

mation she provided to General Stonewall Jackson helped win the battle for the Confederacy. The restored Belle Boyd Cottage is owned by the Warren Heritage Society. Exhibits at the Ivy Lodge Museum, located in front of the Belle Boyd Cottage, interpret the site and contain Civil War artifacts.

Photo right: Belle Boyd Cottage

THE JOHN SINGLETON MOSBY HERITAGE AREA'S DRIVE THROUGH HISTORY

Virginia Highway 50, Middleburg, VA

PHONE: 540-687-6681 (Mosby Heritage Association)

HOURS: Open daily.

ADMISSION: Free; a fee is charged for Sky Meadows State Park (540-592-3556).

John Singleton Mosby, also called the Gray Ghost, is a legend in the Virginia counties of Fauquier and Loudoun. An unknown lawyer at the beginning of the war, Mosby identified the great advantage of guerrilla warfare in northern Virginia. He was first General J.E.B. Stuart's scout then was given his own command which eventually became the forty-third Battalion of Virginia Cavalry. Mosby led his rangers on raids throughout northern Virginia, wreaking havoc among Union lines, then disappearing without a trace. The area between Snickersville, Aldie, the Plains, and Markham became known as Mosby's Confederacy.

In commemoration of Mosby, Route 50 has been named the John S. Mosby Highway. Along the route, historical markers interpret Civil War-era landmarks. The tour, designed by the Mosby Heritage Area Association, begins at the Mount Zion Church located at Route 860 and Highway 50. Built in 1851, the Mount Zion Old School Baptist Church served as a hospital, a prison, a barracks, and a soldiers' burial ground. Other points of interest include the Goose Creek Stone Bridge, the site of a battle between J. E. B. Stuart's Southern troops and Union forces in June 1863; various homes of Mosby's Rangers; the Clinton Retor House where General Lee ordered Mosby to Gettysburg; and other places instrumental in the life of Mosby. The driving tour ends at Paris.

Also of interest is Sky Meadows State Park at Ashby Gap. This was the site of Abner Edmonds home, Bleak House. During July and August reenactments recreate the daily activities of Confederate soldiers during their march to Gettysburg.

WARRENTON CEMETERY

Lee Street, Warrenton, VA

PHONE: Not Available.

HOURS: Open daily.

ADMISSION: Free.

Although Warrenton saw no battle, it was surrounded by skirmishes and major engagements. Thousands of casualties were brought into Warrenton to be nursed or buried. This seven-acre cemetery includes Confederates from Alabama, Florida, Georgia, Louisiana, Mississippi, North Carolina, South Carolina, Tennessee, Texas, and Virginia. Approximately 200 Civil War dead, including Colonel John S. Mosby and many of his family, are interred here. Until recently, 600 Confederate soldiers were unidentified and buried in a common grave beneath a Confederate Memorial to the Unknowns. In 1995 a researcher at the National Archives in Washington, D.C., discovered the names of most of those soldiers, and a memorial wall inscribed with the 520 names now stands on the site.

FAUQUIER HISTORICAL SOCIETY AND OLD JAIL MUSEUM

*10 Courthouse Square, Corner of Ashby and
Waterloo Streets, Warrenton, VA*
PHONE: 540-347-5525
HOURS: Open daily except Monday; closed
major holidays.
ADMISSION: Free.

This museum contains many Civil War artifacts
and includes personal articles from Warrenton
resident, Confederate Colonel John Singleton
Mosby, as well as memorabilia from Mosby's
Rangers. Mosby's life epitomizes the rancor that
existed throughout the nation after the war
ended. As president, Ulysses S. Grant selected
Mosby for a post in the government prompting an
attempt on Mosby's life. Today, Mosby remains a
hero in this area for his brilliant tactics. Books,
maps, and flags relating to the Civil War are for
sale in the Fauquier Historical Society and Old
Jail Museum gift shop.

Old Jail Museum

ARLINGTON HOUSE, THE ROBERT E. LEE MEMORIAL

On the grounds of Arlington Cemetery, Arlington, VA
PHONE: 703-557-0613
HOURS: Open daily; closed Christmas and New Year's Day.
ADMISSION: Free.

On a hill overlooking the grounds of Arlington Cemetery sits the family home of Confederate
General Robert E. Lee. Lee lived here with his wife and their seven children before the outbreak
of the Civil War. Upon his resignation from the United States Army, Lee moved his family deeper
into Virginia. In the early years of the war, there was an attempt to preserve the house, but time
and tension took their toll. Defenses were thrown up around the house, and many who viewed
Lee as a traitor showered their feelings upon the house.

 After the war, Lee's eldest son had the estate restored to the family, but already several thousand Union dead had been buried in the grounds surrounding the home. The U.S. government
then purchased the property from the Lee family for $150,000, and fortifications around the
property were absorbed into Fort Mayer. In 1925 Congress established the Robert E. Lee
Memorial and began restoring the Greek Revival Mansion. The house contains pieces belonging
to the Lee family, as well as period pieces. The home and grounds are open for self-guided tours.

NORTHERN COMMANDER:
Maj. Gen. A. E. Burnside

STRENGTH: 120,000

CASUALTIES: 12,600

THE BATTLE OF FREDERICKSBURG

December 11–13, 1862

The battle at Fredericksburg, Virginia, proved to be the greatest disaster of the war for the Union army.

Fredericksburg, located in northern Virginia between Washington and Richmond, was the site of four major engagements during the Civil War. Within a seventeen-mile radius of the city, more than 100,000 Americans became casualties.

In the autumn of 1862, General George B. McClellan was replaced by Major General Ambrose E. Burnside after McClellan failed to pursue the Confederate army after its defeat at Antietam, Maryland. McClellan was so slow that President Abraham Lincoln was prompted to write in October 24, 1862, "I have just read your dispatch about sore tongued and fatigued horses. Will you pardon me for asking what the horses of your army have done since the battle of Antietam that fatigue anything?"

Burnside wanted to build upon the victory at Antietam by moving toward Richmond. He planned to use pontoon bridges to cross the Rappahannock River at Fredericksburg,

Sunken Road, Fredericksburg Battlefield

then move directly south to the Confederate capital of Richmond. He had to move quickly, however, to reach Fredericksburg before Longstreet and Jackson arrived to support General Robert E. Lee.

The Union army began moving on November 15, and the first division reached Stafford Heights overlooking Fredericksburg on December 17. Bridging equipment had not yet arrived, however, and the Federals were unable to cross the river. In fact, it took more than a week for the pontoons to come, and by that time Lee's army had taken possession of Fredericksburg. Although Burnside knew of Lee's movements, he believed that only part of Lee's army was in position. In truth, 78,000 were there. Burnside pushed ahead, and the disaster that followed ultimately earned him the nickname of "Butcher" Burnside.

On December 11 at 3:00 A.M., Union engineers began placing pontoon bridges in the Rappahannock. At daybreak, they were interrupted by minié balls from Confederate sharpshooters in town. After Union volunteers crossed the river and battled for control of the town, Lee allowed the bridges to be completed. On December 12, Union troops crossed the Rappahannock and plundered Fredericksburg.

On December 13, Burnside still believed he was facing only part of Lee's army and ordered attacks accordingly. One piece of land south of town exchanged sides between North and South throughout the day. Meanwhile, Burnside ordered an assault up Marye's Heights, just behind Fredericksburg, where Lee's men were entrenched in Sunken Road behind a stone wall at the base of the heights. Wave after wave of Union troops swarmed the hill, only to be mowed down by Confederate guns. By the end of the day, 8,000 Union troops, many from the Sixty-ninth New York "Irish Brigade," died attempting to reach the Heights. Men who were wounded froze to death that night in the torrential downpours. Burnside withdrew in defeat. Upon hearing of the loss of Fredericksburg, President Abraham Lincoln remarked, "If there is a worse place than Hell, I am in it."

"It is well that war is so terrible—we should grow too fond of it."

Gen. R. E. Lee
December 1862

SOUTHERN
COMMANDER:
Gen. R. E. Lee

STRENGTH: 78,000

CASUALTIES: 5,300

FREDERICKSBURG BATTLEFIELD

1013 Lafayette Boulevard, Fredericksburg, VA

PHONE: 540-373-6122

HOURS: Open daily; closed Christmas and New Year's Day.

ADMISSION: One fee admits visitors to all sites within the Fredericksburg and Spotsylvania National Military Park.

Kirkland Monument, Fredericksburg Battlefield

The Fredericksburg Visitor's Center offers interpretive exhibits and a slide presentation as well as exhibits and displays concerning the Battle of Fredericksburg. A self-guided driving tour includes the entire battlefield as well as Marye's Heights, a national cemetery, Sunken Road, Chatham Manor, Salem Church, and a monument to the Angel of Marye's Heights, nineteen-year-old Sergeant Richard Kirkland of the Second South Carolina Infantry. Kirkland was so moved by the cries of the wounded Union soldiers that he took as many canteens as he could carry and went among them, giving them some relief through water and compassion. Brochures and maps are available at the Visitor's Center.

FREDERICKSBURG NATIONAL CEMETERY

1013 Lafayette Boulevard, Fredericksburg, VA

PHONE: 540-373-6122

HOURS: Open daily.

ADMISSION: One fee admits visitors to all sites within the Fredericksburg and Spotsylvania National Military Park.

Fredericksburg National Cemetery

Of the 15,243 Union soldiers here, only 2,473 are identified. Local organizations were largely responsible for providing these Union soldiers a final resting place. The cemetery is not organized by state, unit, or campaign, but as the soldiers were brought in for burial. Various monuments do, however, commemorate units and campaigns. Most of the interred are privates; higher ranking officers were often transported home by family members. This cemetery, part of the Fredericksburg and Spotsylvania National Military Park, sits behind the Fredericksburg Battlefield Visitor's Center, and overlooks the Sunken Road.

The Southern dead are interred in the Fredericksburg Confederate Cemetery and the Spotsylvania Confederate Cemetery. Registers for the national cemetery and both Confederate cemeteries can be found in the Fredericksburg Battlefield Visitor's Center.

CHATHAM MANOR

120 Chatham Lane, Fredericksburg, VA
PHONE: 540-371-0802
HOURS: Open daily; closed
Christmas and New Year's Day.
ADMISSION: One fee admits
visitors to all sites within the
Fredericksburg and Spotsylvania National Military Park.

Chatham Manor was used as the
Union headquarters during the
Battle of Fredericksburg and
now serves as headquarters of
the Fredericksburg and Spotsylvania Battlefield Park. The elegant home of William Fitzhugh
and Confederate Major J.

Chatham Manor

Horace Lacey became the Union headquarters at various times for Generals McDowell, Burnside, Sumner, and Gibbon. In May of 1862, Lincoln visited the home.

After the battle of Fredericksburg, Chatham was converted into a hospital where Dr. Mary Walker, Clara Barton, and Walt Whitman attended to the wounded. Graffiti scrawled by Union soldiers is still visible today. Five of its ten rooms are open to the public and contain exhibits and displays.

FREDERICKSBURG WALKING TOUR

1013 Lafayette Boulevard, Fredericksburg, VA
PHONE: 540-373-6122 (Fredericksburg Battlefield Visitor's Center)
HOURS: Open daily; closed major holidays.
ADMISSION: Free.

The National Park Service hosts a two-part walking tour recounting the battle of Fredericksburg. The city is located on the banks of the Rappahannock River which served as a natural defensive barrier. Fredericksburg's position on the north-south rail corridor was strategic in keeping both armies supplied. On four separate occasions, the Union Army of the Potomac fought the Confederate Army of Northern Virginia in and around the city, leaving over 100,000 casualties and a scarred landscape in their wake. The walking tour visits the scenes of the Fredericksburg Campaign of November–December 1862. Many of the buildings on the tour were standing at the time of the battle. Additional historic walking tours are available at the Fredericksburg Visitor's Center.

> "May God have mercy
> on General Lee, for I will
> have none."
>
> *Maj. Gen. J. Hooker*

NORTHERN
COMMANDER:
Maj. Gen. J. Hooker

STRENGTH: 130,000

CASUALTIES: 17,000

THE BATTLE OF CHANCELLORSVILLE

May 1–3, 1863

The Battle of Chancellorsville stands as the greatest Civil War victory for Confederate General Robert E. Lee.

After the crushing defeat at Fredericksburg, General Ambrose Burnside was relieved of his command and replaced by General Joseph "Fighting Joe" Hooker. In the spring of 1863, Hooker made plans to swing around and attack the rear of Lee's army at Fredericksburg. Lee discovered Hooker's plan, however, and fled to Chancellorsville, where he took up position protected by an area called the Wilderness. This terrain had dense and impenetrable underbrush, which provided excellent defense for the badly outnumbered Confederates. Hooker followed Lee and made for a high plateau marked by Zoan Church. Lee daringly split his small command in two and sent one group under General Jackson to meet Hooker. Jackson arrived at the ridge in time to drive Hooker back to Chancellorsville.

Hazel Grove, Chancellorsville Battlefield

Ruins of Catharine Furnace, Chancellorsville Battlefield

SOUTHERN COMMANDER: Gen. R. E. Lee

STRENGTH: 60,000

CASUALTIES: 12,800

That night Lee and Jackson further divided their force, and Jackson attacked Hooker's rear on the second day. Late that afternoon, Jackson's men roared out of the Wilderness, rolled over the Union army, and destroyed half of Hooker's line. On the third day, Confederate artillery aided the infantry surging across the fields around Chancellorsville and victory was secured.

Although Chancellorsville was a great victory for the Confederacy, elation soon mixed with mourning. On the evening of May 2, Jackson and his staff were reconnoitering the area. As they rode back to the Confederate lines, a North Carolina unit believed they were being attacked and fired on the Jackson group. Jackson was hit twice in the left arm and once in the right hand. His left arm was amputated that night.

Upon hearing that Jackson was wounded, Lee said, "He [Jackson] had lost his left arm, but I [Lee] have lost my right arm." Jackson died eight days later in Fredericksburg from pneumonia.

FREDERICKSBURG AREA MUSEUM

907 Princess Anne Street, Fredericksburg, VA
PHONE: 540-371-3037
HOURS: Open daily; closed major holidays.
ADMISSION: A fee is charged; children are discounted.

Fredericksburg Area Museum is located in the 1816 Town Hall and Market House that survived the destruction of the Civil War. Permanent and changing exhibits describe the significance of Fredericksburg during the Civil War.

Fredericksburg Area Museum

 # CHANCELLORSVILLE BATTLEFIELD

9001 Plank Road, Fredericksburg, VA
PHONE: 540-786-2880
HOURS: Open daily; closed Christmas and New Year's Day.
ADMISSION: One fee admits visitors to all sites within the Fredericksburg and Spotsylvania National Military Park.

There are 1,252 acres of Chancellorsville Battlefield remaining. The Visitor's Center presents a twelve-minute slide presentation as well as numerous exhibits. A six-mile driving tour is marked with stops as a continuation of the Fredericksburg Battlefield.

Jackson Monument, Chancellorsville Battlefield

Stops include the ruins of the Chancellorsville Inn, Lee-Jackson Bivouac Site (the last time Lee would see Jackson), Catharine Furnace ruins, and the Visitor Center itself which marks the spot where Stonewall Jackson was hit by his own infantry. During the summer, a thirty-five minute guided walking tour is conducted to the site where Jackson was shot.

STONEWALL JACKSON SHRINE

Virginia Highway 606, Guinea, VA

PHONE: 804-633-6076

HOURS: Open daily second week in June–Labor Day; closed Wednesday and Thursday, October; open Saturday–Monday, November–March.

ADMISSION: One fee admits visitors to all sites within the Fredericksburg and Spotsylvania National Military Park.

During the Battle of Chancellorsville, Stonewall Jackson was wounded by his own infantry in the darkness. Doctors at the field hospital amputated his left arm. Jackson was then taken about twenty-seven miles to a plantation in Guinea. There, an outbuilding that served as the plantation's office was converted into a small cottage for Jackson's recovery. Unfortunately, with his wife and young daughter by his side, Jackson died of pneumonia on May 10, 1863. The six-room cottage is furnished as it appeared at Jackson's death.

Stonewall Jackson Shrine

NORTHERN COMMANDERS:
Lt. Gen. U. S. Grant
Maj. Gen. G. B. Meade

STRENGTH: 118,769

CASUALTIES: 18,000

THE BATTLE OF THE WILDERNESS

May 5–6, 1864

The terrible battle fought in the thickest and roughest of terrain, the Wilderness has been called the "beginning of the end" for the Confederacy.

The Wilderness was a region ten miles west of Fredericksburg twelve miles wide and six miles deep, running along the south bank of the Rapidan River. It had been called the Wilderness since the first colonists to settle the area discovered that it could not be tamed. With Lieutenant General Ulysses S. Grant and his men advancing upon them in the spring of 1864, General Robert E. Lee saw the wild entanglement of the Wilderness as a possible ally. It was there that Lee would meet the Union advance.

Fighting began in the early afternoon of May 5 in the north and slowly spread southward as the Union forces came into line. By nightfall the Confederate line was solid in the north and ragged in the south. Lee, however, had only two-thirds of his army engaged. Reinforcements were due early the second day but were slow in arriving. When they did come, the

140th New York Monument, Sounders Field, Wilderness Battlefield

Monument to Texans, Wilderness Battlefield

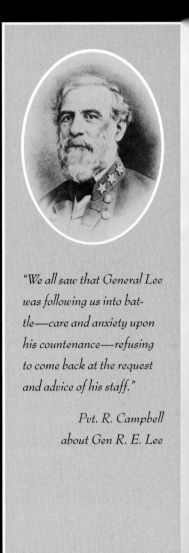

Confederate counterattack brought the Union to a standstill.

The Wilderness, which in the beginning was a friend to the Confederates, became a foe for North and South. The fighting was so fierce in the dry underbrush that fires broke out all over the battlefield, confusing the men on both sides. Fires were so strong that soldiers too wounded to move were burned to death. Both North and South suffered terrible losses and the battle itself was not a victory for either the Union or Confederacy, but Grant was the first Union general to press on south despite the number of casualties. The North, with far greater numbers, could endure the losses, unlike the South, whose every man was irreplaceable. The Civil War had become a battle of attrition; and the Wilderness sounded the death knell of the Confederacy.

SOUTHERN COMMANDER:
Gen. R. E. Lee

STRENGTH: 62,000

CASUALTIES: 10,800

WILDERNESS BATTLEFIELD

Virginia Highway 20 (Old Orange Turnpike), 16 miles west of Fredericksburg, VA

PHONE: 540-786-2880 (Chancellorsville Visitor's Center)

HOURS: Open daily; closed Christmas and New Year's Day.

ADMISSION: One fee admits visitors to all sites within the Fredericksburg and Spotsylvania National Military Park.

The Chancellorsville Visitor's Center provides brochures and maps for self-guided tours of Wilderness Battlefield, and there is an exhibit shelter with a historian on duty. Nearly 2,000 acres of the battlefield's dense woods remain. Confederate trenches along the Hill-Ewell Drive are still visible. During the summer months, a forty-five-minute guided walking tour is available. It leaves from the Wilderness Exhibit Shelter; stops include the Gordon Flank Attack, Tapp Farm, and Brock Road-Plank Road Junction.

Saunders Field, Wilderness Battlefield

SPOTSYLVANIA COURT HOUSE BATTLEFIELD

Virginia Highway 3 to County Highway 613 (Brock Road), Spotsylvania, VA

PHONE: 540-786-2880 (Chancellorsville Visitor's Center)

HOURS: Open daily; closed Christmas and New Year's Day.

ADMISSION: One fee admits visitors to all sites within the Fredericksburg and Spotsylvania National Military Park.

Ohio Monument at Bloody Angle, Spotsylvania Court House Battlefield

The Battle of Spotsylvania followed directly after the Battle of the Wilderness and was a continuation of General Grant's overland campaign toward Richmond. While Grant headed toward Richmond, the Confederates marched toward Spotsylvania Court House. The two forces met on Spindle Farm, May 8, 1864. On May 12 at Mule Shoe Salien, close firing and hand-to-hand combat in the pouring rain resulted in what is known as "Bloody Angle." With Confederate bodies filling the trenches, the sight was terrible and ghastly. Both sides were unsuccessful after thirteen days and 28,000 casualties.

Today, 1,448 acres of the battlefield remain. A self-guided driving tour includes stops at Bloody Angle, McCoull House, and the restored Spotsylvania Court House. During the summer, a forty-five-minute guided walking tour leaves from the Bloody Angle stop. Although there is no Visitor's Center at the battlefield, the Visitor's Center at Chancellorsville provides maps for self-guided tours of Spotsylvania Court House Battlefield. It also has information on those buried at the Confederate Cemetery.

SHENANDOAH VALLEY CIVIL WAR CENTER

2 North Cameron Street, Winchester, VA

PHONE: 540-722-6367

HOURS: Open daily.

ADMISSION: Free; a fee is charged for guided tours.

Stonewall Jackson once remarked, "If this [the Shenandoah] valley is lost, Virginia is lost." The Shenandoah Valley Civil War Center commemorates the importance of the valley through "Shenandoah: Crossroads of the Civil War," a permanent feature of the center. The exhibit chronicles the Shenandoah Valley's importance between 1861 and 1865 a brief overview of its fifteen military engagements and a summary of Stonewall Jackson's valley campaigns. A Visitor's Center, a gift shop, and brochures are available. Brochures include self-guided walking tours of the historic area of Winchester. Guided walking tours are also available. Booklets that outline driving tours along routes of many Civil War sites in the Winchester area can be purchased at the gift shop.

NEW MARKET BATTLEFIELD MILITARY MUSEUM

9500 Collins Drive, New Market, VA

PHONE: 540-740-8065

HOURS: Open daily March–December.

ADMISSION: A fee is charged.

This military museum rests on the grounds of the Battle of New Market where cadets from VMI in Lexington fought and died alongside seasoned veterans. A thirty-five-minute film orients visitors to the overall history of the Civil War and the Battle of New Market. The museum's extensive collection of over 2,500 original artifacts are chronologically arranged in 130 displays and include Stonewall Jackson's Bible. A self-guided walking tour of the battle site is also available. An extensive book and gift shop is located in the museum.

Lee Chapel and Museum at Washington and Lee University

Jefferson Street, Washington and Lee University, Lexington, VA

PHONE: 540-463-8768

HOURS: Open daily; closed Thanksgiving and the day after, Christmas Eve, Christmas, and New Year's Day.

ADMISSION: Free.

After the war, Gen. Robert E. Lee became president of Washington University; the name later changed to Washington and Lee, in his honor. Lee Chapel contains the Lee family crypt in which Lee, his wife, mother, father, and children are interred. Lee's horse, Traveller, is buried just outside the chapel. The museum contains exhibits on namesakes Generals Lee and Washington.

Photo above: Lee Chapel, Washington and Lee University

Photo left: Recumbent statue of Lee, Lee Chapel, Washington and Lee University

Virginia Military Institute Museum

U.S. Highway 11, Letcher Avenue, Lexington, VA

PHONE: 540-464-7232

HOURS: Open daily; closed during Virginia Military Institute's Christmas vacation.

ADMISSION: Free.

The VMI Museum is located on the institute's campus in Jackson Memorial Hall. Before earning his nickname "Stonewall," Thomas Jackson was a professor at VMI. The institute honors its famous alumnus at the VMI Museum. Among the museum's exhibits are the raincoat Jackson was wearing when he was shot; the hide of Jackson's horse, Little Sorrel; and uniforms and weapons used by cadets in the Battle of New Market.

VMI's grounds are home to three notable monuments: Jackson Statue, Cadet Battery, and the New Market Statue. The Jackson Statue depicts General Jackson as he surveyed the field at

Chancellorsville shortly before his death. Little Sorrel's bones are buried next to the statue. The guns preserved in the Cadet Battery monument were cast in 1848 and used by Jackson in cadet artillery training. The New Market Statue, also called "Virginia Mourning Her Dead," is a memorial to the VMI cadets who fought at the 1864 Battle of New Market. This battle was the only incident when an entire school formed a single unit in battle. The statue honors the ten students who died in battle; six of the cadets are buried beneath the New Market Statue. Each year in mid-May, a commemorative ceremony, open to the public, is held at the site.

VMI Museum

STONEWALL JACKSON HOUSE

8 East Washington Street, Lexington, VA

PHONE: 540-463-2552

HOURS: Open daily; closed major holidays.

ADMISSION: A fee is charged.

Stonewall Jackson House

The Stonewall Jackson House was home to Thomas Jackson and his wife. The modest brick town house was the only home Jackson ever owned. Stonewall Jackson taught natural philosophy for ten years at VMI. The 1801 house and garden have been restored and include period furnishings and Jackson's personal belongings. Guided tours of the museum are available.

HALL OF VALOR CIVIL WAR MUSEUM
NEW MARKET BATTLEFIELD STATE HISTORICAL PARK —

Virginia Highway 305 (George Collins Parkway), New Market, VA
PHONE: 540-740-3101
HOURS: Open daily; closed major holidays.
ADMISSION: A fee is charged.

On May 15, 1864, 8,940 Union troops clashed with 5,335 Confederates for possession of the only road across the Massanutten Mountain Range to the Union capital. Confederate General John Breckinridge reinforced his line with 247 cadets, fresh from the classrooms of nearby Virginia Military Institute. Although initially in a defensive mode, General Breckinridge took the offensive before Sigel could bring up his entire command. When a gap suddenly developed in the center of the Confederate line, the VMI cadets were ordered in. Whereas the VMI cadets proved to be a morale booster for the Confederate troops, Sigel's commands given in German sealed the victory for the South.

Hall of Valor Civil War Museum

The Battle of New Market resulted in over 1,300 casualties, including ten cadets. Nearly 300 acres of the New Market Battlefield are preserved by VMI in honor of those fallen cadets. Memorials on the battleground were erected by veterans of the battle. The park includes an orchard commemorating the battlefield site and the Hall of Valor Civil War Museum. The museum features two films: one details the battle, the other focuses on Professor Thomas Jackson, later General Stonewall Jackson. Jackson took the VMI Cadet Corps to Richmond where they became drill instructors for the Confederate army.

Also located on the grounds is the Bushong home which was used as a hospital, the wheelwright and blacksmith shops, a loom house, and a summer kitchen. Every year a reenactment of the Battle of New Market takes place.

CEDAR CREEK BATTLEFIELD

8437 Valley Pike, Middletown, VA

PHONE: 540-869-2064

HOURS: Open daily April–October; closed major holidays.

ADMISSION: Free; a fee is charged for the Visitor's Center and guided tours, as well as reenactments; children 12 and under are free.

On October 19, 1864, the Union dug in at Cedar Creek, not concerned about Confederate forces whom they had defeated at Kernstown and Fisher's Hill. General Sheridan, in fact, departed for a conference in Washington. Confederate General Early needed a quick victory to bolster his dwindling supplies and so tested the Union lines. Although this alerted acting Commander Wright of the Confederate intentions, the Union slowly gave ground until Sheridan's return inspired the Northern soldiers to regroup. In a counterattack, the Confederate line broke, and they fled south. Two future U.S. presidents, Rutherford B. Hayes and William McKinley, fought in the battle along with George Armstrong Custer. A museum, a Visitor's Center, a self-guided tour, and two battlefield monuments provide information on the battle. Each October, Cedar Creek Battlefield Foundation hosts a reenactment on the 158-acre site.

Cedar Creek Battlefield

"I again repeat that I am not responsible for this, and I say it with the earnestness of a general who feels in his heart the loss of every brave man who has been needlessly sacrificed today."

Maj. Gen. G. B. McClellan

NORTHERN COMMANDER:
Maj. Gen. G. B. McClellan

STRENGTH: 91,200

CASUALTIES: 16,000

SEVEN DAYS' BATTLES

June 25–July 1, 1862

Seven hard days of bloody battles saved the Confederate capital at Richmond from capture by the Union.

In May 1862, Federal forces were only seven miles from the Confederate White House in Richmond. Union commander, Major General George B. McClellan, was cautious and did not attack immediately. Instead, he waited for reinforcements. While McClellan waited, the recently appointed commander of the Confederate Army of Virginia, General Robert E. Lee, worked to fortify Richmond. Eventually, the Union initiated the Battle at Oak Grove on June 25.

This small battle commenced a week of fighting which would be known collectively as the Seven Days' Campaign.

Watt House, Gaines' Mill site, Richmond National Battlefield Park

*Union cannon overlooks battlefield from Malvern Hill,
Richmond National Battlefield Park*

*"Yes, he will get away
because I cannot have my
orders carried out."*

Gen. R. E. Lee
about McClellan's retreat

Particularly fierce fighting took place at Gaines' Mill. Here, McClellan's troops under General Porter were entrenched along the Beaver Dam Creek with military bridges linking them to the main force. To attack, the Confederates charged across a cultivated field, down wooded slopes, and through Boatswain's Creek. Fighting that day was fierce, including hand-to-hand combat before the Confederates fell back for the evening. The second day saw what may have been the heaviest fighting of the war. Lee ordered an all-out assault, asking General Hood if he could break through Union lines. Hood succeeded with such force that a general Northern retreat ensued.

The seven days of fighting ceased at Malvern Hill on July 1. Confederate reconnaissance saw that the Malvern Hill plateau was suitable to mass its artillery against Union forces. This, combined with cannon on the left, would catch the Union in a deadly crossfire. Confederate artillery, however, could not get into position due to the wooded and swampy area and heavy Union fire. Lee began to look for another plan of attack but failed to notify his commanders of changes. Throughout the day, the Union prevented the Confederacy from serious assault. The next day, the Northern Army of the Potomac withdrew, relieving the Confederacy of any immediate threat to its capital, but at an extremely high price to the South. Lee lost one-fourth of his men, and the Confederate capital was again put out of the Union's reach. It would be three years before the Union got as close to Richmond.

**SOUTHERN
COMMANDER:**
Gen. R. E. Lee

STRENGTH: 95,500

CASUALTIES: 21,000

RICHMOND NATIONAL BATTLEFIELD PARK

3215 East Broad Street, Richmond, VA

PHONE: 804-226-1981

HOURS: Open daily; closed Thanksgiving, Christmas, and New Year's Day.

ADMISSION: Free.

Approximately 800 acres of Richmond National Battlefield Park are divided into ten units: Chickahominy Bluff, Beaver Dam Creek; Gaines' Mill (Watt House); Glendale (Frayser's Farm) where Union forces warded off Confederate forces; Malvern Hill, Drewry's Bluff, Cold Harbor, Garthright House, Fort Harrison, and Parker's Battery. A Visitor's Center sits on Chimborazo Hill, the site of a Confederate hospital, and offers orientation of the total park. An eighty-mile self-guided auto tour follows the Seven Days' Battles in chronological order. Audio tapes which narrate the tour are available to purchase.

CHICKAHOMINY BLUFF

Chickahominy Bluff was a part of the outer Confederate line that formed Richmond's defense. Here, overlooking Mechanicsville and the Chickahominy River Valley, General Robert E. Lee watched the beginning of the Seven Days' Battles. The original earthworks are still intact.

BEAVER DAM CREEK

Ellerson's Mill, in the valley of Beaver Dam Creek, marks the point at which Lee's attack was stopped. The Confederates attacked the three-mile-long Union front here, but few Confederates crossed the stream due to heavy Union artillery and infantry fire.

COLD HARBOR

On May 31, 1864, Grant continued his incessant march toward Richmond, consistently driving around Lee's right to ensure that his army was resupplied from the tidal rivers; the next key was at the crossroads of Cold Harbor. The Southern cavalry reached Cold Harbor first, but General Phil Sheridan and the Union troops drove them out. Confederate General Anderson then advanced against Cold Harbor with two divisions. Sheridan, upon hearing this news, withdrew but returned under General Meade's order to hold the intersection at all costs, and Union forces retook it.

Although Cold Harbor was secured for the Union, Grant felt it necessary to attack again two days later, in an attempt to force Lee to retreat across the Chickahominy River. Nothing went well on June 3, to the extent that Grant "always regretted that the last assault at Cold Harbor was ever made." Lee was able to stave off the Union attacks and drive them into a stalemate until Grant requested a truce on June 7. Although the Union advanced deeper into Virginia through another route that led to Petersburg, it was at a tremendous loss of life, half of which occurred that third day.

Cold Harbor is a unit of the Richmond National Battlefield Park. There are 149 acres remaining of the battlefield. There is a mile-long walking trail through trenches with explanatory stops to detail the fighting. Another walking trail winds through the Union lines nearby. Cold Harbor National Cemetery is close, as is the cavalry battlefield at Trevilian Station.

Forest and Confederate Breastworks, Cold Harbor, Richmond National Battlefield Park

GARTHRIGHT HOUSE

The Garthright House was built in the early 1700s and served as a Union field hospital during the Battle of Cold Harbor. The house is restored but not open to the public; it can be viewed from the outside.

GAINES' MILL (WATT HOUSE)

Gaines' Mill was the site of extremely heavy fighting. During the summer of 1862, Lee ordered an all-out assault in an attempt to force the Union army back from Richmond. Hood found a gap in the Union line and penetrated with such force that a Union retreat ensued. The restored Watt House, built in 1835, was used as Union General Fitz-John Porter's headquarters. A walking trail connects the home with the site where Texas and Georgia troops broke through the line and hastened Union withdrawal.

Photo right: Watt House at Gaines' Mill

DREWRY'S BLUFF

Northern troops referred to Drewry's Bluff as Fort Darling. The bluff was the guardian of the James River and prevented the capture of Richmond by water. Five Federal vessels attacked the bluff, including the ironclad *Monitor*, but all were driven off. During the Civil War, this area served as the Confederate Naval Academy and Marine Corps Camp of Instruction. A self-guided trail gives details of the bluff's rich history.

Across the river from Fort Darling is Fort Brady, constructed by Union forces after the Battle of Fort Harrison. Fort Brady was built to anchor the Federal line from Fort Harrison. An overlook at the fort affords a panoramic view of the James River.

FORT HARRISON

Union soldiers captured Fort Harrison on September 29. After Cold Harbor, Grant, who had been deterred from capturing Richmond, crossed the James

Boatswain's Creek, Gaines' Mill, Richmond National Battlefield Park

River and began a push against Petersburg. Union forces occupied and enlarged the fort, forcing a realignment of Richmond defenses. Several regiments of African-American Union troops were recognized on September 29, 1864, for gallantry, and fourteen received Congressional Medals of Honor.

A self-guided trail through Fort Harrison uses exhibits and plaques to provide details of the battle and the fort. In addition to Fort Harrison, the following sites—Battery Alexander, Forts Gilmer, Gregg, Johnson, and Hoke—contain remnants of Confederate defense works connected by miles of breastworks. Union soldiers are buried in Fort Harrison's national cemetery.

MALVERN HILL

On July 1, 1862, the last battle of the Seven Days' Battles took place at Malvern Hill. The Union army positioned itself between the steep slope of Malvern Hill and the swamp bottoms. The attacking Confederates were forced to advance across open ground. The Northern Army of the Potomac did not dig trenches but, instead, stood in parade-ground, line-of-battle formation across the gently sloping fields. Their artillery and infantry fire shattered the ranks of attacking Southerners. One Confederate officer later remarked, "It was not war—it was murder." A short self-guided tour is available.

GLENDALE (FRAYSER'S FARM)

On June 30, Union troops protected the crossroads at Glendale while McClellan's retreating army pushed south toward Malvern Hill. Throughout the afternoon, Confederates repeatedly assaulted Glendale but failed to take it.

PARKER'S BATTERY

Parker's Battery, a Confederate artillery works, was part of the defense of Richmond until the capital was abandoned in April 1865.

THE MUSEUM OF THE CONFEDERACY AND WHITE HOUSE

1201 East Clay Street, Richmond, VA

PHONE: 804-649-1861

HOURS: Open daily.

ADMISSION: A fee is charged.

The Confederate White House was home to Jefferson Davis and his family while he was President of the Confederate States of America. The museum's three levels of galleries feature period furnishings, including pieces of furniture which belonged to the Davis family. The Museum of the Confederacy contains over 500 flags, Lee's Appomattox sword, and a large collection of Lee's personal belongings. Self-guided tours are available.

South Patio, The Museum and White House of the Confederacy

Center Parlor, The Museum and White House of the Confederacy

THE VIRGINIA HISTORICAL SOCIETY

428 North Boulevard, Richmond, VA
PHONE: 804-358-4901
HOURS: Open daily; closed major holidays.
ADMISSION: A fee is charged; children and seniors are discounted. Members are free.

The Virginia Historical Society building houses the murals *The Four Seasons of the Confederacy* and *The Story of Virginia.* The society's permanent collection contains many Civil War exhibits and features an impressive collection of Civil War artifacts, including General Lee's uniform and an extensive collection of Confederate-made weapons.

The Virginia Historical Society

HOLLYWOOD CEMETERY

412 South Cherry Street, Richmond, VA
PHONE: 804-648-8501
HOURS: Open daily, office open weekdays; closed major holidays.
ADMISSION: Free; a charge for brochure.

Hollywood Cemetery opened in the summer of 1849. Each day of the Civil War, bodies arrived from 10:00 A.M. until noon for burial. Confederate soldiers were buried free of charge until the spring of 1862. As casualties mounted, however, the cemetery began charging one dollar to bury each soldier. Because of Northern blockades during the war, marble could not be obtained for headstones, and wooden markers were used. An estimated 14,000 Confederate soldiers are buried here in a Confederate soldiers' section marked by a pyramid dedicated to the women of the Confederacy who were prevented from being buried with their husbands and were interred elsewhere on the grounds. Other Confederates buried on the grounds include Generals George Pickett, J. E. B. Stuart, and Confederate President Jefferson Davis and his family. A bronze statue stands in memory of Davis, and a marble angel for Winnie, his daughter. Presidents James Monroe and John Tyler are also interred here.

VALENTINE MUSEUM

1015 East Clay Street, Richmond, VA
PHONE: 804-649-0711
HOURS: Open daily.
ADMISSION: A fee is charged.

The Valentine Museum is dedicated to the life and history of the city of Richmond and includes artifacts from the Civil War era, as well as busts of many Confederate leaders. The museum's park is located on the site of Tredegar Ironworks. Half of all Confederate cannon were produced at this site.

Valentine Museum

BELLE ISLE

An island in the James River, Richmond, VA
PHONE: Not Available.
HOURS: Open daily.
ADMISSION: Free.

Belle Isle is located in the James River and was the site of the Belle Isle prison camp for Union soldiers. A pedestrian bridge off Tredegar Street leads to what is now a city park.

NORTHERN COMMANDER:
Lt. J. L. Worden

STRENGTH: 7000

CASUALTIES: 178

THE BATTLE OF HAMPTON ROADS

March 8–9, 1862

The first use of ironclad ships in battle.

At the beginning of the war, the South had naval personnel but no ships. The first logical step was to capture the Norfolk, Virginia, Naval Yard, a strategic port with all the resources to maintain a fleet. Following the attack on Fort Sumter in April, the Union chose not to risk valuable resources in protecting Norfolk. On April 20, 1861, Union troops set fire to the Norfolk Naval Yard. Northern forces left too early, however, and the Confederates hurried in, saved the dry dock, most of the important facilities, and the USS *Merrimac*. Although the ship had been burned to the water line, her hull and engines were only slightly damaged. She was hoisted up, repaired, and given the new name: CSS *Virginia*.

Now converted to the first armor-plated, cannon-mounted ship, the *Virginia* took its shakedown cruise to Hampton Roads, Virginia. There, the Union had instituted a blockade consisting of the sailing frigate *Congress,* the sailing sloop *Cumberland,* and the steam frigates *Minnesota* and *Roanoke*. The *Virginia* rammed the *Cumberland* below her waterline, sinking the Union sloop but tearing off the *Virginia*'s ram. The *Virginia* turned to the *Congress,* which had run aground in shoal water, and brought all its firepower on the helpless ship. Within an hour, the *Congress,* struck her colors, but when Confederate boarding parties approached, Union batteries fired upon them. Angered, Captain Franklin Buchanan ordered hot shot to be poured into the Union ship, setting it aflame. The *Virginia* then left the burning *Congress* and the other disabled ships for the next day.

When battle resumed the following morning, the *Virginia* encountered "the strangest looking craft we had ever seen before . . . an immense shingle floating in the water with a gigantic cheese box rising from its center; no sails, no wheels, no smokestack, no guns." This was the *Monitor*, the Union's answer to the Confederate ironclad. Its "cheesebox" was, in actuality, a revolving turret in which two cannon were mounted. The

The Monitor *and the* Merrimac

"It is my intention . . . to appear before the enemy off Newport News at daylight on Friday next. . . . My object is first to destroy the frigates Congress *and* Cumberland, *if possible, and then turn my attention to the destruction of the battery on shore and the gunboats."*

Cpt. F. Buchanan
(pictured above)
to Lt. J. R. Tucker

barely seaworthy craft arrived at the entrance of the Chesapeake Bay on the evening of March 8. It took its position next to the disabled *Minnesota* and waited until morning.

On March 9, the *Virginia* began firing on the *Minnesota*, ignoring the shots from the *Monitor* for the first part of the morning. When the *Virginia* began exchanging shots with the *Monitor* they were from fifty to 100 yards apart, sometimes close enough to scrape each other. Although the *Monitor* was more maneuverable, the *Virginia* could reload and fire faster. Neither vessel was seriously damaged after four hours of firing, at which time the *Virginia* broke off the combat and headed for Norfolk; the Battle of Hampton Roads was a draw. By its presence, the *Virginia* was able to prevent Union forces from using the James River for an offensive move into Richmond that spring.

Ironically, when Norfolk was abandoned in May 1862, the *Virginia* ran aground and was destroyed by her crew. The *Monitor* was lost in a storm off Cape Hatteras at the end of 1862 as she was being towed to waters off Charleston. The Battle of Hampton Roads ushered in a new type of naval warfare, one which the Union, with its resources, would dominate.

SOUTHERN COMMANDERS:
Cpt. F. Buchanan
Lt. C. Jones

STRENGTH: 600

CASUALTIES: 27

FORT BOYKIN HISTORIC PARK

7410 Fort Boykin Trail, Smithfield, VA
PHONE: 757-357-2291 (County Parks and Recreation)
HOURS: Open daily.
ADMISSION: Free.

Fort Boykin is located near the mouth of the James River and was initially constructed in 1623 to protect English settlers from the Spaniards. During the Revolutionary War, the colonists refortified the fort and used it again in 1812. At the start of the Civil War, the Confederates reinforced Fort Boykin to protect Richmond. In

Fort Boykin Historic Park

May 1862, Union gunboats sailed up the James River, fired upon Fort Boykin, and forced the Confederates to retreat. A walking trail includes remainders of Civil War gun salients and magazines. Confederate artifacts were excavated from a well and are on display in the park's museum.

 # HAMPTON ROADS NAVAL MUSEUM

1 Waterside Drive, Norfolk, VA
PHONE: 757-322-2987
HOURS: Open daily; closed major holidays.
ADMISSION: Free.

Naval exhibit, Hampton Roads Naval Museum

This specialized naval history museum displays material on the battle of the ironclads at Hampton Roads, as well as other Civil War actions. An exhibit, which includes models of the *Monitor* and the *Merrimac,* help interpret the Battle of Hampton Roads. Some uniforms are also on display.

THE CASEMATE MUSEUM

Bernard Road, Fort Monroe, Hampton, VA
PHONE: 757-727-3391
HOURS: Open daily; closed Thanksgiving, Christmas, and New Year's Day.
ADMISSION: Free.

Fort Monroe was built between 1819 and 1834 to protect Hampton Roads, the entrance to Chesapeake Bay, and Washington, D.C. Ironically, when Robert E. Lee was in the Corps of Army Engineers, he helped complete the fort's construction. The fort was held by the Union throughout the war and served as the beginning point for the Union Peninsula Campaign. The fort currently serves as the headquarters for the United States Army Training and Doctrine Command.

The Casemate Museum

Located on the grounds of Fort Monroe and surrounded by a moat, The Casemate Museum's exhibits include the cell where Confederate President Jefferson Davis was incarcerated, weapons, uniforms, coastal artillery models, and drawings of Fort Monroe at the time of the Civil War. A self-guided walking tour of Fort Monroe is available.

THE MARINERS' MUSEUM

100 Museum Drive, Newport News, VA
PHONE: 757-596-2222
HOURS: Open daily; closed Thanksgiving and Christmas.
ADMISSION: A fee is charged; students are discounted and children under 5 are free.

The Mariners' Museum protects the *Monitor* shipwreck sanctuary located off the coast of Cape Hatteras, North Carolina, and serves as the official repository for artifacts recovered from the Union's ironclad. Part of the museum is dedicated to the clash of the ironclads, and items on display include the *Monitor*'s anchor, lanterns, mustard jars, and, a recent find, the propeller. A new exhibit features a reconstruction of the *Monitor*'s turret and the "Geer Letters," a display of letters written by a crew member of the *Monitor* to his wife.

Crabtree Collection of Miniature Ships, The Mariners' Museum

Virginia War Museum

9285 Warwick Boulevard, Huntington Park, Newport News, VA

PHONE: 757-247-8523

HOURS: Open daily; closed Thanksgiving, Christmas, and New Year's Day.

ADMISSION: A fee is charged; children and seniors are discounted.

The Virginia War Museum contains artifacts from all of America's wars. Civil War exhibits include items from the Peninsula Campaign, handguns, uniforms, and a flag from the Confederate raider, the CSS *Florida*, which was captured, held at Newport News Point, and then scuttled by Union forces.

Lee Hall Mansion

163 Yorktown Road, Newport News, VA

PHONE: 757-888-3371

HOURS: Open daily; closed major holidays.

ADMISSION: A fee is charged; children and seniors are discounted.

Lee Hall Mansion was built by Richard D. Lee (no relation to Robert E. Lee), who was a wealthy planter in the area. During the war, the mansion was used as a Confederate headquarters by Generals Magruder and Johnston. The original earthworks which surrounded the house are visible. The house features a Peninsula Campaign exhibit and rooms decorated with period furnishings.

Lee Hall Mansion

ENDVIEW PLANTATION

362 Yorktown Road, Newport News, VA

PHONE: 757-887-1862

HOURS: Restoration completion tentatively scheduled for April 1, 2000.

ADMISSION: Free.

Built in 1760, Endview Plantation served as a hospital for both Union and Confederate forces during the 1862 Peninsula Campaign. The plantation hosts several events of Civil War interest throughout the year. During the summer, children learn about the war during four-day Civil War camps. In December, reenactments of Christmas in the field are held on the property. In April the house is the site of a reenactment of the Peninsula Campaign.

A Living History Museum which focuses on the events of 1862 and a complete restoration of the house are scheduled to be completed by the spring of 2000.

BERKELEY PLANTATION

12602 Harrison Landing Road, Charles City, VA

PHONE: 804-829-6018

HOURS: Open daily; closed Christmas.

ADMISSION: A fee is charged.

Berkeley Plantation was the final stop of McClellan's Union Peninsula Campaign and served as the general's 1862 headquarters and as a base for 140,000 soldiers. President Lincoln visited

Berkeley Plantation

Berkeley on two occasions during McClellan's encampment. In 1862 Gen. Daniel Butterfield composed "Taps," the now-familiar retreat played at every military funeral. Civil War artifacts are on display in the main house.

PORTSMOUTH NAVAL SHIPYARD MUSEUM

2 High Street, Portsmouth, VA
PHONE: 757-393-8591
HOURS: Open daily June–September, closed Monday November–May.
ADMISSION: A fee is charged.

The Portsmouth Naval Shipyard Museum includes Civil War weapons, uniforms, swords, medals, manuscripts, and documents. The museum also contains an exhibit on the Gosport Navy Yard, the forerunner of the Norfolk Naval Shipyard. Gosport was one of the major Confederate shipyards during the Civil War. The museum also displays a gun carriage from the CSS *Virginia* and a model of the ironclad.

STRATFORD HALL PLANTATION

Virginia Highway 214, Stratford, VA
PHONE: 804-493-8038; 804-493-8371 weekends and holidays
HOURS: Open daily.
ADMISSION: A fee is charged.

Built in the late 1730s by Thomas Lee, Stratford Hall Plantation is the birthplace of General Robert E. Lee. The home features many eighteenth-century furnishings of American and British design. Several of the property's outbuildings have been restored, including a workshop, a coach house, the stables, the slave quarters, and a burial vault. Gardens flanking the home have also been restored to their original splendor.

A Visitor's Center provides information concerning the plantation's history and the Lee family. Guided tours are available. Gifts, including fruitcakes, plum puddings, and cookies are on sale at the plantation store, and visitors can eat lunch in the Plantation Dining Room.

Chamber where Robert E. Lee was born (his crib is near the window), Stratford Hall Plantation

Great House, circa 1738, Stratford Hall Plantation

ISLE OF WIGHT MUSEUM

103 Main Street, Smithfield, VA
PHONE: 757-357-7459
HOURS: Open daily, closed Monday.
ADMISSION: Free.

The Isle of Wight Museum houses Indian artifacts, Civil War relics, and fossils from the James River. One of the museum's main attractions is the Golden Eagle from the Union gunboat, *Smith Briggs*. Confederate Captain Joseph Norsworthy removed the eagle as a trophy when the crew of the *Smith Briggs* surrendered in the Battle of Smithfield.

Golden Eagle from the Smith Briggs, *Isle of Wight Museum*

NORTHERN COMMANDERS:
Lt. Gen. U. S. Grant
Maj. Gen. G. B. Meade

STRENGTH: 109,000

CASUALTIES: 12,000

THE BATTLE AND SIEGE OF PETERSBURG

June 15, 1864–April 1, 1865

The fall of Petersburg came only days before the surrender of the Confederate capital at Richmond and the end of the Civil War at Appomattox Court House.

Petersburg, located on the south bank of the Appomattox River, was a major Virginia shipping port. The Richmond and Petersburg Railroad funneled all major railroad lines into the city. Control of Petersburg was essential to a Union capture of Richmond.

Lieutenant General Ulysses S. Grant began his campaign to capture Petersburg in June 1864. General Robert E. Lee was aware of Grant's intentions and set up a horseshoe defense around Petersburg with its ends on the Appomattox River. When Grant attacked, his Eighteenth Corps captured a section of the Confederate line but did not press their success. The Confederates then built a new line, which could not be directly assaulted; thus Grant planned a siege of Petersburg.

Six major battles and numerous engagements, skirmishes, and assaults marked the siege. Throughout the summer and fall, Grant continued to hammer away at Lee, who had his

Battle of Fort Stedman, Petersburg National Battlefield

The Dictator, Petersburg National Battlefield

59,000 men spread over a thirty-five-mile line. Grant finally gained control over the rails and forced Lee to supply his men by wagons. When winter set in, the men created log cities to protect themselves from the sleet and snow.

On March 25, 1865, Confederate forces stormed Fort Stedman on the north flank but were driven back with 5,000 casualties. On March 29, Grant ordered an all-out attack. After five days of fighting, Lee evacuated Petersburg on the evening of April 2, and by three o'clock on the morning of April 3, Grant occupied Petersburg.

Like Petersburg, Richmond was also evacuated and formally surrendered on April 3, 1865. The Confederate capital was in Union hands, and the Civil War was within days of its end.

The Crater, Petersburg National Battlefield

"We must stop this army of Grant's before he gets to the James River. If he gets there it will become a siege, and then it will be a mere matter of time."

Gen. R. E. Lee

SOUTHERN COMMANDER:
Gen. R. E. Lee

STRENGTH: 45,000

CASUALTIES: 7,600

PETERSBURG NATIONAL BATTLEFIELD

Virginia Highway 36, next to Fort Lee, Petersburg, VA

PHONE: 804-732-3531

HOURS: Open daily; closed Christmas and New Year's Day.

ADMISSION: A fee is charged.

Petersburg National Battlefield contains 2,460 acres of the original battle and siege area, including City Point, Five Forks, the battlefield itself, the siege line, and Poplar Grove National Cemetery. Information on a four-mile battlefield tour, a sixteen-mile siege-line tour, a driving tour and short walking tours which include wayside

Five Forks Battlefield

exhibits and audio stations are available at the Visitor's Center. Points along the driving tour include Battery 8, captured by U.S. African-American troops and renamed Fort Friend; Battery 9, which U.S. African-American troops captured during the first day of fighting; Harrison Creek; Fort Stedman, the focus of Lee's attack on March 25, 1865; Fort Haskell, where Union artillery and infantry fire stopped the Confederate southward advance during the Battle of Fort Stedman; Taylor Farm; and The Crater, which marks the site where a Union mine exploded beneath a Confederate fort. During this episode, the Forty-eighth Pennsylvania Infantry, many of whom were coal miners before the war, dug a tunnel toward a Confederate fort. The explosion destroyed the artillery battery and left a crater about 170 feet long, sixty feet wide, and thirty feet deep. Union troops, instead of going around the crater, plunged directly into it and were unable to go any further. Confederate counterattacks retook the position, inflicting more than 4,000 Federal casualties. As part of the Interpretative History Program, artillery demonstrations occur during the summers.

A roster of the soldiers interred at Poplar Grove is at the Visitor's Center. Of the 6,178 Union soldiers buried at Poplar Grove, only 2,139 are identified.

PETERSBURG VISITOR'S CENTER

425 Cockade, Petersburg, VA

PHONE: 804-733-2400

HOURS: Open daily; closed Christmas.

ADMISSION: Free.

Petersburg's ten-month siege was the longest siege of any American city, and much of historic Petersburg is devoted to this period. The Visitor's Center offers information on walking tours of historic Petersburg along with maps that detail the Civil War Trail, an eighty-mile driving tour that follows the 1864–1865 overland campaign of Lee and Grant.

PAMPLIN HISTORICAL PARK AND THE NATIONAL MUSEUM OF THE CIVIL WAR SOLDIER

6125 Boydton Plank Road, Petersburg, VA
PHONE: 804-861-2408
HOURS: Open daily year round.
ADMISSION: A fee is charged; children and seniors are discounted.

Pamplin Historical Park's two miles of walking trails feature reconstructed soldier huts, original picket posts, well-preserved earthworks, and artillery emplacements. A reconstructed military encampment contains costumed soldiers drilling, cooking, and performing general camp duties. A renovated and refurbished 1812 plantation home, Tudor Hall, is also on the trail. Costumed guides greet visitors at the entrance to the museum. The museum's collection focuses on the life of an ordinary Civil War soldier, and exhibits range from a chaplain's sermon at a camp revival to a wounded and imprisoned soldier.

The National Museum of the Civil War Soldier, Pamplin Historical Park

SIEGE MUSEUM

15 West Bank Street, Petersburg, VA
PHONE: 804-733-2400
HOURS: Open daily; closed major holidays.
ADMISSION: A fee is charged.

Exhibits at the Siege Museum interpret the affects of the siege on the people of Petersburg. During the ten-month siege, supplies were scarce, and a chicken could sell for as much as fifty dollars. The museum's displays interpret life in Petersburg before, during, and immediately after the siege.

Siege Museum

BLANDFORD CHURCH

319 South Crater Road, Petersburg, VA
PHONE: 804-733-2396
HOURS: Open daily; closed Thanksgiving, Christmas, and New Year's Day.
ADMISSION: A fee is charged.

Blandford Church was built in 1735 but was abandoned after the Civil War. In 1901 a local woman's group restored the church and commissioned a series of stained glass windows to commemorate Southern soldiers who died in the Civil War. Each of the fifteen former Confederate states contributed money to purchase a stained glass window crafted by Louis Comfort Tiffany and dedicated to their state's dead. Approximately 30,000 Confederate soldiers are buried on the grounds, although only 2,200 are identified.

Photo right: Blandford Church

CITY POINT UNIT

Far end of Cedar Lane and Pecan Avenue, Hopewell, VA
PHONE: 804-458-9504
HOURS: Open daily; closed Christmas and New Year's Day.
ADMISSION: A fee is charged.

The City Point Unit is a part of the Petersburg National Battlefield and features Appomattox Manor. The home originally belonged to the Epps family, but during the war it served as General Grant's headquarters from June 1864 to April 1865. An orientation film and guided tours of Appomattox Manor are available.

Appomattox Manor, City Point Unit

WESTON MANOR

400 Weston Lane at the corner of 21st Avenue, Hopewell, VA

PHONE: 804-458-4682

HOURS: Open daily April–October.

ADMISSION: A fee is charged.

Built in 1789, Weston Manor briefly served as Union Gen. Philip Sheridan's headquarters during the final siege of Petersburg. During the Civil War, twelve-year-old Emma Wood lived there with her family. Later, at the age of seventy-five, Wood wrote her memoirs. The home features these experiences in period furnishings, and a guided tour is available.

Weston Manor

CITY POINT NATIONAL CEMETERY

15th Avenue N, City Point, VA

PHONE: 804-795-2055

HOURS: Open daily.

ADMISSION: Free.

More than 5,100 Civil War Union and Confederate soldiers are buried at the City Point National Cemetery. The interred Federal soldiers include more than 1,000 African-Americans.

STAUNTON RIVER BATTLEFIELD STATE PARK

1035 Fort Hill Trail, Randolph, VA

PHONE: 804-454-4312

HOURS: Open daily May–October; open Wednesday–Sunday November–May; closed mid-December–mid-February.

ADMISSION: Free.

One of the many minor engagements in the Siege of Petersburg, the Staunton River Battle occurred on June 25, 1864, when 492 old men and young boys from Southside, Virginia, joined fewer than 300 Confederate soldiers against 5,000 Union cavalry for control of the Staunton River railroad bridge. Although the Union wreaked havoc, they could not destroy the Staunton River Bridge. The bridge was burned during General Lee's retreat to Appomattox Court House but was rebuilt by the railroad within weeks of the end of the war. The current steel bridge was constructed in 1902 on the original stone piers. The park offers a walking tour of the battlefield, which includes remnants of earthworks, an earthen fort, and the rebuilt bridge. The Visitor's Center features exhibits and brochures on the history of the bridge and the battle.

"*General Sheridan says, 'If the thing is pressed I think that Lee will surrender . . . ,* 'Let the thing be pressed.'"

Pres. A. Lincoln to Gen. U. S. Grant, April 7, 1865

NORTHERN COMMANDER:
Gen. U. S. Grant

STRENGTH: 63,285

CASUALTIES: 164

THE SURRENDER AT APPOMATTOX COURT HOUSE

April 9, 1865

This was last Civil War battle in the east and the site of General Robert E. Lee's surrender.

After the battle of Sailor's Creek, General Robert E. Lee split his Army of Northern Virginia into two parts and headed to North Carolina to meet with General Johnston's army. The Union pursued and captured 8,000 Confederates, including most of Ewell's Corps and Anderson's Corps. Lee pushed on. Tired and low on rations, he and his men rested around Appomattox Court House, where they hoped to find the supplies Lee left at Farmville after the Battle of Sailor's Creek.

Lee soon found himself surrounded by Union forces in the west, south, and east. On April 7, General Ulysses S. Grant sent Lee a note suggesting surrender. Lee declined but asked about the terms. Grant replied on April 8 that the Confederates should give up their arms never to fight again and go home. Lee asked to meet and talk, but Grant said he would only meet if it were to discuss surrender. The last message of Grant's did not reach Lee until the morning of April 9. In the meantime,

Appomattox Courthouse, Appomattox Court House National Historic Park

Lee's Surrender to Grant, *Artist Unknown*

"There is nothing for me to do but go and see General Grant. I would rather die a thousand deaths."

Gen. R. E. Lee

Lee met with his commanders to discuss options. Lee agreed to advance his cavalry to the front, attack, and possibly break through Union General Sheridan's line in the west. When the Confederates attacked, Sheridan pulled back, not out of weakness, but to allow Gibbon's infantry to join. Lee was forced to withdraw and called off the engagement.

Just after noon on April 9, Grant met Lee at the home of Wilmer McLean. (Ironically, McLeans' former home was located on the battlefield at Manassas. After the battle, he moved to Appomattox Court House to get away from the war.) At the McLeans' house, Grant proposed the same terms as in his message and, at Lee's request, added that the Southerners could take their horses with them. Grant also authorized rations for Lee's men. The formal surrender ceremony was held April 12, 1865. Brigadier General Joshua Chamberlain, famous from Gettysburg, was given the honor of receiving Lee's surrender.

Only 22,000 Confederates were there to lay down their arms and furl their flags for the last time. Chamberlain formed his troops on either side of the road and saluted their enemies, who were once again their countrymen. Confederate General Gordon ordered his men to return the salute.

Although it would be another four months before all fighting ceased, Lee's surrender to Grant at Appomattox Court House symbolically ended the war.

SOUTHERN COMMANDER:
Gen. R. E. Lee

STRENGTH: 31,900

CASUALTIES: 500

APPOMATTOX COURT HOUSE NATIONAL HISTORIC PARK

Virginia Highway 24, Appomattox, VA

PHONE: 804-352-8987

HOURS: Open daily; closed Thanksgiving, Christmas, and New Year's Day.

ADMISSION: A fee is charged.

Over twenty buildings in the Appomattox Court House Village have been restored to their 1865 appearance. This national historic site commemorates General Robert E. Lee's surrender to General Ulysses S. Grant. Not all the buildings are open to the public, but those open include the Appomattox County Court-

Parlor of McLean House, Appomattox Court House National Historic Park

house, the McLean House where the surrender terms were written, and Lee's and Grant's head-

McLean House, Appomattox Court House National Historic Park

quarters. Orientation videos, maps, and self-guided walking tours of the village are available at the Visitor's Center. During the summer, costumed interpreters conduct tours. A small Confederate cemetery is also located inside the park.

OLD CITY CEMETERY

401 Taylor Street, Lynchburg, VA
PHONE: 804-847-1465
HOURS: Open daily; office open Monday–Friday.
ADMISSION: Free.

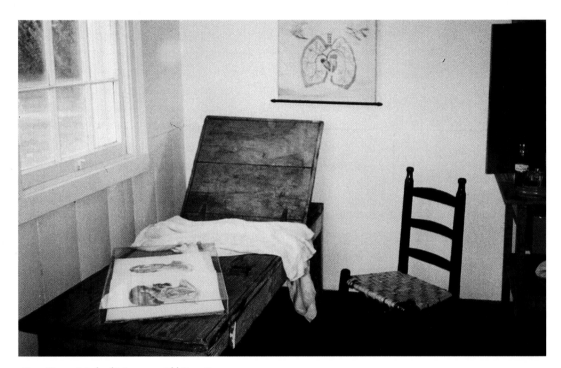

Pest House Medical Museum, Old City Cemetery

The Old City Cemetery contains the cemetery, the Pest House Medical Museum, a Potter's Field, and the site of the Quartermaster's Glanders Stables. A greenstone arch marks the entrance to the Civil War section where over 2,200 soldiers from fourteen states are interred and provides the setting for the 125-year tradition of the Memorial Day service. Eleven slaves who worked in the hospital are buried in the Confederate section. Two African-American soldiers, one Confederate, and the other Union, also rest in the cemetery. Originally, the cemetery contained the remains of 187 Yankee prisoners. Although their bodies were moved in 1866, their names still appear on a commemorative plaque.

The Pest House Medical Museum, next to the Confederate Section, relives the time of the smallpox epidemic and Dr. John Jay Terrell's successful efforts to stop the deadly disease. A self-guided tour is available with recorded narratives. Inside, tours are available by appointment.

WASHINGTON, D.C.

During the Civil War, the nation's capital was surrounded by a series of sixty-eight forts and ninety-three batteries with 837 guns to protect it from the foreign nation across the Potomac River. Although only one skirmish took place near Fort Stevens, Washington, D.C., was forever changed by the Civil War. Even the Washington Monument, the 555-foot obelisk that has come to symbolize our country, was affected by the war. Begun in 1848, construction was halted by the Civil War. When construction resumed, builders used marble from a different quarry, resulting in a noticeable color difference.

Directly west of the monument is the Lincoln Memorial. Lincoln's Gettysburg Address and Second Inaugural Speech are carved into the walls surrounding Lincoln's statue. The Emancipation Proclamation rests in the National Archives, only a few blocks away. Lincoln's presence is also felt nightly at Ford's Theatre, the site of his assassination.

Also situated on the Mall, the city's symbolic center, is the Smithsonian Institution's National Museum of American History. Items ranging from military relics to Civil War-era life are housed in the massive collection. Nearby, the National Portrait Gallery contains a number of Mathew Brady's Civil War photographs. Brady documented the battles and their terrible aftermath in photographs. Brady's work can also be seen at the Library of Congress.

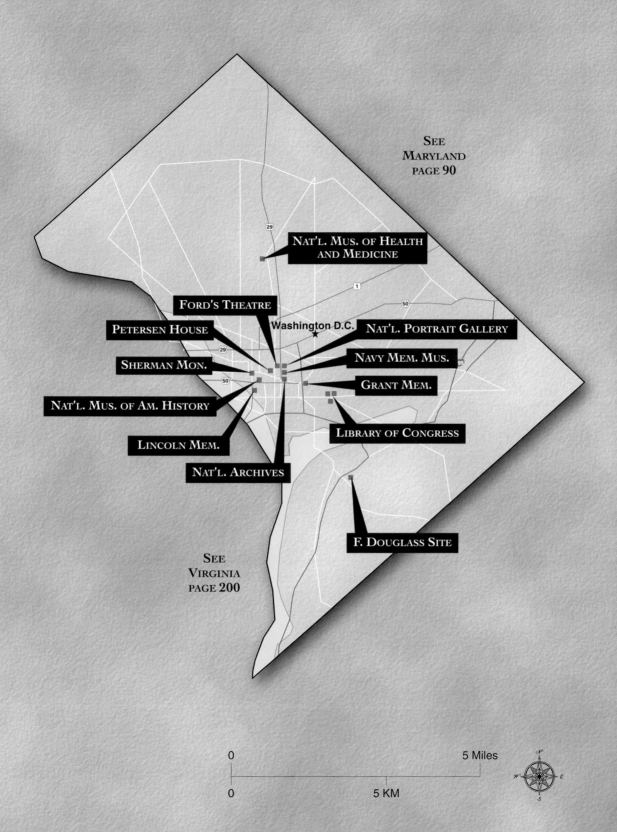

SEE
MARYLAND
PAGE 90

NAT'L. MUS. OF HEALTH
AND MEDICINE

FORD'S THEATRE

Washington D.C.

PETERSEN HOUSE

NAT'L. PORTRAIT GALLERY

SHERMAN MON.

NAVY MEM. MUS.

GRANT MEM.

NAT'L. MUS. OF AM. HISTORY

LIBRARY OF CONGRESS

LINCOLN MEM.

NAT'L. ARCHIVES

F. DOUGLASS SITE

SEE
VIRGINIA
PAGE 200

0   5 Miles

0   5 KM

N
W   E
S

NATIONAL MUSEUM OF HEALTH AND MEDICINE

In Walter Reed Army Medical Center, 6825 16th Street NW, Washington, DC
PHONE: 202-782-2200
HOURS: Open daily; closed Christmas.
ADMISSION: Free.

The National Museum of Health and Medicine contains a great deal of information pertaining to Civil War medical practices. Among the exhibits are many Mathew Brady photographs and a model of the *Captain January*, the first hospital on water. This boat was used to transport the injured from one side of the Mississippi River to the other side. A popular exhibit, entitled "The Bullet That Killed Lincoln," features the bullet fired at Ford's Theatre, casts of Lincoln's hands, and a description of the assassination. Another popular exhibit is a display of General Sickle's leg and the cannonball that blew the leg off. After its amputation, Sickle donated his leg to the U.S.; later he wanted the leg returned. He was told that it was now the property of the U.S. government. Until his death, Sickle made regular trips to visit his leg.

SHERMAN MONUMENT

Pennsylvania Avenue and 15th Street NE, Washington, DC
PHONE: Not Available.
HOURS: Not Available.
ADMISSION: Free.

Sherman Monument stands on the spot where, in 1865, General William T. Sherman reviewed his victorious army. The monument is located east of the White House and south of the Department of Treasury.

NATIONAL MUSEUM OF AMERICAN HISTORY

14th Street and Constitution Avenue NW, Washington, DC
PHONE: 202-357-2700
HOURS: Open daily; closed Thanksgiving, Christmas, and New Year's Day.
ADMISSION: Free.

The National Museum of American History is one of the museums of the Smithsonian Institute, and it houses permanent exhibits on Civil War weaponry, uniforms, and related relics. The flag of the Eighty-fourth Regiment U.S. Colored Infantry, which fought in many campaigns of the Civil War in Louisiana and Texas, is also on display. Included among the models of ironclads are the *Monitor* and the *Virginia*, better known as the *Merrimac*. Union Gen. Philip Sheridan's horse is also on display. Sheridan rode the horse, named Rienzi, to the town of Winchester in northwestern Virginia to turn a potential defeat for the Union forces into a victory. Rienzi was later renamed Winchester.

One of the main attractions of the museum is the 1814, fifteen-star, fifteen-stripe flag that inspired Francis Scott Key to write *The Star-Spangled Banner*.

LINCOLN MEMORIAL

23rd Street NE (west end of the Mall), Washington, DC
PHONE: Not Available.
HOURS: Open daily.
ADMISSION: Free.

The classical columns of the Lincoln Memorial anchor the eastern axis of the Mall. The white marble statue of Lincoln, designed and sculpted by Daniel Chester French, surveys the Reflecting Pool and, beyond it, the Washington Monument. On the walls, the words of Lincoln's Gettysburg Address and Lincoln's Second Inaugural Address serve as a constant reminder of the sixteenth president's place in national history. Ironically, the 1922 dedication ceremony, which was attended by Lincoln's son, Robert Todd, was segregated; African-Americans, including Booker T. Washington who gave a speech, watched from across the road. In 1963, Martin Luther King, Jr. chose the site to deliver his stirring "I Have a Dream" speech.

Lincoln Memorial

PETERSEN HOUSE

516 10th Street NW, Washington, DC
PHONE: 202-426-6830
HOURS: Open daily; closed Christmas.
ADMISSION: Free.

Across the street from Ford's Theatre National Historic Site is the house where Lincoln died. After the shooting, Lincoln was moved across the street to the Petersen boarding house. The bedroom where Lincoln died and the front parlor where Mrs. Lincoln sat through the night have been restored. Also on display is the back parlor in which Secretary of War Edwin Stanton interviewed witnesses to the assassination.

Petersen House

FORD'S THEATRE NATIONAL HISTORIC SITE

511 10th Street NW, Washington, DC
PHONE: 202-426-6924
HOURS: Open daily; closed Christmas.
ADMISSION: Free.

On April 14, 1865, John Wilkes Booth fatally shot President Abraham Lincoln at Ford's Theatre. The interior is now restored as closely as possible to the building's original appearance. The president's box looks as it did on the night of the assassination, although the pieces of furniture are reproductions. The murder weapon and other memorabilia are on exhibit in the Lincoln Museum located in the basement of the theatre.

Ford's Theatre National Historic Site

NATIONAL PORTRAIT GALLERY

8th and F Streets NW, Washington, DC
PHONE: 202-357-2700
HOURS: Open daily; closed Christmas.
ADMISSION: Free.

The National Portrait Gallery is a view of history as seen through the eyes of various portrait painters. This national museum contains portraits of many Civil War leaders including Lincoln, Grant, and other generals. Also on display in the Meserve Gallery is a large display of Mathew Brady's Civil War photographs.

NAVY MEMORIAL MUSEUM

901 M Street SE, Building 76, Washington Navy Yard, Washington, DC

PHONE: 202-433-4882

HOURS: Open daily; closed Thanksgiving, Christmas, and New Year's Day.

ADMISSION: Free.

The Navy Memorial Museum features various items that illustrate the long and varied history of the U.S. Navy. Of particular interest is a Civil War 100-pound cannon taken from the CSS *Atlanta* which was captured by the U.S. monitor *Weehawken*.

NATIONAL ARCHIVES

7th Street and Pennsylvania Avenue NW, Washington, DC

PHONE: 202-501-5400

HOURS: Open daily except Sunday; closed major holidays.

ADMISSION: Free.

The U.S. Constitution and Bill of Rights are on permanent display at the National Archives. The Emancipation Proclamation is housed here and is displayed in January to coincide with the Martin Luther King, Jr., holiday.

National Archives

GRANT MEMORIAL

East end of the Mall, Washington, DC
PHONE: Not Available.
HOURS: Open daily.
ADMISSION: Free.

At the time of the statue's dedication in 1922, the Grant Memorial was the largest cast sculpture in the United States. Today, it remains as the city's largest statue dedicated to a general. The 252-foot-long sculpture features a calm General Grant surveying seven charging horsemen and three horses hauling cannon through mud.

LIBRARY OF CONGRESS

101 Independence Avenue SE, Washington, DC
PHONE: 202-707-5000
HOURS: Open daily except Sunday; closed Christmas and New Year's Day.
ADMISSION: Free.

The Library of Congress holds over 1,200 Civil War photographs, most of which were made under the supervision of Mathew B. Brady. They include scenes of military personnel, preparations for battle, and the aftermath of battle. The collection also includes portraits

Main Reading Room, Library of Congress

Jefferson Building, Library of Congress

of both Confederate and Union generals. Guided tours, which include the Main Reading Room in the Jefferson Building, leave from the Madison Building.

FREDERICK DOUGLASS NATIONAL HISTORIC SITE

1411 W Street SE, Washington, DC
PHONE: 202-426-5961
HOURS: Open daily; closed major holidays.
ADMISSION: A fee is charged.

Born a slave, Frederick Douglass was one of the most ardent and eloquent speakers of abolition before and during the Civil War. Douglass purchased this, his final home of Cedar Hill, in 1877 and expanded the house from fourteen to twenty-one rooms. In addition, he purchased the adjoining land to expand its acreage. Ninety percent of the furnishings at Cedar Hill are original from Douglass's time, and the house contains many of Douglass's personal possessions. Tours are available and begin with a film at the Visitor's Center.

Douglass's Study, Frederick Douglass National Historic Site

Frederick Douglass National Historic Site

WEST VIRGINIA

At the beginning of the Civil War, both the South and the North began military operations to secure that region of Virginia which is now known as West Virginia. On May 14 , 1861, General George McClellan was assigned to command the Department of the Ohio which included the area of Western Virginia. McClellan's success in securing the area for the Union during the summer of 1861 led to his being named to command all of the Union armies.

During the remainder of the war, West Virginia saw fighting in its mountains and sent troops into battle under the banner of "The Army of West Virginia." The area was officially admitted as a state June 20, 1863, although the transfer of Berkley and Jefferson counties from Virginia to West Virginia was not recognized by Congress until March 10, 1866.

Today, West Virginia protects its rich Civil War heritage, through sites such as Harpers Ferry National Historical Park, where John Brown captured the city in 1859, and the Monongahela National Forest, which contains remnants of both Northern and Southern forts.

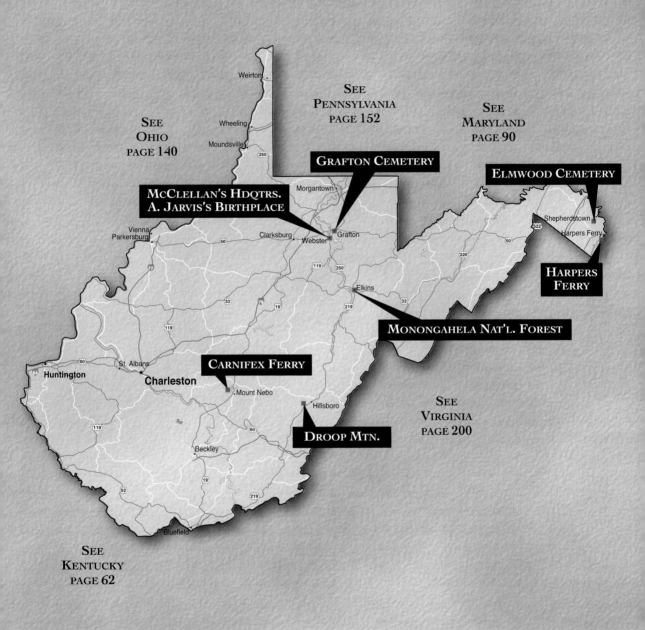

Weirton

SEE
PENNSYLVANIA
PAGE 152

SEE
MARYLAND
PAGE 90

SEE
OHIO
PAGE 140

Wheeling

Moundsville

250

GRAFTON CEMETERY

ELMWOOD CEMETERY

Morgantown

**McCLELLAN'S HDQTRS.
A. JARVIS'S BIRTHPLACE**

Shepherdstown

522

Harpers Ferry

Vienna
Parkersburg

50

Clarksburg

Webster

Grafton

50

**HARPERS
FERRY**

119

250

220

33

Elkins

219

33

MONONGAHELA NAT'L. FOREST

119

L

19

St. Albans

60

CARNIFEX FERRY

Huntington

Charleston

Mount Nebo

Hillsboro

SEE
VIRGINIA
PAGE 200

119

Toll

60

DROOP MTN.

Beckley

19

52

219

Bluefield

SEE
KENTUCKY
PAGE 62

0   100 Miles

0   100 KM

NORTHERN COMMANDERS:
Gen. H. W. Halleck
Col. D. S. Miles

STRENGTH: 14,000

CASUALTIES: 12,700

BATTLE OF HARPERS FERRY

September 13–15, 1862

Harpers Ferry changed hands eight times during the war. Its railroad junction, its arsenal, its armory, and its location on the border between North and South made this small town strategically important to both sides.

Harpers Ferry is probably best known as the site of abolitionist John Brown's raid on a Federal arsenal in 1859. Brown saw himself as a prophet and messenger of God whose purpose was to free the slaves. In 1855, he followed his sons to Kansas with a large load of weapons to aid in keeping Kansas free but in the process helped the state earn the title of "Bloody Kansas." While there, Brown and four of his sons deliberately murdered five men on the banks of the Pottawatamie.

On October 16, 1859, Brown and twenty-one men came to Harpers Ferry, seized the armory and railway bridge, and took possession of the town. In addition, Brown had control of 100,000 weapons from the arsenal. When asked why and on what authority he acted, Brown replied, "To free the slaves, and by the authority of God Almighty."

Local militia blocked Brown's escape, and a company of marines, led by Colonel Robert E. Lee came to put down the uprising. Brown was captured and ten of his men were killed.

View of Harpers Ferry from Maryland Heights

Shenandoah Street in the Harpers Ferry National Historic Park

Brown was tried for treason; and on December 2, 1859, he was hanged at Charlestown. Among the soldiers observing the hanging was John Wilkes Booth. Northern sympathizers considered John Brown a martyr, and he became the hero of the song "John Brown's Body."

Three years later, in September of 1862, Lee, by then a Confederate general, returned to Harpers Ferry with his Army of Virginia, hoping to capture the arsenal himself on his way into Northern territory.

Lee divided his men into three columns, the first commanded by General Stonewall Jackson, the second by Brigadier General John G. Walker, and the third by Major General Lafeyette McLaws. These units advanced on the Union force led by Colonel Dixon S. Miles from three directions. In order to hold their lines, Union troops posted brigades on the high ground surrounding the city. After three days of siege, 12,000 Federal troops surrendered. An additional 1,400 Union cavalry had escaped under cover of darkness. Colonel Miles was killed by one of the last Confederate cannonballs to be fired as he prepared to offer surrender.

Lee then continued on to Antietam, Maryland. Only days after his defeat at Antietam, Lee abandoned Harpers Ferry to the Union and retreated into Virginia.

SOUTHERN COMMANDERS:
Gen. R. E. Lee
Maj. Gen. T. J. Jackson
Maj. Gen. L. McLaws
Brig. Gen. J. G. Walker

STRENGTH: 24,000

CASUALTIES: 286

MONONGAHELA NATIONAL FOREST

200 Sycamore Street, Elkins, WV

PHONE: 304-636-1800

HOURS: Visitor's Center open weekdays; closed holidays.

ADMISSION: Free.

The 909,000-acre Monongahela National Forest contains Camp Allegheny and Cheat Summit Fort. The park's Visitor's Center provides free brochures detailing self-guided tours of the Civil War sites.

Cheat Summit Fort, Monongahela National Forest

CHEAT SUMMIT FORT

Cheat Summit Fort, also called Fort Milroy, was built by the order of Gen. George B. McClellan in July 1861. The fort, intended to stop a Confederate invasion, was believed to be impregnable by artillery or frontal assault from infantry or cavalry. Confederate Gen. Robert E. Lee attacked the fort on September 12, 1861, dividing his force to isolate and capture the fortification. Because of the density of the forest, neither side was aware of the strength of the other. The Southern troops of 1,500 believed they were outnumbered by the Northern troops, who, in actuality only consisted of 200 men. The Confederate forces retreated, leaving weapons and equipment. Although skirmishes continued for the next two days, Cheat Summit Fort was never captured. The main fortification of Cheat Summit Fort is well-preserved. Surface features, such as pit and parapet earthworks, cabin sites, and earthen mounds representing collapsed chimneys, are visible.

CAMP ALLEGHENY

Camp Allegheny, also known as Camp Baldwin or Camp Johnson, is a Civil War-era Confederate fortification located astride the Staunton-Parkersburg Turnpike in Pocahontas County, West Virginia. Camp Allegheny was built in the summer of 1861 by Confederate forces in an attempt to control the turnpike (which is now County Route 3). They hoped to bar Federal advances toward Staunton, Virginia, and the Shenandoah Valley. At an elevation of approximately 4,400 feet above sea level, the fortification is the highest in the eastern theater of the Civil War. The fort was constructed on the farm of John Yeager, and a large sugar maple grove supposedly was cut down for building cabins. Following the October 3, 1861, Battle of Greenbrier River at Camp Bartow (nine miles northwest), Confederate Gen. Henry R. Jackson moved his forces to this position. Here the Confederate army established winter quarters.

Camp Allegheny is extremely well-preserved and looks today much as it did in 1861. The area includes three rows of stone piles and surface depressions representing the remains of at least thirty-five cabins. The hillside above this point contains a shallow trench which indicates the location of General Milroy's attack during the December 13, 1861, battle.

CARNIFEX FERRY BATTLEFIELD STATE PARK

Carnifex Ferry Road, off West Virginia Highway 129, 5 miles west of U.S. Highway 19 near Mt. Nebo, WV
PHONE: 304-872-0825
HOURS: Park open daily; museum open weekends Memorial Day–Labor Day.
ADMISSION: Free.

Carnifex Ferry Battlefield State Park commemorates the September 10, 1861, battle where Union troops led by General Rosecrans forced the Confederates to evacuate their entrenched position on the Henry Patteson farm overlooking Carnifex Ferry. Confederate Gen. John B. Floyd retreated to Meadow Bluff near Lewisburg. This Civil War battle represented the failure of a Confederate drive to regain control of the Kanawha Valley; and as a result, the movement for West Virginia statehood proceeded without serious threat from the Confederates.

Carnifex Ferry Battlefield State Park

A small museum contains exhibits on the area's history. Several self-guided hiking trails are available. Each year the park hosts a Civil War Weekend during the weekend after Labor Day. The two-day program features reenactors portraying Civil War camp life complete with Confederate and Union camps, morning reveille, skirmishes, infantry and artillery drills, and other living history demonstrations.

DROOP MOUNTAIN BATTLEFIELD STATE PARK

HC 64, Box 189, Hillsboro, WV
PHONE: 304-653-4254
HOURS: Open daily.
ADMISSION: Free.

Droop Mountain Battlefield, West Virginia's oldest state park, was dedicated on July 4, 1929, as a memorial to the men who took part in what is generally considered to be the largest Civil War battle fought on West Virginia soil. Located in Pocahontas

Droop Mountain Battlefield State Park

County, five miles south of Hillsboro, the park offers scenic mountain vistas, hiking and picnicking but is most noted for its historic significance as the site of a fierce struggle which took place between the North and the South on November 6, 1863. The battle resulted from the movements of the Union army of Gen. William Averell, whose intent was to clear Confederate troops in the southeastern section of West Virginia and then strike at the Virginia and Tennessee Railroad. He was successful in forcing the army of Gen. John Echols into Virginia but failed to reach the railroad.

A museum contains exhibits of firearms, uniforms, canteens, and other Civil War artifacts. The park features Civil War trenches, a lookout tower, memorials, and walking trails that include Musket Ball Trail, Minié Ball Trail, and The Horse-Heaven Trail, where all the dead horses from the battle were tossed in the ravine. In October of even-numbered years, the park hosts a reenactment of the battle.

GRAFTON NATIONAL CEMETERY

431 Walnut Street, Grafton, WV
PHONE: 304-265-2044
HOURS: Open daily.
ADMISSION: Free.

Grafton National Cemetery was established in 1865 for the purpose of having all the Civil War dead reburied in a location accessible from all parts of the state. More than 1,250 of both Union and Confederate troops were exhumed and reburied here. Records in the cemetery office indicate the location from which

Grafton National Cemetery

all bodies were disinterred. The 664 unknowns buried here are marked only by number. The cemetery also has the distinction of having interred the first casualty of the Civil War, Private Thornsberry Bailey Brown; a special monument commemorates his grave.

GENERAL McCLELLAN'S HEADQUARTERS/ ANNA JARVIS'S BIRTHPLACE

U.S. Highway 119/250 S, Webster, WV
PHONE: 304-265-5549
HOURS: Open daily, except Monday, April–December.
ADMISSION: A fee is charged; children are discounted.

Here in June 1861, soon after the Battle of Philippi, Gen. George B. McClellan established his headquarters and began to prepare for the Battle of Rich Mountain. The headquarters was the first field headquarters of the Civil War. This house was also the childhood home of Anna Jarvis, whose efforts to honor her mother resulted in the founding of Mother's Day.

ELMWOOD CEMETERY

West Virginia Highway 480, Shepherdstown, WV

PHONE: 304-876-6440

HOURS: Open daily.

ADMISSION: Free.

Elmwood Cemetery is the final resting place of 577 Confederate soldiers, most from the Battle of Antietam, Maryland. Brochures describing the Confederate officers burial sites are available.

HARPERS FERRY NATIONAL HISTORICAL PARK

West Virginia Highway 340, Harpers Ferry, WV

PHONE: 304-535-6298

HOURS: Open daily; closed Christmas.

ADMISSION: A fee is charged.

Because of Harpers Ferry strategic location on the Baltimore and Ohio Railroad at the northern end of the Shenandoah Valley, Union and Confederate troops moved through Harpers Ferry frequently. The town changed hands eight times between 1861 and 1865. When the Federals returned to Harpers Ferry after the Battle of Antietam, they began transforming the surrounding heights into fortified encampments to protect both the town and the railroad. In 1864 Union Gen. Philip H. Sheridan used Harpers Ferry as his base of operations against Confederate troops in the Shenandoah Valley.

The expansive park features five museums, each focusing on a different era of Harpers Ferry's history. The Civil War museum contains a large collection of Civil War artifacts. Guided walking tours and self-guided tours are available at the Visitor's Center. The John Brown Museum offers short films which detail the town's pre-Civil War history.

Harpers Ferry National Historical Park

INDEX

PHOTO CREDITS

Page 16, 17(top, bottom): Michael H. Henderson. 18: AL Bureau of Tourism & Travel, Karim Shamsi Basha. 19: Michael H. Henderson. 24: Pea Ridge NMP. 25: Jeff Gnass. 27, 28 (top): Eastern National. 30: Old State House. 31 (top): Eastern National. 32, 34, 35 (top, bottom): FL Park Service. 36: NPS, E. H. Albrecht. 36 (top): Eastern National, E. H. Albrecht. 36 (bottom): Museum of FL History. 37, 38: FL Park Service. 39:Key West Art & Historical Society. 44–47: Bob Keebler. 18, 19: Kennesaw Mountain NBP. 54, 55: Jeff Gnass. 62: Springfield CVB. 65: Corey Wilson. 67 (top): NPS. 67 (bottom), 68 (top), 69 (top, bottom),71–72: KY Dept. of Travel. 73: NPS. 76, 77: Robert Buquoi, LA State Parks. 78 (top): LA Office of Tourism. 83 (bottom): Lewis Morris. 84: LA Office of Tourism. 85: Jeff Gnass. 86 (right, left): Query Photography. 88 (bottom), 89 (top): Eastern National. 89 (bottom): Sarah McKee. 94: International Stock, Mark Newman. 95 (top): MD Office of Tourism. 95 (bottom): International Stock, Andre Jenny. 96, 97: © 1998, Parks & History Assoc., Chuck Wasson. 100 (top): NPS. 102: MD Office of Tourism. 110–112: Eastern National. 114 (bottom): Old Capitol Museum of MS History. 118, 119: Jeff Gnass. 121 (bottom), 123, 124 (top): NPS. 125: MO Dept. of Natural Resources. 129: George H. H. Huey. 134: NC Historic Sites & the NC Division of Archives & History. 135–7: NC Historic Sites & the NC Div. of Archives & History. 138 (bottom): Brownie Harris. 139: International Stock, Andre Jenny. 143 (top, middle), 145: OH Historical Society. 148: Corbis-Bettman. 149: Superstock. 149 (inset): Archives & Manuscripts Div, OK Historical Soc. 154–157: NPS. 160: Superstock. 162 (bottom): SC Dept. of Parks, Recreation, and Tourism. 164–165 (top): Corbis-Bettman. 166: SC Dept. of Parks, Recreation, and Tourism. 174–176: James Pat Bagsby. 185: Kevin Daley. 187 (top left, right): Christine Landry. 188–191 (top): Bob Keebler. 202: Jeff Gnass. 204–207: The Prince William County/Manassas CVB. 208: Fort Ward Museum, City of Alexandria. 211: VA Tourism Corp. 217: Eastern National. 224 (left), 225 (top): VA Tourism Corp. 227: Connie Toops. 228–231 (top): Jeff Gnass. 231 (bottom): NPS. 232: Superstock. 235: VA Tourism Corp. 237: Hirz/Archive Photos. 239 (top): Hampton Conventions & Tourism. 241: Bicast Publishing, Williamsburg, VA. 242: Stratford Hall Plantation, Stratford, VA, Christopher Cunningham. 243: Stratford Hall Plantation, Stratford, VA, Richard Cheek. 247 (top): Jay Paul. 247 (bottom), 248 (top): VA Tourism Corp. 251: Superstock. 257 (top): NPS, National Capital Region, Bill Clark. 257 (bottom), 258: ©1998, Parks & History Assoc., Carol M. Highsmith. 259, 260 (top): Washington, D.C. CVB. 260 (bottom), 261 (top): ©1998, Parks & History Assoc., Carol M. Highsmith. 261 (bottom): NPS, Harpers Ferry Center and Parks & History Assoc. 264: WV Division of Tourism, Steve Shaluta, Jr. 265: Jeff Gnass. 266: Monongahela National Forest, M. Ledden. 267 (top): Carnifex Ferry, Ron Snow. 269:WV Divison of Tourism, David Fattaléh.Our sincere thanks to Ron & Linda Card whom we could not locate for the Pettersburg National Battlefield images. All portraits of commanders courtesy of National Archives except for the following: page 22: Archive Photos. 23: AL Dept. of Archives & History. 34, 35: FL State Archives. 55: NPS. 128, 129: CO Historical Society. 135: NC Division of Archives & History.197: TX State Library & Archives Commission.